ined the army in

Lieutenant Edmund Halsey in a photo taken soon after he 1862 (Rockaway Historical Society Collection)

BROTHER AGAINST BROTHER

The Lost Civil War Diary
of
Lt. Edmund Halsey

Edited by Bruce Chadwick

A BIRCH LANE PRESS BOOK
PUBLISHED BY CAROL PUBLISHING GROUP

A Birch Lane Press Book
Published by Carol Publishing Group
Birch Lane Press is a registered trademark of Carol Communications, Inc.

Editorial, sales and distribution, and rights and permissions inquiries should be addressed to Carol Publishing Group, 120 Enterprise Avenue, Secaucus, N.J. 07094.

In Canada: Canadian Manda Group, One Atlantic Avenue, Suite 105, Toronto, Ontario M6K 3E7

Carol Publishing Group books may be purchased in bulk at special discounts for sales promotion, fund-raising, or educational purposes. Special editions can be created to specifications. For details, contact Special Sales Department, Carol Publishing Group, 120 Enterprise Avenue, Secaucus, N.J. 07094.

MANUFACTURED IN THE UNITED STATES OF AMERICA
10 9 8 7 6 5 4 3 2 1

Library of Congress Cataloging-in-Publishing Data

Halsey, Edmund Drake, 1840–1896.
    Brother against brother : the lost Civil War diary of Lt. Edmund Halsey / edited by Bruce Chadwick.
        p. cm.
    "A Birch Lane Press book."
    Includes bibliographical references and index.
    ISBN 1-55972-401-3
    1. Halsey. Edmund Drake, 1840–1896—Diaries. 2. United States—History—Civil War. 1861–1865—Personal narratives. 3. Halsey family. 4. United States. Army. New Jersey Infantry Regiment, 15th (1862–1865) 5. New Jersey—History—Civil War, 1861–1865. 6. Soldiers—New Jersey—Diaries. I. Chadwick, Bruce. II. Title.
E521.5 15th. H35   1997
973.7'449—dc21   97–7214
                                                                        CIP

CONTENTS

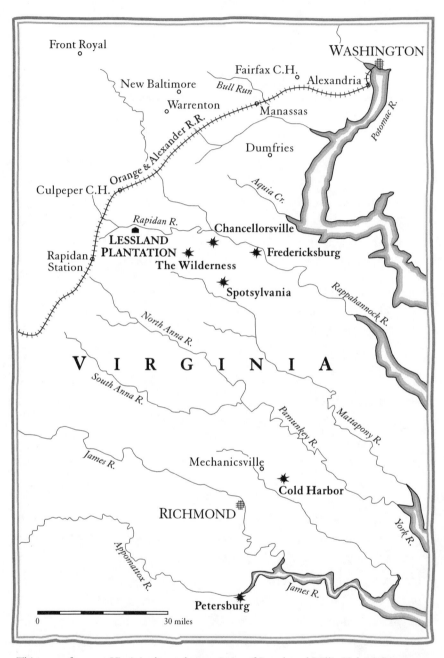

This map of eastern Virginia shows the proximity of Joseph and Millie Halsey's home—Lessland Plantation—to the sites of some of the many important battles in which Edmund Halsey's regiment fought.

AUTHOR TO READER

The diary and papers of Lt. Edmund Halsey, an ancestor of World War II naval hero Adm. William "Bull" Halsey, were the work of a highly educated and polished writer who enjoyed a unique vantage point from which to view the Civil War. Enlisting in the Union army at the age of twenty-one, Edmund was at first made an adjutant, or clerk, and supervised all the papers of his regiment, the Fifteenth New Jersey Volunteers, and delivered its orders on and off the battlefield. He learned everything that was going on throughout most of the Army of the Potomac. He quickly became an infantryman and saw heavy action in many of the key battles of the war, including Fredericksburg, Chancellorsville, Gettysburg, the Wilderness, Spotsylvania, Cold Harbor, Petersburg, and the Shenandoah Valley. He fought for nearly three years and was almost killed on more than a dozen occasions.

His father, sisters, and brothers constantly sent him money to buy clothes, books, and food, and that enabled him, with other officers from well-to-do families, to move about in the areas around camp and to buy meals at the homes of local residents—North and South. This gave Halsey a chance to learn about the war from the bystanders, and the victims, particularly Southerners—a chance few officers had, including generals.

He began to write letters to newspapers back in New Jersey shortly after the Fifteenth's first battle because he thought his comrades-in-arms were not getting the notice they deserved in the press. Editors were impressed with his style and encouraged him to keep writing letters for publication in their newspapers, and he produced a number of vivid, widely read letters.

Another unique backstage view he had of the war was in the courtroom. Lawyers and law students were made judge advocates (combination prosecutors and defense attorneys) and supervised courts-martial. Halsey became a judge advocate in 1863 and tried fifty-seven cases. Through these cases he saw the army's justice, and injustice, and through testimony had a broad-based view of the dark side of war within an army: soldier thievery, brawls, drunkenness, desertions, and the never-ending feuds between officers and enlisted men. He learned army politics, saw bungling firsthand, and observed quickly how the law could be twisted and circumvented by the powerful.

He had a view of the war from the home front, too, which few soldiers enjoyed. His family in Rockaway wrote him constantly about the solid support for the war in his hometown. Life for his girlfriend in Newark, Mary Darcy, however, was quite different. Her family's business was nearly ruined by the war, and her hometown was a hotbed of Copperhead, or anti-war, feeling. Feedback from both towns gave Halsey a more complicated view of the war than that of any other soldier who kept a diary or wrote memoirs.

There was a melodramatic family dimension to Halsey's days in the army, too, since his older brother, Joseph, who lived on a Virginia plantation with his wife, Millie, and their five children, fought for the Confederacy. Joseph exchanged numerous letters with Ed and his father before the war, heated letters in which the Halseys, North and South, argued about the social and political issues that had brought on the war, particularly slavery. Throughout the conflict, Ed had an understanding about the South and its cause—through his brother—that few Union soldiers possessed. Also included in this book are excerpts from letters and notebooks of Joseph and Millie Halsey, which give a marvelous and gritty look at how a prosperous Southern plantation was ruined by the war and how Millie worked day and night and continually risked her life to keep her family safe as her sprawling plantation was occupied several times by the Confederate Army and raided once by the Yankees. There are also riveting notes on his slave-trading business from Joe's father-in-law.

It is the combination of all these elements that makes Halsey's papers so interesting. Halsey wanted to write a book when the war ended, but so did cousin and close friend Alanson Haines, his regiment's chaplain. Halsey backed off from his own plans and helped Haines with his memoir.

Halsey's diary and letters were lost from time to time over the years. In 1975, when Halsey's hometown of Rockaway celebrated its two hundredth anniversary, town elders asked the Halseys to look for the diary for the inclusion of some notes from it for an anniversary book. They replied that the papers were lost. A family attorney was retiring about that same time and, in cleaning out his office, found the diary and a treasure trove of letters in the bottom of a vault.

Small notes from the diary have been used in books about regiments in the war, such as Alanson Haines's 1882 memoir *The History of the Fifteenth New Jersey Volunteers,* and Joseph Bilby's *Three Rousing Cheers: A History of the Fifteenth New Jersey From Flemington to Appomattox* (Longstreet House Press, 1993). No one ever used the diary (updated by Ed Halsey in 1882), letters, newspaper columns, and courts-martial notes as a collective record of the war and the foundation for a vastly different and interpretive work.

Now, putting together all the papers and the never-before-published papers of Confederate brother Joseph Halsey, it is possible to see the Civil War in a most unusual and comprehensive way, from the view of two brothers fighting in it.

ACKNOWLEDGMENTS

This work was not a book as much as it was a treasure hunt. It all began with the story of the "lost" Halsey papers from Mary Robinson, a member of the Rockaway, New Jersey, Historical Society. I would like to thank her and Bill Monroe, another member of the society, who trekked back and forth to churches and libraries with me in search of the missing pieces of the Halsey Papers puzzle. I had considerable help on the history of the Northern wing of the Halsey family from Dan Morris, one of the family's descendants and a historian himself. On the Southern side, Mildred Tyner, a descendant of Joe Halsey's, who lives at what is left of Lessland Plantation, was extremely helpful, as was her cousin Alice Bartlett.

Thanks to Ervin Jordan, Christina Deane, and the staff at the University of Virginia's Alderman Library Special Collections Room, and to Theresa Tironi of the Rockaway Borough Library, Leslie Douthwaite of the Morristown Library, and Marie Heagney at the Morris County (N.J.) Library.

Thanks to John Kuhl, a historian whose ancestor fought with Ed Halsey in the Fifteenth New Jersey Volunteers, for letting us use his photos, and to the staff at the archives of the New Jersey State Department.

Thanks for resource suggestions to professors Cliff Landers and Carmela Karnoutsis at Jersey City State College and Kurt Piehler at Rutgers University.

Special thanks goes to my literary agent, Carolyn Krupp, of IMG Literary, for seeing that this is a very different book from most works on the Civil War. I thank the editor of this book, Hillel Black, for seeing the human melodrama behind the cannon fire and charges of Blue and Gray and for helping me to stitch together the many elements of the book into a good story.

INTRODUCTION

Nowhere in the Union was the Civil War's call to arms answered with more enthusiasm and patriotism than in Rockaway, New Jersey, nestled snugly on the banks of the gently rushing Rockaway River, Edmund Halsey's hometown. Between 1861 and 1865, this tiny village, thirty-five miles west of New York City, sent one in every three of its healthy adult men—over 350 of them—off to the Civil War. Men too old to work anymore enlisted alongside sixteen-year-old boys who lied about their age. College graduates marched alongside blacksmiths. Lawyers fought next to ironworkers. No village in the United States sent its boys off to war with more pride and bravado than Rockaway. Ministers from every church in town blessed the departure of the men for battle, local newspapers heralded their enlistment, and thousands lined the streets to cheer loudly all along their route to join the Union Army.

Perhaps no village in the country, North or South, suffered such grief and sorrow as Rockaway, either. One-third of those who went off to war never came back. Anson Waer, Tom Tinny, and Eliphalet Sturtevant died at Gettysburg; Tom Jefferson Hyler, Dan Palmer, and Felix Cash were killed at Chancellorsville; and Abe Earls, Ed Zeek, William Thompson, Bill Shores, and Lemuel Smith died at Petersburg. Jeremiah Haycock Sr. was killed in Tennessee, and his son Jeremiah Jr. was killed in Virginia. Many died of disease, some in makeshift hospitals, some in ambulances bouncing down crude dirt roads, and some in their rickety, windblown tents.

The boys from Rockaway were victims of two of the greatest single tragedies of the war. The first was the May 6, 1863, mass drowning in the Cumberland River, when nineteen boys from the village were swept off boats and drowned in the turbulent waters of the river as thousands watched in horror from the shores. The second was the battle of Spotsylvania, when nearly one-third of the regiment was wiped out in the infamous charge at the "angle" of Confederate breastworks, the second single highest one-day regimental loss in the entire Union Army during the war. Deaths in the fighting at Spotsylvania and in other battles of the Wilderness Campaign were so heavy that at one point in the spring of 1864, just after Cold Harbor, the First New Jersey Brigade, made up of the Rockaway men, had lost half its men.

Rockaway's Joshua Beach, Gil Blanchard, Cyrus Talmadge, Sam Kitchel, and George Crim died in the South's wretched Andersonville Prison. Several others died at Salisbury Prison and Libby Prison. Two hundred forty-seven men were killed from the Fifteenth New Jersey Volunteers, the twelfth-highest number of fatalities in the more than two thousand regiments in the Union Army. The Fifteenth was a killing field. The village lost so many men in the war that the local cemetery, where Edmund Halsey worked as a busy gardener before the war, had to be expanded to accommodate all of their coffins.

To the people of Rockaway, it was a sacrifice they had made before—during the American Revolution, the War of 1812, the Black Hawk War, and the Mexican War—and a sacrifice they would make again in World War I, World War II, Korea, Vietnam, and the Persian Gulf War. Rockaway was one of thousands of tiny towns in the United States that were beginning to grow when the Revolution got under way. The town took shape as the nation went through the great religious revivals of the 1790s and 1820s.

Rockaway was a forerunner of the industrial revolution, which tightened its grip on America as the Civil War loomed, a town, like so many others, that took great care to keep its churches and its public schools strong. Some people lived in great mansions and some in small shacks. Some went to college and some never got out of grade school.

It was a town, on the eve of the Civil War, that was typical of many others from one end of the nation to the other. Like all of them, its residents publicly cheered the soldiers going off to war and privately wept and prayed for them, knowing that they had to go, that an awful apocalypse was about to take place that would change their communities and country forever.

HISTORICAL
BACKGROUND

HEAD QUARTERS.

First Brigade, First Division, Sixth Corps.

Camp near Middletown Oct 26 1864

My Dear Brother

The mail leaves this evening at Eight and I drop you a line to say if you have not sent me the money I asked for in my last or more than one installment of it. I wish you would send your check for $20.00 to Marcus L. Ward Newark to the credit of Chaplain Haines. I borrowed that much of him to day. money he intended to send home for some men. As a general thing there are always men having funds to send and there is no need of risking the transportation twice. I thought when I wrote you that Lieanson would probably go home with the Major's body but Major's Broker in law took the remains to New Jersey in his place. I have a bill for services in Court Martial made out for $37.00 which I gave Emison to get cashed and taking his own account of 15.00 out send me the balance but I have not seen him since and wrote to him yesterday to return the bills and I would get them cashed myself if possible. It is not so easy to get the money as it depends on the

... ville Plains
... & 12
... think it is
... le there
... ur front

... i getting
... if you
... taken?
... ne-
... morrow or
... who went
... call at
... r account
... has been a

... teacher" the
... at be nearly

ready. Give my love to all and write (as you before have done) regularly, to

Your Affectionate Brother
Ed.

Very few of the more than three hundred letters that Ed Halsey wrote during the war were, like this one, on army stationery. Most of them were on blank or lined paper that was mailed to him or that he picked up in a town. (Rockaway Borough Library)

1

THE HALSEYS OF
ROCKAWAY

One of the boys who marched off to the Civil War from Rockaway was young Edmund Halsey, twenty-one. The tall, thin, 130-pound, clean-shaven young man was a graduate of the College of New Jersey at Princeton (renamed Princeton University in 1896), who was studying to become a lawyer like his brother Joseph and his father, Samuel Halsey. He was born in Rockaway and attended its public school. He spent most of his time as a boy exploring area caves, his favorite hobby, and just as much time swimming in the hundreds of rivers and lakes that dotted Rockaway and Morris County. As he grew older, he spent some time each summer working as an apprentice to his father on the family farm and in its grist-mill business. Now, in the summer of 1862, young Ed Halsey had disobeyed his father's urgent pleas to stay home with him and had joined the army. He was in so much of a hurry to leave that the only possessions he took with him were a single, thin valise with some badly folded clothes and his empty diary. Most of his clothes would be worn out and tossed away by the time Gen. George Pickett staged his charge at Gettysburg, but Ed Halsey's diary would be with him until the end of the war.

Edmund Halsey was the latest in the long line of Halseys who had lived in Rockaway, through their own family and the Jackson family, since the 1720s. The Jackson-Halsey family had helped to found the tiny village and, as its "first family," had helped to develop every aspect of its life, from churches to recreation to schools to government. The Jacksons and Halseys and their relations, through legal and business affairs, also became leading figures in their county, state, and nation, serving in the state legislature, the governor's mansion, and the U.S. Senate and House of Representatives.

3

Several Halseys became ministers, and others were university professors. Some were adventurers. The Halseys, dozens of them, had fought hard for the United States in the American Revolution, the War of 1812, the Black Hawk War, and the Mexican War. Another dozen, from different states, would fight in the Civil War. Their descendants, including World War II naval hero Adm. Bull Halsey, would fight in later conflicts. The story of the Halseys, just like that of Rockaway, was the story of the nation.

The Halseys were not just the founding family of Rockaway. In a sense, they were one of the founding families of America. Thomas Halsey, of Hertfordshire, England, whose family had prospered in Great Britain since the reign of Henry VIII, was one of the Pilgrims at John Winthrop's Massachusetts Bay Colony, arriving in 1637. Thomas Halsey, like so many others, had fled religious persecution in England. A successful businessman with some money, which he brought with him, Halsey helped others build up the colony at Plymouth and then, in 1644, decided to move off on his own and sailed south to Long Island, where he became one of the founders of the town of Southampton. The descendants of Thomas Halsey moved off into other towns in New York, Connecticut, and New Jersey. In New Jersey, the Halseys prospered and married into several prominent local families. The men and women of the Halsey family became involved in numerous businesses, from iron mining to law. Many, imbued with Thomas Halsey's fierce need for religious freedom, became ministers. The Halseys flourished in America, but they always knew that success and freedom had a high price.

The Halseys first fought for their country in the American Revolution, when nearly a dozen took up arms with the Continental Army to fight the British. Among them were Luther Halsey, Daniel Halsey, and Elias Halsey. Jacob Drake, who would later marry into the family, was a colonel. Aaron Lindsley, who also married one of the Halsey women, was a lieutenant. Many of the Halseys living in northern New Jersey joined the Morris County Militia, part of the army. The busiest was Capt. Isaac Halsey, who led the company. Joining him in it were twelve other Halseys. Silas Halsey was a male nurse who died of smallpox when an epidemic broke out in the army's camp in Morristown in 1777.

Some achieved distinct notoriety. Jeremiah Halsey was an officer with Ethan Allen's Green Mountain Boys, the New England guerrilla band, when they captured Fort Ticonderoga in upstate New York. He was promoted to colonel and was later named the United States' first naval commander when he was put in charge of all U.S. frigates on Lake George and Lake Champlain. Matthew Halsey was a private with the Continental Army in the harsh winter of 1778–79 at Valley Forge. He volunteered for a secret mission to New York City when he learned that the Hudson River had frozen over, preventing boat traffic. Halsey knew how to ice-skate, he told George Washington, and crossed the Hudson on skates to deliver messages.

One of the youngest Halseys was one of the bravest. Isaac Halsey, orphaned at four when both his parents died, was captured by Indians and held captive at a small Indian village in Wyoming, Pennsylvania, for several months in 1777 when he was twelve. He escaped in the winter, one of the most brutal in history, hid in thickets of trees in the hills around Wyoming, crossed the Delaware River, then rode and walked his way back to Morris County. The young boy somehow survived the journey, which left him lame the rest of his life. He wandered into the camp of George Washington's army in Morristown, under a foot of snow, and joined it as a wagon boy.

The Halsey women in the Revolution were just as tough as the men. Sarah Halsey, recently married to Lt. Matthias Ross of the Continental Army, hid the members of her family on their farm in Springfield during the 1780 battle there. A group of British soldiers burst into her farmhouse and demanded to know where the family was. She refused to tell them, and when an officer thrust a sharp bayonet against her slender throat, Sarah told him to go ahead and kill her, that she would sooner die than betray the Continental Army (the redcoats left).

The most notable Halsey in the Continental Army, though, was the handsome and dashing Col. Stephen Jackson. Born in 1744, Stephen was one of the most successful businessmen in New Jersey when the Revolution began. He owned three large iron forges (he bought a fourth and fifth in 1778) and several hundred acres of property. Just before the war began, Stephen Jackson was one of five men on a political action group in the area, the Committee of Safety, which called for the establishment of a provincial government (the Continental Congress) and a county militia (the "Minutemen"). Jackson led a recruitment drive that eventually resulted in 177 volunteers for the army. Jackson, a marksman and an accomplished horseman, volunteered with the first wave of men and was made a colonel and trained his own regiment, mostly made up of men from Rockaway.

Jackson and George Washington became fast friends when Washington brought his army into winter camp at nearby Morristown in a bitter January in 1777 for the first of many winters there. Washington worked with

Jackson and other iron-forge owners to produce needed cannon and shot for the Continental Army (when the army trudged into Morristown, decimated by disease and desertion, it was outgunned by the British, three hundred to eighteen). They manufactured enough cannons and shot to give the army firepower sufficient to keep it on the field with the British throughout the war. Outside of Morristown, a "West Point" school for artillerists was set up at the same time by Gen. Henry Knox to train soldiers to load and fire the cannons of Jackson and his Rockaway neighbors.

Washington had formed such a firm friendship with Col. Stephen Jackson that he put him in charge of several attacks against the British in central New Jersey and at Elizabethtown and, the ultimate compliment, made him commander of his corps of personal bodyguards. Jackson, who admired Washington intensely, led several risky missions in the Short Hills and Elizabethtown areas during the winters and came down with a pneumonia that almost killed him in 1779. He nearly died a second time in 1782, and his health was bad for years after the war.

The success of the Revolution did not end the service of different Halsey men to the newly formed United States. Many fought in the armed forces in later wars. Silas Halsey became a hero in the War of 1812 when he tried to fire the very first torpedo into the side of a British warship. Isaac Sandford Halsey fought in the Black Hawk War against the Indians in 1832. Daniel Baker Halsey died fighting for the U.S. Army in the Mexican War in 1846. Joseph Armstrong Halsey served in the navy with Admiral Perry when he visited Japan in 1854, but was killed on his way home when pirates attacked his ship in the China Sea.

It was the iron business that made Stephen Jackson prosperous after the war and the iron business that served as the foundation of prosperity for the entire Jackson-Halsey family through the end of the nineteenth century. Jackson, who owned several ironworks, bought a large grist mill in 1783 and later built a second, which were successful for more than seventy years. Jackson also used his money to buy up the entire village of Rockaway, then consisting of two dozen or so buildings, and an additional two thousand acres of land that hugged the Rockaway River.

Located eight miles north of Morristown, Rockaway grew as Stephen Jackson's family increased over the next century. The town and the family were always intertwined. The Jacksons, and later the Halseys, saw their personal service in government, business, and education as instrumental in the development of the town, and the townspeople saw the Jackson-Halsey family and its wealth as the key to their own growth. Stephen Jackson began a long family tradition of community service in Rockaway and spent thousands of dollars of his own funds to help improve the town. Jackson funded the very first grade school in Rockaway, built a "high school" nearby, helped subsidize one of its two churches, and spent whatever money he could for bridges and roads in the town.

Stephen Jackson had fourteen children. One of them, William, married Susan Halsey, beginning the Jackson-Halsey family line. William took over his father's business with his brother Joseph but eventually left the state to live in western New York. He was the first of several Jacksons and Halseys, infused with the adventurous spirit, who left the friendly confines of Rockaway for the mountains, glens, and winding rivers of the rugged frontier. Joseph Jackson went on to become one of the most prominent business and political figures in New Jersey, and the fortunes of Rockaway grew almost in direct proportion to his. During his lifetime Rockaway grew from a tiny village to a prosperous town.

Col. Joseph Jackson, born in 1774, left high school at age twenty after studying surveying in order to work in his father's mining business. In 1802, he married Elizabeth Ogden, a niece of New Jersey governor Aaron Ogden.

Like his father, Joseph Jackson was instrumental in developing Rockaway. He succeeded in getting the U.S. government to build a post office in Rockaway in 1793 (he served as voluntary postmaster from 1798 until 1843). He became one of the hardest workers in the local Presbyterian Church, and his second wife, Electa, the former sister-in-law of Gov. Mahlon Dickerson, whom he married in 1808 after his first wife died, founded the Sunday school there. (The Colonel considered himself a God-fearing man, but had no room in his life for the evangelical tide that swept the nation in the 1820s and 1830s and resulted in the building of the town's first Methodist church in 1832, a church that quickly became one of the stops for the evangelical fire-and-brimstone young ministers who rode the religious "circuit" to bring the new wave of religion to the people. The church had to be built because Joe Jackson booted the Methodists out of the schoolhouse, where they first met.)

The Colonel spent hundreds of hours working on committees and small corporations entrusted with the development of Rockaway. The family was involved in other aspects of Rockaway life, also. Jackson's son John was the manager of one of the two hotels that opened in Rockaway during the 1830s. The Jacksons even supplied Rockaway's only doctor, Dr.

J. D. Jackson, who made house calls at every hour of the day to any stricken resident in town.

Joe Jackson, a tall, thin man with an angular face, was left one-third of his father's estate in 1812 and proceeded to expand on the Jackson fortune by buying another grist mill, three more iron mines, several farms, and thousands of acres of forest. His men spent much of their time digging shafts into the sides of hills throughout his land in attempts to hit more rich iron veins, and often they did. By 1841 he owned nearly two thousand acres and his businesses were among the most successful in the state.

Like his father, Colonel Jackson was very patriotic. From 1801 until 1812 he served as colonel in the local militia (the title stuck), always on call for duty. That duty came in 1812, when war broke out again between Great Britain and the United States. Jackson's company was activated by the U.S. Army and went into combat against the British. After the war, Jackson became a local judge and justice of the peace for Rockaway. Those positions served as springboards into politics, which he saw as community service as his father had, and as a means to further his business ends, which were growing. Jackson was elected to the New Jersey legislature as an Andrew Jackson Democrat in 1828 and reelected in 1829 and 1830. He worked hard for the election of other Democrats and was instrumental, through campaigning and fund-raising, in the election of his relative Gov. Mahlon Dickerson to the U.S. Senate. He switched to the Whig Party in 1831 after the national Democratic leadership insisted on antitariff policies he felt were ruinous to his iron business.

Rockaway village grew and prospered as the Jackson-Halsey family prospered through the 1820s, 1830s, and 1840s, mainly because of the Morris Canal, a water route from Pennsylvania to Newark. The construction of the canal in 1832, pushed hard by the Jacksons, put Rockaway on a new and successful waterway. The Jacksons managed to get the canal to build its first major lock, which raised and lowered boats, in Rockaway, thus requiring all boats traveling the canal to stop at the village. The success of the canal doubled Rockaway's population and made it one of the most important small towns in the state. The canal also served as the impetus for the creation of the town's business district, which complemented Rockaway's single school and two churches, four stores, including a general store, grist mill, sawmill machine shop, three blacksmith shops, two cabinet shops, and two carriage makers, plus the various mines, ironworks, and iron forges. The village had soon grown to one hundred families and four hundred residents, most of whom worked in the Jackson ironworks, by 1840, the year Edmund Halsey was born.

Colonel Jackson prospered throughout the 1830s, but in 1839 his entire empire was threatened with ruin. Engineers of the newly built Morris Canal had diverted Rockaway River water at Dover, north of Rockaway, leaving the Jackson ironworks on the river with insufficient water for use as power and for other manufacturing operations. The Colonel sued the Morris Canal in a legal action that drew considerable press attention. He faced economic catastrophe unless he could field a strong legal team to take on the wealthy and politically well-connected operators of the canal, defended by two of the nation's best lawyers, Samuel Southard and Henry Ford. Fortunately, by that time Samuel Beach Halsey had come into his life.

Samuel Halsey grew up in quiet Fishkill, New York, the son of a local physician. His mother died when he was nine, and his father soon married the niece of Dr. Jacob Green, of Hanover, New Jersey, the fiery Revolutionary-era abolitionist and politician who wrote New Jersey's Revolutionary-government constitution, and brought her to live in Fishkill.

Samuel Halsey studied with a local tutor and was sent off to Columbia College in New York City as a freshman in 1809. In New York, he quickly discovered politics and taverns. He began to go to taverns to argue politics and argued politics in order to go to taverns. He became so engrossed in both that for years Columbia students told of the night he arrived back at the college and opened the door of its stable to put in his horse when he remembered that he had left the horse at the tavern.

His parents may have heard the story, too, because Sam was taken out of Columbia and, through family connections, given a job as a clerk in the Firemans' Insurance Company. He was sent to live with his uncle Isaac so that someone in the family could watch over him. Isaac, the Revolutionary War wagon boy, had amassed a small fortune through a dry-cleaning business and street-grading company in booming Manhattan, which enabled him to successfully dabble in midtown-Manhattan real estate. He had become quite prosperous. Many of his business virtues rubbed off on young Halsey. By 1811, Isaac was convinced that young Sam should have another chance for a college degree and sent him back to Fishkill. He and his brother Abraham studied under a local tutor in Poughkeepsie for two years and were then together matriculated at Union College in upstate New York, where Sam, more mature and determined to study, earned a degree.

The new college graduate decided to become a lawyer and clerked for James Tallmadge, in Poughkeepsie, until 1818, when he passed the New York bar exam. Some of his first cases involved indigent people cheated out of their homes and life savings by unscrupulous companies who used loop-holes in the law to their advantage. Halsey, always impressionable, felt bitter about the law almost as soon as he started to practice it.

His life took a sudden turn a year later when he started to visit his older sister Susan, who had married William Jackson and moved to Rockaway. The community was smaller than the more established Fishkill, but it had much in common with the New York town. Rockaway, too, had a river running through it, thousands of acres of thick forests, cool mountain breezes, and large, flat meadows. It was pretty in summer and, when snow was on the ground, gorgeous in winter. Halsey liked it.

At one of the large Jackson-family gatherings, the muscular, six-foot-two-inch, blue-eyed Halsey, a handsome man with fine facial features, high forehead, and a proud, long, wide Roman nose and wavy jet-black hair, met Sarah Jackson, the daughter of Colonel Jackson, and fell hope-lessly in love with her on the spot. Sarah, a slight, rosy-cheeked, and beau-tiful young woman, was swept off her feet by the stunning young New York lawyer. The couple tumbled into a whirlwind courtship that became legendary throughout Morris County. They were married a year later and were driven all the way from Rockaway back to Fishkill in a two-wheeled carriage, waving and smiling to every single person or couple they passed on the ninety-mile journey. Over the years, Sam and Sarah would have seven children: Joseph, Sam junior, Edmund, Susan, Abe, Cornelia (nicknamed Sill), and Anne.

Sam Halsey's friends began to urge him to get into politics, an idea that had drifted in the back of his mind since his student days at Columbia. Encouraged, he ran for the state legislature as a Whig in 1826 and was elected to a four-year term. He was reelected in 1830 despite a general Democratic landslide. He spent several months in Albany, the state capital, each year, to the dismay of his wife, but enjoyed government work. As a legislator, he was an influential leader of the temperance movement and became friendly with state senator William Seward, who would later become governor of New York, a U.S. senator, the lightning rod for the national abolitionist movement, and a key player in the political drama that would result in Sam's losing his youngest son, as yet unborn, to the army.

Sam Halsey's life received a sudden jolt in 1834. Someone offered to buy his farm at the same time that Colonel Jackson asked him to move to New Jersey and become the lawyer for the family's iron empire. Sam's wife, Sarah, eager to return to Rockaway, where she had such fond childhood memories, encouraged the move, and the Halseys moved to Rockaway at the end of the year. Samuel, already an established lawyer, temperance leader, and political figure, was fiercely independent and refused to simply go to work for the J. Jackson Co. He wanted to help the family, but insisted that he be viewed as an independent lawyer and retained on a case-by-case basis by the Jackson iron companies. However, within a year he was practically running the iron business. His first important contribution to the family company came within two years when, as a partner with the Colonel and Stephen Jackson, a cousin, he reorganized the J. Jackson Co. into the Rockaway Manufacturing Company to make it more profitable. The first officially organized mining and ironworks company in the town, it became enormously successful.

Sam Halsey always liked Rockaway and enjoyed the move. His wife was happy to be home with family and friends after living away for twelve years. The Colonel and his brother William helped Halsey build a home at the far end of his property. It was there, in 1840, that Edmund was born. The Colonel's other brother, Dr. John Jackson, Rockaway's physician for four decades, delivered the baby.

William Jackson, born with a pioneer spirit and bored by the family business, finally quit the firm and moved to a small farm buried in the dramatic Adirondack Mountains of northern New York in 1836, taking his wife (Sam's sister) with him. Samuel bought his entire estate from him—land, buildings, and stables—for $6,000 and made mental plans to build a grist mill on the grounds.

It was not long before Sam's legal abilities were tested. The Morris Canal case was one of the most important in New Jersey legal history up to that time, testing whether an enterprise that was good for the entire state superseded the good of a single ironworks. The high-powered legal team for the Morris Canal argued effectively that the Rockaway River water was desperately needed for the canal, and that without the canal hundreds of businesses would collapse and hundreds more, in the planning stages, would go bankrupt. If a single ironworks could be allowed to get in the way of the canal, they argued, then all of the dozens of ironworks nearby would file similar suits and the canal would simply lock up its locks and go out of business.

At first, a local legal team represented the ironworks, but the Colonel was not pleased with the courtroom attack they planned. He turned to his son-in-law, who he knew was a good lawyer and an effective politician, two elements that frequently worked in a controversial courtroom case. He soon put Sam Halsey in charge of the case. His instincts also told him that since it was a family case, Sam's ardor would be greater than any outside lawyer's. Halsey took the case to court after nearly a year of extensive research and preparation. The trial was one of the most publicized of the year in the state, and most legal experts thought the canal, which had become a political power as a transportation waterway, would win. They were wrong. Their legal team called witness after witness and read document after document to the court, but young Sam Halsey, arguing that no monolithic company had the right to restrict the rights of any small company, especially one that employed so many local residents, beat them.

Sam's victory, widely covered in statewide newspapers, once again propelled him into politics. He was elected to the New Jersey Assembly as a Whig in 1841 and reelected in 1843. Since he was a veteran legislator in New York, it was easy for him to learn the ropes of the New Jersey Assembly, form alliances, and achieve quick effectiveness in getting bills passed. His legislative abilities were so respected, and his political savvy so finely tuned, that in 1843 Halsey was elected Speaker of the House. Halsey formed strong political alliances in the House that would last a lifetime.

Sam Halsey was another in a long line of Jackson-Halsey family men to serve in state and national legislatures. Stephen Jackson was the first. Sam's uncle Silas Halsey was the second. He was a U.S. congressman from New York from 1804 to 1806.

Samuel Halsey was an effective Speaker, impressing the Democrats as well as the Whigs, and the Whig Party nominated him to run for Congress against Hugh Kirkpatrick. Halsey carried most of the counties in his congressional district, but lost all-important Morris, a Democratic stronghold, and the election.

The loss, and pressure from his wife, constantly worried about his sagging health, convinced Halsey to get out of politics when he finished his term as Speaker in 1845. He suffered from annual bouts of pleurisy. From October through the spring, his body was racked with a nagging cough. He complained of chest and heart problems, too, and friends and family worried constantly about him.

Despite his health, the 1840s were good years for Sam Halsey. He dabbled in land speculation and bought and sold several large farms at considerable profit. He worked to improve conditions in the iron industry, which had slowed considerably since British and European iron began to flood the U.S. market, where American iron was not protected by a strong tariff.

He localized all of his political and civic attention. He was named a Common Court pleas judge for Morris County in the late 1840s and served with distinction for years. Like his father-in-law, he had come to love Rockaway and worked hard to develop the town. He was easily elected to the town committee, where he served for years and ran the town's finances, and he spent several years as the town's superintendent of schools.

He was influential in the town's Presbyterian church. He became an elder there in 1841, the year after Edmund's birth, and spent his entire life on the church board. He contributed thousands of dollars to the church over the years and in the 1850s gave the church two large plots of land that he owned, adjacent to it, for the construction of a parsonage for a permanent minister. He also donated a large sum of money for the construction of the parsonage.

Through the church, Sam Halsey heard of dozens of people in town, most ironworkers, in dire financial straits and quietly helped them with money and/or food. He worked hard for Rockaway because over the years his family had become an integral part of the fabric of the community, and hundreds of people in town worked for his different businesses. Sam and his family had something to do with just about every building constructed in town, every job offered through the mines, manufacturing, farming, or the grist mills, the churches, the schools, recreation, and the roads and bridges.

Sam and the other Halseys and Jacksons in Rockaway were instrumental in getting the brand-new Morris and Essex Railroad, which began service between Newark and Morristown in 1838, to extend the line and put a train depot in Rockaway in 1848. The railroad connected Rockaway to Newark and New York and the rest of the world. The depot opened up rail routes for the Halseys' iron and grist-mill business, too, in addition to the tonnage being shipped on the Morris Canal, and made it easy for the Halseys and others in town to visit relatives and friends in other New Jersey towns, particularly Newark, and to travel to and from New York for business and entertainment. By the late 1840s, when Edmund Halsey was just starting grade school, the Halseys and Rockaway had become one.

Education was important to Halsey. He wanted his children to get the best possible schooling and had the money to assure it. His eldest son, Joseph, who wanted to follow in his father's footsteps as a lawyer, graduated from Princeton in 1842. Second son Abe went to Princeton in 1847. Third son Samuel Jr. graduated Princeton in 1855. His youngest son, Edmund, enrolled there in 1857. Daughter Anne was educated at a women's school in Bethlehem, Pennsylvania; Susan at Mrs. Cooke's School, in Bloomfield, New Jersey; and Cornelia at Mrs. Willard's Seminary, at Troy, New York.

The 1850s, though, were a time of upheaval and trouble for the Halseys, just as they were for the nation. The American iron business, unable to compete with imported iron and unable to get federal tariff help from a Democratically controlled Congress, went into a severe depression in the early part of the decade.

Halsey wrote to his brother Silas in 1859: "I see no chance for forge owners in this country to clear themselves from their embarrassment, and predict that in two years without the protecting care of government they must all go down and the business be abandoned at least for a time. We have been struggling long against the current of hard times, but there must be an end of it even with us unless relief comes soon. I am daily more and more satisfied of the truth of father's notions about the iron business. He always advised me against embarking in it, and I have in some measure, indeed as far as I could, regarded and followed his advice. It is not on my account that I ever had anything to do with it, and even now am only connected in being associated with those who are in it."

Halsey's dire predictions came true. The Rockaway Manufacturing Company and all of its iron properties plunged into bankruptcy in 1852 and might have ruined the entire family if Sam Halsey had not put together a brilliant business and legal plan to slip his aging father-in-law out of the economic noose in which he found himself. Colonel Jackson died in 1855, and within months Sam Halsey closed out the family iron business and added a grist mill to the farming business for his own income and left the mines and manufacturing forever.

The grist mill and farming business were not easy. In 1856, Sam fretted that it took nearly a year to construct a new 36-by-24-foot grist mill and months more to make it operational. The new mill did become successful, but in the fall of 1856 only brought in a profit of $15 a week. Sam's farms, too, prospered in land value, but only because Sam senior, with the help of Sam junior and Edmund, worked hard at maintenance and upkeep. As an example, one farm he'd bought for $2,500 in 1855 had grown in value, Sam senior wrote in his books, to $7,000 by 1859, but, Sam noted, underlining the sentence, only with extremely hard work by everyone in the family. During that same period, the family of Sam Halsey moved into the huge home of the late Col. Joseph Jackson and slowly began to make it their own with some additions, a new stable, gardens, added furniture, and an organ for Anne to play beautiful music that wafted through the small town in the early hours of the evening when people took advantage of spring breezes and walked along the bank of the river.

Sam Halsey had enormous personal problems in the 1850s, too. For years, he had sent thousands of dollars to his free-spirited brother Abraham, who lived in various cities throughout America and Europe without establishing any occupation and rarely working. Abraham lost money in just about every investment he ever made and, after marrying the daughter of a Choctaw Indian chief, lost her money and property in 1840 when the entire tribe was victimized by land swindlers. Abraham went to California in 1849 after the gold rush there and died in Panama in 1852.

Sam's brother Silas, another free spirit, moved to Michigan in 1837 to begin a pioneer community in the wilderness. He was constantly destitute and borrowed money from Sam for years—most of it never repaid. Sam's older sister, Susan, had left Rockaway with her husband, William Jackson, in the 1830s and settled in northern New York. Sam Halsey, growing old in the late 1850s, desperately missed them all.

His children were grown and had moved away from home. His eldest son, Joseph, had moved to Virginia in 1843. Son Abe followed his uncle to the gold fields of California in 1849. He moved to a Chinese mining camp in 1852, in Tuolumne County, where he lived for twenty years. He married in 1857, but his wife died just a year later. Sam junior became a lawyer and moved to Morristown, but his business had not gone well. He started out in a partnership with another lawyer, but it dissolved with little money made by either man, and Sam talked about quitting the law and even moving to the California gold fields, ideas that greatly distressed his father. Susan married Dr. Columbus Beach, a wealthy physician, and was living in Beach Glen, the Beach family's sprawling estate, in another part of Morris County.

Tragedy struck in 1859 when Sam's wife, Sarah, died at the age of fifty-seven. For years, she had struggled with crippling rheumatism. Just a few months later, daughter Anne, age thirty-two, was struck with it, too. Bedridden, she required constant care. Just a few months after his wife's death, Dr. John Jackson, the Colonel's brother and a close friend and adviser to Sam Halsey for twenty-five years, also died. Only Cornelia, who was by then spending most of her time caring for a bedridden Anne, and young Ed remained at home.

Edmund was a teenager when Colonel Jackson died and his father took the Halseys out of the manufacturing business. Sam, watching his grown children going off to school as he cared for his ill wife, turned all of his love and attentions to his youngest son. They had precious times together. Edmund was just old enough to enjoy Sam's company as both a father and a friend, and Sam was old enough to be more lenient with his youngest son than he had been with his other children. The timing was perfect for a strong and loving father-son relationship to blossom, and it did. Edmund had become the joy of Sam's life in perhaps the worst time of it.

A lifelong politician who understood the tide of historical events and the moods of people, Sam Halsey, then sixty-four, feared that civil war was coming. North and South could not resolve their differences over slavery. The Kansas-Nebraska Act, passed in 1854, permitting slavery in new territories via voter approval, not only started a firestorm, but brought about the death of Sam's old Whig Party. The Supreme Court's Dred Scott decision, which again upheld slavery, caused another uproar. Then, in 1859, abolitionist John Brown attacked Harpers Ferry, in Virginia, and brought the country to the edge of rebellion.

The strife reached deep into Sam's own family. His son Sam junior had become a fire-eating, antislavery Republican and was one of the county leaders in the Republican presidential campaigns of John C. Frémont in 1856 and Abraham Lincoln in 1860. Edmund was even more ardently opposed to slavery than Sam and talked endlessly about his hatred of slavery and the need to keep the Union together. Halsey's close friend Dr. John Jackson became so incensed over the North-South disputes that in 1855, after a twenty-year hiatus from politics, he jumped back in, became a Republican, and was once again elected to the State Assembly. The divisive slavery issue had fractured Sam Halsey's family, though, with the children in the North against it and Sam's son Joseph, who owned slaves in Virginia, fervently for it.

Friends said that in 1860 and 1861, Sam Halsey, aging, afflicted with pleurisy, lonely and depressed, sat in front of the large fireplace in his Rockaway home at night and talked endlessly of doom and despair. He was convinced that a terrible civil war was going to split the country in half, that years of bloodshed were ahead. At the end of all his conversations was a dread fear that the war would sweep up his hotheaded son Joseph and take his beloved youngest son, Edmund, away from him.

2

EDMUND HALSEY

Edmund Halsey had the best of all worlds as the youngest son of a large and wealthy family in Rockaway. His sisters doted on him, buying him presents whenever they went shopping, and often brought him shopping with them (he made up stories for his friends to explain his shopping trips with his sisters in order to preserve his manly reputation). His brother Sam, with whom he was close, served as his mentor and protector as he grew up. His mother was still in good health during Ed's early years and, with domestics to help her with housework, spent as much time with the tall, thin boy as she could. Rockaway, and the surrounding towns, were full of members of the Jackson and Halsey families. Essex County and Newark, the state's largest city, were home to several dozen more Halseys. The opening of the Morris and Essex Railroad made it easy for the Halseys of Rockaway to frequently visit relatives, such as the Darcys of Newark. All of these relatives served as a loving support system for young Ed as he grew up.

His greatest support was his father. Samuel Beach Halsey adored Ed. Sam Halsey enjoyed bringing Ed to his office in Rockaway and another office the family had in Morristown. Whenever Sam senior traveled through his property to survey it, a hobby of his, he brought Ed along. He also frequently took Ed on the train with him for business trips to Newark. He usually took the boy on the final day of a business negotiation, when some papers would be signed and Sam would profit, so that he could show off to his son, and then, always, the two enjoyed a celebratory dinner at the city's largest hotel.

Sam senior also took young Ed with him to New York on frequent shopping and business trips and brought him along to listen to political speeches by some of the leading public figures of the day, particularly those delivered by then U.S. senator William Seward (whom everybody felt

17

would soon be president), an old friend of Sam's from his New York legislative days. Sam senior also took Ed to New Jersey state Whig and
Democratic conventions when he was thirteen so he could get an insider's
look at politics and brought him along to dozens of other political meetings
and picnics. At sixteen, through Sam (and his older brother), Ed got a firsthand look at insider politics during the 1856 Republican presidential campaign of John Frémont.

Sam was determined that Ed have the broadest possible social and cultural upbringing and often took him, sometimes with Sam junior, to New
York for a weekend. The father and sons would stay at a fancy hotel, dine
in the best restaurants, and attend exhibitions of some kind or take in a
play. Dinners would be consumed with long and detailed discussions about
business and politics, and the boys had a chance to learn about both from
one of the nation's better businessmen and politicians.

Sam Halsey constantly brought iron ore samples from the Jackson-
Halsey mines to show Ed, and the two would spend a long time analyzing
them and packaging them for further study. Sam enjoyed bringing home
baskets of food from the family farm and asked Ed to inspect them for quality. Ed, in turn, made his father a full partner in his gardening empire, cajol-
ing him to kneel down in the soil next to him and plant row after row of
plants, vegetables, and flowers in the enormous gardens at the rear of the
large, white clapboard family house. Sam senior probably did not enjoy it
very much, but put in countless hours just to be next to his son.

The Halseys had numerous horses, buckboards, and carriages in their
long, rectangular stables, which ran parallel to the river, so it was easy for
Ed to move about the town and county to see friends and relatives. It took
him less than five minutes to walk to the Morris and Essex train station to
board a train for Morristown or Newark. He belonged to an inordinately
large family, which had relatives throughout the county, whom Ed, an out-
going, friendly boy, loved to visit. His cousins remained fast friends all of his
life, and he made numerous visits to the camps of those who fought in the
Union Army later. He also became friendly with the friends of his cousins.
In Rockaway, he had dozens of fellow students from school as friends.

Among his responsibilities around the home was caring for all of the
animals, and there were dozens. His pride and joy was a long, rectangular
wood-and-wire chicken coop he and his father had built. Ed cared for all
the chickens in it, making sure they were properly fed. His delight as a
youngster was to watch chicks hatch from their eggs and then to run into
the house to drag his father outside to watch. He wrote a long, sad story in

his diary about the death of one, which showed how he was slowly growing from a teenager into a sensitive young man.

He was also in charge of the family cat, whom he adored but regretted spanking one day for grabbing one of the young chickens and racing about the yard with it in his teeth. He was also put in charge of the family gardens, a chore that fascinated him. He spent countless hours pruning bushes, planting flowers, and arranging plants in the gardens. He was so obsessed with the garden that he kept copious notes on when he planted each group of seeds and when flowers bloomed or vegetables were ready to eat. He even measured some plants, such as peas, and kept lists on the length of each pea pod. Later, at the minister's request, he became the volunteer gardener for the Presbyterian Church cemetery, located just behind the old red-brick building and framed by long lines of oaks and chestnuts—where so many of his childhood friends would later be buried.

Young Halsey was a good athlete. He played baseball and football with town teams whenever he could and was an ardent gymnast, practicing a variety of somersaults and handstands on the flat portion of the yard behind his house. He used the easy-flowing Rockaway River to its fullest in learning how to become a strong swimmer. He began to play chess at an early age and became quite proficient at it as a teenager.

He worked hard at school and around the house and played hard at sports. He loved to relax, though, and absolutely reveled in inventing excuses to stay home from school, pretending he had farmwork that was crucial, and take it easy. Some of his fondest memories as a teenager were of simply lounging about the house with his sisters, particularly on a rainy day. Anne and Cornelia were hopeless social lions, even as teenagers, and Ed loved to sit on the edge of the porch and just listen as they sat next to him and spent hours planning a picnic of some kind. When it rained, Ed and Anne would retreat to the large, spacious living room and plop down in chairs, opposite each other, and read novels as the rain pelted the roof. Sometimes he would lounge on the sofa and close his eyes as Anne played the organ for hours.

He was a boy obsessed with details. He kept lists of everything he and everyone else in his family did. Just about every day he made up a list of where he went, with whom, and what they did. He even added up the number of miles he traveled each day and kept track of his meals, when and what he ate. He kept lists of things other people did, even when they did not want them. His sister Cornelia, nicknamed Sill, like Ed, loved to write and penned hundreds of short essays. Ed went over them and made up a list of the subjects of these essays. This attention to detail would make his wartime diary invaluable.

Ed, like all of the Halseys, had a disciplined, religious upbringing. Members of the Halsey family had served as ministers throughout the New York–New Jersey area for over a hundred years, and some were considered among the top theologians of their era. In July 1862, Ed's cousin Samuel P. Halsey became the minister at the Rockaway Presbyterian Church, where the Halseys had worshiped for 104 years. Ed not only went to services at this church his family had helped fund and build, but attended Sunday school there right after services every Sunday and then, after dinner, went with his family to Bible meetings either in Rockaway or nearby Dover. His deep belief in God would help get him through the war.

The early 1860s were a difficult time for all young men, including Ed Halsey. It was a time when people of a community, such as Rockaway, worked together to make the community strong. When boys reached manhood, in their early twenties, they were expected to take their place as a member of the community. Service to the community, the kind of service the Halseys had given to Rockaway for eighty years, was an important part of a man's life in the middle of the century. It was expected of young Halsey just as it had been expected—and received—from his father and brothers.

The early twenties were also a time in midcentury Victorian America when men were expected to move beyond boyhood into manhood by becoming independent. They were expected to get jobs, find professions, and live outside the home until they married and made a home of their own. Ed Halsey was trying to seek independence from home and father— through a career in law.

Halsey found himself a man in a maze as he turned twenty-one. He was desperately trying to serve his community and live independently, yet the dark forces swirling around the American landscape in the early 1860s were pushing him into a deep vortex where he would not be able to achieve anything, a vortex of time and space that would not only delay society's normal tests of manhood, but test his manhood in the most awful way.

Ed Halsey had two great loves: exploring and writing.

Rockaway was riddled with hundreds of abandoned mine shafts that had been dug into the deep hills of the town, and the county, for over a hundred years. Some paid off in iron ore and some were useless. A finished shaft, whether played out or empty, was shut down by the Rockaway

Manufacturing Company and its entrances closed with nailed-up boards or rocks rolled in front of them.

As a young boy, Halsey began to explore the abandoned mines of the town. Pulling away boards or scrambling between rocks, he went as far into each shaft as he could, or as far as he felt safe, with small torches. Sometimes he explored by himself and sometimes he went with friends. He kept notes on what mines he explored and what he found in them. He was just as eager to probe the long, dark, winding passages of the caves that dotted the entire countryside, which sat in the foothills of the Allamuchy Mountains. It was a hobby he continued when he fought in the Civil War, exploring dozens of caves throughout Virginia, in the rich Luray Cavern area, while the army was in camp.

A spirit of adventure ran through the blood of many Halseys, going back to Stephen Jackson, who loved to ride throughout the county with George Washington in the afternoons and discover new forest trails and deep glens. Halseys had served in the army and the navy over the years. Sam senior's brother Abe traveled throughout the world and was one of the first New Jersey adventurers to go to California for the 1849 gold rush. Ed's older brother Abe, as adventurous as his uncle, followed him to California a few months later and remained, eking out an existence in the rough-and-tumble mining camps that sprang up alongside rivers and creeks where gold nuggets were found. Abe found the life intoxicating and reveled in the shabbiness of the camps and towns, enjoying the dance halls, the streets filled with bars, and the all-night gossip sessions with prospectors who had descended on the rolling hills of California from all over the world in search of fortunes. He sent back photographs and newspaper clippings and illustrations of the mining camps where he lived, which Ed placed in a prominent spot in the Halsey living room and showed off with great pride whenever visitors arrived.

Ed Halsey's real love, though, was writing. Encouraged by teachers, he wrote as often as he could. His first interest was poetry. He amused his father by writing funny little poems about lawyers and wrote other poems for his sisters. By the time he was thirteen he had moved into journal writing. That year saw the production of a 137-page journal, kept from winter through fall, which chronicled his daily life. He took notes on just about everything that happened to him, jotting down the days he began and finished books, noting the weather every single day, and keeping a list of the different people he met. Though nothing particularly notable was in the journal entries, they offered a nice, soft reflection of life in the 1850s from a teenager's eyes. They also served as sturdy training for the diary he would keep during the Civil War, a diary that would turn out to be one of the richest chronicles of the conflict.

Halsey was one of the brightest students at the Rockaway School, which offered instruction from grade through high school, and teachers there moved him through classes quickly. He went to Phillips Academy, in Massachusetts, for his final year and then, a year early, entered college. There was no doubt about where he would go to college. More than a half dozen of his cousins and uncles had earned degrees at Princeton, and so did his brothers Joseph and Sam. Three of his great-uncles were professors there.

Halsey was a superb student at Princeton. He graduated seventh in a class of ninety and earned philosophical oration (honors). He not only did well in the courses he took, but audited additional courses each semester he was in school with no purpose other than to learn as much as he could in as many subjects as possible. He also quickly showed his expertise as a writer. His years of letter writing, diaries, and journals had improved his skills considerably. He was such a good writer that during his first two years he served as one of the writers on the *Nassau Literary,* the college magazine, and in his senior year was elected one of its editors, a prestigious post in Ivy League circles, akin to being an editor at the *Harvard Law Review*.

Princeton was located almost on top of the Mason-Dixon line, and the college had just as many students from Southern states as Northern states. Halsey's days there, particularly his senior year, were filled with discussions about national politics and whether or not the country would split apart in a civil war.

Ed's brother Sam Halsey Jr. had graduated from Princeton in 1855 and argued the slavery question there endlessly. He opposed slavery and any ideas of Southern independence and got into heated arguments with classmates from the South over the subjects. "The doctrine of secession and nullification is a deformed child of some years' growth," he told Southerners sarcastically. "Can Southern states succeed [on their own]? South Carolina has one hundred thousand more Negroes than white people. If she should drift out to sea and be obliged to take care of herself, she would surely go to the devil."

Young Ed Halsey hated slavery all of his life and was even more of a fire-eater than brother Sam junior. By 1856, Ed had formed strong and remarkably learned, complex opinions about politics for someone still in high school, and the backbone of his political views was a loathing for slavery. "I believe slavery to be an unmitigated curse, socially, morally and politically," he wrote his slaveholding brother, Joseph, in Virginia that year.

Ed finished high school as the Republican Party was formed as a reflex of many to the Kansas-Nebraska Act, which permitted slavery in those territories if approved by the residents. Ed was against the act and the spread of slavery anywhere and helped his brother and father campaign for the Republicans that year.

The Halseys never called themselves abolitionists and frequently denounced them, but they were clearly very radical Republicans. All were vehemently opposed to the Kansas-Nebraska Act and saw it as opening the door to slavery in all the territories (although they did not object to current slave states continuing their practices, which was the view of most Northerners).

Sam junior deplored bondage of any kind. "Negro slavery is a curse, a slow, consuming cancer. . . . I don't believe slavery can be justifiable by Scripture, [that] God intended to punish the Negro race. Show me your papers with God's seal saying that you may traffic in the lives, liberties, and souls of men who unfortunately happened to be born on the wrong side of a territorial line and with a little darker skin," he said.

Sam junior and Ed, who were close to each other, agreed that slavery had to be kept out of the new territories and any states that might be formed there. Ed wrote to his brother Joseph, in Virginia: "We do not want this fair land [Kansas], a tract composed of 81 million acres and large enough for three states, to be blighted with a curse which has tied down the energies and been a blight upon the commercial, agricultural, social, educational and religious prospects of our southern brethren."

Ed was vehemently opposed to the Kansas-Nebraska Act and expressed it poignantly in letters to his brother Joseph. "I would vastly prefer to see the principle of American Institutions carried out [in Kansas] by an industrious population of free Irishmen or Germans who would soon make themselves rich and educated, than to see the rich and productive prairies of the west thinly settled by a few miserable negro [slaves] who never can rise and who belong body and soul to a few haughty lazy slaveowners. The North will pitch them [slaveowners in Kansas] out whether the government is with or against them."

Ed argued against slavery and states' rights in logical, informed letters backed up with dozens of historical references. In one letter to his brother Joseph, he listed a long line of respected Southern political leaders, including Thomas Jefferson, George Washington, and Henry Clay, and cited speeches by each in which they opposed slavery. He concluded that "it looks bad for all of your greatest men to be on our side."

Ed graduated from Princeton in the spring of 1860 and returned to Rockaway to prepare for his bar exams.

Ed went to work for his older brother Sam, who had his one-man law office just a block from the Green in Morristown and had great difficulty getting clients because thirty other lawyers were within two blocks, all with considerably more experience. Ed lived at home with his father and sister. The family had moved into the Colonel's huge, white clapboard manor house after his death in 1855. Ed walked to the train depot a few blocks away each morning and took the Morris and Essex Railroad to Morristown, then walked two long blocks to the law office, located a block from the site of Arnold's Tavern, which had served as George Washington's headquarters during the first winter of the American Revolution.

Morristown was the county seat and the site of the county courthouse. All legal business was done in the town, and any lawyers trying cases in the county had to travel to Morristown to do their work. In 1860, when Edmund went to work for Sam, Morristown was a busy community of over four thousand people that served as the business and shopping hub for a half dozen nearby small towns. Morristown had two hotels, the United States Hotel and the Mansion House, three bakeries, two bookstores, twenty-one dry goods and grocery stores, a dozen carriage makers, several banks, seven schools, seven churches, and a growing free-black community of two hundred people, who had their own church.

The first two years that Edmund worked as a clerk for his older brother were fertile training ground for the fledgling lawyer-to-be, even if neither of the Halseys were making much money.

Edmund Halsey tried to enlist in the Union Army when the war broke out, but his father, terrified of losing him, talked him out of it, convincing him that the war would be over in a few months. His father persuaded him to forget about the conflict and to continue his preparations to become a lawyer, something Ed had wanted to do since childhood. (Sam senior was able to talk older son Sam into not going into the war, too, convincing him that he could do as much for the cause in politics at home as he could on the battlefield in 1861. Then, after Sam junior was married in 1862, Sam senior talked him out of going because he had a wife and planned to start a family.) His father persuaded Ed that he was needed at home to help with the family business and to help run the farm since his sister Anne was practically bedridden with rheumatism and his sister Cornelia spent most of her time caring for her. Sam argued, too, as so many did, that the war would be over soon. Despite his eagerness to get into the fight, Halsey stayed home—reluctantly, a victim of his father's guilt trip—continually pushing out of his mind the images of his great-grandfather fighting with George Washington in the Revolution and his uncles in the War of 1812.

When Halsey did get into the war, he was already an accomplished diarist, having begun a journal in 1853. His father had taught him how to write "field books," or surveyor's charts, when he was a boy (Sam senior studied surveying in college). Ed and his father and brother Sam had filled out dozens of them over the years, most outlining the land, rocks, and streams on the Halsey properties and mines. This skill became useful in the war, when Ed drew careful and incredibly accurate maps and charts of various battles to explain the movements of the army to his family in his letters. ·

Ed wrote numerous letters home and to his brother Joseph in Virginia when he was a student at Princeton. He spent numerous hours as a teenager trying to write novels and short stories, many of them military adventures. His diary writing showed his eye for detail and definition, but his short stories about the military displayed his sense of heroic narrative and his belief that the individual fighting for the right cause would prevail. All of his prewar writing not only developed his writing skills, but gave him an eye for color and detail—and a feel for people—that few soldiers had.

Some of his accounts of battle, such as Grant's order for the fatal charge at Spotsylvania—made into a rebel fire so hot that the trees above the soldiers' heads were cut in half by the bullets—were so vivid that relatives who read the work later claimed they could not only see the charge, but hear all the sounds of battle. His account of the Union retreat at the first battle of Winchester was so full of action that it reads like a screenplay. Other accounts were infused with pathos and tragedy, such as Halsey's eerie walk among the dead the day after the battle of Gettysburg and his emotional, circular walk around the limp body of a soldier executed for desertion.

His letters, written at night by campfire or by day in his adjutant's tent, were much richer than his diary because he had time to compose them. Some were nearly two thousand words long. They were detailed and full of strong, descriptive writing. In his letters, he had the ability to set the stage for a story, including a complete description of the scene where the story would take place. Some of his portrayals were quick and effective, but others were long and languid, and powerful, such as his description of the devastation in what used to be the beautiful Shenandoah Valley and his story about the long lines of freed black slaves, some packed into wagons and some walking, who marched out of captivity with the Union Army, a long line of stragglers following a blue-uniformed Moses out of slavery and toward the promised land.

His letters, and his diary entries about his family, show a thick lifeline of love from back home, whether from family at Rockaway or from Mary Darcy in Newark, a lifeline that helped him keep his sanity throughout the long and terrible conflict.

Slender, lovely, educated, and sophisticated Mary Darcy, Halsey's distant cousin, was more than a correspondent. Every soldier seemed to have a girl he left behind, and Mary Darcy was Ed Halsey's. They knew each other all of their lives, growing up through grade school and puberty together. The Halseys frequently visited the Darcys in Newark, and Dr. Henry Darcy and his daughters visited the Halseys in Rockaway. The Darcys were just as prosperous as the Halseys. Dr. Darcy's father had arrived in Newark as a young man in 1831 and became a local hero when he helped save hundreds of lives during the cholera epidemic of 1832 that swept through the city. Later, he became the founder of a major New Jersey railroad and went to California in the gold rush and returned even wealthier.

His son Henry, Mary's father, whose great-grandfather fought in the Revolution, became a leading business and civic figure in Newark. He was the owner of a large clothing business that exported goods all over the United States and was a leading figure at St. Barnabas Hospital, the Newark Public Library, and a director of the State Bank. He was a key figure in the growth of Newark just before the Civil War, a growth chronicled in the works of New Jersey historian John Cunningham.

Whenever Ed was home in New Jersey on furlough during the war, he managed to visit Mary. His diary is full of notes about visits to Newark. He would stop off there for a day on his way home to Rockaway or, on his way back to the war, take a train to Newark first to see Mary and then take another train to Washington and then to the war. He became more and more attached to her as the war progressed.

Unfortunately, since all his letters to the Darcy house were read by Mary's sister and parents, there is little romance in them, except for a few lines here and there and a few coded messages of some kind. Clearly, though, his growing love for Mary, and her growing admiration for him, helped sustain him through every battle. She was the girl he was going home to.

His religion helped, too. By 1860, the Second Great Awakening, a nationwide revival of evangelical religion begun in the 1820s, which resulted in the founding of the Methodist church in Rockaway in 1838, had run its course. New churches and ministries were everywhere following the evangelical tide, but the fervor had died down, and all of the Protestant religions, some changed substantially and some just a little, settled into structures that would last generations.

Many Americans in the mid nineteenth century transferred religious fever to politics, though in a natural bridge between God's will and public good. Hundreds of thousands of Americans became abolitionists in the 1840s and 1850s and pushed hard for the elimination of slavery in the South. Most became staunch Republicans and helped the Republican Party, only established in 1854, grow so quickly that by 1858 the party dominated the House of Representatives and, in 1860, controlled the Senate and White House, too.

Others, such as Edmund, although not abolitionists, believed the Northern free-labor system and the Southern slave-labor system could not coexist as the industrial revolution grew and America began to turn from an agrarian society into an industrial nation. These people used their religious fervor by joining political parties and pushed for changes in their own states and in the nation. They couched their political feelings in religious terms and frequently quoted the Bible. Ed Halsey, as an example, when referring to wrongs done by the South toward slaves or toward the North—unpunished—always quoted Scripture: "The wicked fly and no man pursueth."

Although not providential firebrands on slavery like the abolitionists, the Halseys saw the entire slave system as unjust and unfair—in both a labor, civic, and Christian way—and worked hard in politics to unhinge it. Few families in America were as strong in their belief in the power of religion—they had had to flee England because of it—as the Halseys of Rockaway.

America in 1860 was in the middle of the Victorian age, an era of great progress but also of individual disenchantment and personal reevaluation. The people of Rockaway, where the industrial revolution took hold early in the mines and ironworks, were typical. As the industrial revolution grew and large companies formed, the average person felt more and more removed from the river of American life. All of the institutions they valued, whether the general store, the small farm, or the village church, had grown huge and, many felt, left the individual behind. To prevent that separation of individual from larger life, Americans at the time of the Civil War

worked hard through civic institutions and politics. They used the political
storms of the day as a way to be useful in a civic sense but also in a moral
and religious fashion.

Successful elimination of slavery would validate Americans in the
North politically and religiously, and just as important, that elimination,
and the fight to do it, validated each of them as individuals, whether they
fought at Chancellorsville or stayed home and supported the cause. All of
these moral and religious modes, channeled toward civic participation and
a yearning for self-validation, propelled Edmund Halsey as it did so many
others.

That religious spirit certainly inspired Lt. Ed Halsey. He attended
church, Sunday school, and evening religious meetings for years as a child
and teenager and was a devout Christian at the outbreak of the war. He
was a staunch Presbyterian who went to at least one church service every
Sunday during the war and sometimes attended two, one in the morning
and one in the evening, and was the cousin and best friend of the regiment's
chaplain, Alanson Haines. He was so interested in religion during the war
that he kept notes on all of Haines's and other chaplains' sermons and a list
of sermon titles. He read the entire New Testament of the Bible during the
first winter of the war. He was not a religious zealot, but his diary and letters were full of references to Providence and his sincere belief that God
would watch over him. Despite the deaths and maiming of so many of his
friends, men who had stood next to him and prayed with him in chapel, he
never lost his faith in God or faulted God for the apocalypse around him.

He always had money to spend and bought just about every newspaper
sold in camp. There are constant references to accounts of battles he found
in newspapers. He read so many newspapers that he even functioned as a
wartime librarian, advising his family which newspapers offered the best
accounts of a particular battle that involved the Fifteenth (he thought most
war correspondents got their facts wrong).

He was an absolute devourer of books. He constantly asked his father,
sister, and Mary to send him works of fiction and nonfiction. He bought
books from bookstores in cities the army captured and occupied, or towns
the army passed through. He bought books from the wagons of the Sanitary
Commission, a volunteer group that supplied books, newspapers, and other
items for the men on the front lines, and the always present sutlers, who
sold just about anything to the soldiers. He read an average of one book a
week. Some were classics, such as the works of Shakespeare, and some were
popular bestsellers of the day, such as Victor Hugo's *Les Misérables*. He read

books in his tent, by the campfire, on his horse, and even while lying on the ground about to go into battle. He formed the Adelphi Literary Society, a reading group, with Chaplain Haines. Members read the same books and then talked about them and also wrote essays about national topics and discussed each other's work. The Adelphi Literary Society tried to meet every Wednesday night, but meetings were often canceled when the regiment was hurled into battle.

His strong ties to his family and hometown, religion, books, diary, letters, and friendships in the army worked as a buffer against the awful war he was fighting. He could plunge into his letters or ride to see friends or bury himself in great books to put himself, for a while, in a peaceful and enchanting universe that ran parallel to the fatal furnace he fought in every day. It enabled him to get through the war even though as an infantryman he was one of the rebs' easiest targets and his regiment, through twisted fortune, became one of the hardest-fighting units in American military history, in the thick of just about every major battle in the Eastern theater.

Halsey was a tolerant man, but even he continually railed against the constant bungling by Union generals and officers and the ineffectiveness of politicians. The regiment was ordered to be ready to march at 3 A.M. on countless occasions, yet never budged. Hundreds of men lay in fields waiting to move into battle all day long until late afternoon, when the 3 A.M. order was finally canceled. The regiment was often moved into battle and then held in reserve. Orders were delivered and then, an hour later, countermanded.

Halsey's diary chronicles all of the bungling, chaos, and confusion and, more than any other book about the war, gives a vivid and comprehensive picture of camp life as seen from the bottom rung of the soldiers. They were not concerned about mismanagement at the top. Despite the wrongheaded battle plans, incompetent generals, short food rations, and constant sickness, their view of the war, and his, was the same: they had come to fight for the Union and that's what they intended to do.

His odd position as an adjutant, judge advocate, foot soldier, and officer gave him a look through many keyholes to see the entire operation of the Union Army, a view not found in any other wartime papers. He saw incredible courage, such as that of a friend from Rockaway, on the ground dying at Chancellorsville, telling his men to give the rebels hell, or the different charges the Fifteenth and other regiments made into a hailstorm of cannon shot at Fredericksburg, the turning back of Pickett's charge at

Gettysburg, the heroic stand of men under withering fire at Cold Harbor, and the remarkable ride of Gen. Philip Sheridan in the Shenandoah.

From these different vantage points, he also witnessed just about every one of the warts of the Union Army—court-martial interference, bungled attacks, confusing orders, arrogant officers, meddling politicians, poor supplies—and yet he never lost his faith and admiration for the generals, colonels, captains, sergeants, corporals, and privates around him, for all the men of what he called "the greatest army on the face of the earth."

3

THE HALSEYS OF
VIRGINIA

On a bluff behind a thick forest in Orange County, Virginia, over-looking the Rapidan River rolling through stands of trees below, sits Lessland Plantation. Its majestic Georgian-style, brick manor house is high-lighted by four towering white columns that hold up its large white portico. Lessland is a five-hundred-acre plantation that, on the eve of the Civil War, was home to Edmund's older brother Joseph, thirty-eight, a rich Southern planter who had married into one of the wealthiest families in Virginia.

Joseph Halsey fought for the Confederate Army and was as strident in his defense of slavery as Edmund was against it. He firmly believed that the Congress of the United States had become a runaway abolitionist train and that something had to be done to stop it before the Northern politi-cians devoured the Southern states and eliminated slavery forever. The South's reasons for fighting the Civil War were Joe Halsey's reasons and Joe Halsey's reasons were the South's. The South, and Joe, were sick and tired of Northerners, in Joe's case his own father and brothers, telling them that the slave system they had profited by for two hundred years was evil and that all Southerners were evil because of it. Joe Halsey believed in slav-ery and the slave-driven economic system. It had made his wife's family rich and prominent and would do the same for him. He was willing to give his life in a horrible civil war to preserve it.

Joseph Halsey's conversion to the slave system did not happen quickly, but it was complete. He first set foot on the soil of a slave state, Virginia, in 1843, and within a decade he had been converted to the slave system through his marriage to Millie Morton. Joe went South like many other Princeton graduates because some of his best friends lived in the South, and

31

like most of his Northern friends at school, he deplored slavery but believed that if Southerners wanted it, they could keep it. He looked for work as a college professor at the College of William and Mary and some other schools and wound up as the principal of a high school in Fredericksburg. He had made up his mind to pursue a career in education, although he was also interested in law.

Joe was a handsome man—tall, thin, with a high forehead and a thick thatch of hair that was parted on the right and swept back to the left. He had a thin mouth, large eyes, and a long, wide Roman nose. Photos of Joe and his father, Sam, in their early twenties show that they were dead ringers for each other. Girls gravitated toward Joe with ease.

Through his circle of friends, he met and married in 1845 the lovely, slender Mary Glassel, whose family lived on a large slave plantation near Culpeper, Virginia. The couple, neighbors said, was one of the handsomest pairs in Virginia high society. It was a tragic match, though. The young marrieds did not even have time to furnish a home before Mary died of congestive fever just six weeks after the wedding. During his courtship of and marriage to Mary, Joe met all of her cousins and friends and, after she died, fell in love with her cousin Millie Morton, the daughter of Jeremiah Morton, one of the richest men in the South.

Millie was an attractive, slight woman with large eyes, high cheekbones, and a large, expressive mouth. She wore her dark brown hair in a series of shoulder-length braids. Joe was smitten by her just as he had been by Mary. They were married in Philadelphia in 1846, and Joe then decided to get out of higher education and become a lawyer in Culpeper. They had five children, two girls and three boys, when the Civil War began.

His marriage into the Morton family broadened into his absorption into Virginia high society, state politics, and the slave system. Joe's father-in-law, Jeremiah Morton, owned a six-thousand-acre tobacco and corn plantation, one of the largest in the South (over a thousand acres larger than Thomas Jefferson's), which spread over much of the valley south of Culpeper and stretched to the Rapidan River on the north side. The plantation's centerpiece was sprawling Morton Hall, a large and unusually designed manor house with two huge two-story wings connected by a large one-story center building. It was an architectural wonder. Morton Hall was the center of business and social life in the Culpeper area, where women showed off their finest gowns at balls held in the Morton Hall ballroom and men retired to various ornately furnished sitting rooms for cigars after dinner to discuss politics. All of the latest books were discussed at Morton Hall parties, young men were paired off with ladies from the finest Virginia families, and everyone caught up on the local gossip.

Jeremiah Morton had a number of businesses, all directed from his plantation office. He had stock in several railroad companies and owned land in New Orleans. Morton Hall was one of three Virginia plantations he owned. The other two were Moreland (more land) and Stillmore (still more land). Morton was a member of the Texas Board of Trustees of the Southern Pacific Railroad and a speculator in coal-mine deeds in the far western sections of Virginia (later to be the state of West Virginia). He was one of the three largest stockholders in the luxurious hotel at White Sulphur Springs, in the Blue Ridge Mountains, a prosperous resort community where thousands of Virginians trekked on vacation each summer to escape the heat of the lowlands and to partake of the "waters." There, at party after party and dinner after dinner, Jeremiah Morton hosted and courted businessmen and politicians as he built his empire.

The most profitable division of that empire was the slave trade. Morton had become, by the mid-1850s, one of the South's top buyers and sellers of slaves, working as an agent for dozens of planters. Over the years, his success at bringing in high prices for slaves—women and children as well as men—had impressed planters throughout the South, not just Virginia. Morton was soon running slave auctions in Virginia, New Orleans, and in Mobile, Alabama, and made enormous profits. He usually sold off thirty to forty slaves at each auction (always keeping families together) and priced them according to what the market could bear, in many cases up to $1,500 for a slave in excellent physical condition (some $30,000 in today's money).

He graded each slave for the sale, and his comments on each helped to sell them and get his price. At a March 9, 1859, sale he rated Anthony Williams, twenty-six, "black . . . good size" and asked, and received, $1,500. He also noted deficiencies in slaves for his buyers, whom he serviced again and again and had to deal with fairly. At the same sale, for instance, he asked $1,500 for Pete Williams, thirty-three, and noted that he was "stout, ugly and very valuable." He asked for and received $1,500 for a slave who called himself General Williams, but noted in his ledger that Williams drank too much. A slave named Colonel Lindsay, twenty-five, tabbed "confidential" on Morton's ledger, brought $1,500, too. Others brought less because of problems. John Mulloy, twenty-one, who only had one leg, fetched just $800.

Morton's 10 to 20 percent profits on the sales, usually held about once a month in different places, were impressive. That March 9, 1859, sale brought in a gross of $46,000. A March 1844 sale, when prices were lower, totaled $11,370. A May 4, 1860, sale of thirty-four slaves brought in $33,600. An October 1860 sale grossed $54,400. Morton wrote in his papers that in a typical calendar year he earned a commission of close to $30,000 in slave trading (some $500,000 a year in today's money).

Morton was well connected politically and used those connections to make more money. He was elected to Congress in 1849, three years after Joseph Halsey married his daughter. He only served one term in Congress, but later, in 1861, was appointed to the Virginia Secession Convention. In 1860 he wrangled himself a commission as a captain in the Virginia Cavalry, at the time an honorary post but one that enabled Morton to bring in hundreds of other gentlemen in the honorary cavalries for vacations and conventions at White Sulphur Springs, where they spent considerable money at his hotel.

Morton, a thin man with wavy, sandy hair, a broad forehead, small mouth, and wide eyes, had always been a snappy dresser, even in his college days at Washington University in northern Virginia. He began life as a lawyer in 1822, but over the years devoted his interests to the plantations and politics. He was completely committed to the slave system (he owned several dozen slaves himself), and his entire fortune and income were tied up in it. He slowly but surely convinced Joseph Halsey it was a good thing, too, particularly after construction on Lessland began in 1848.

Morton, like all fathers, wanted nothing but the best for his daughter. He "mortgaged" to Joe and Millie five hundred acres of Morton Hall for their own plantation, Lessland (so named because it was smaller than Moreland), where a dozen slaves transferred by Morton worked to grow corn for markets in Fredericksburg. Lessland quickly became a large and profitable slave plantation.

The manor house was a four-thousand-square-foot white stucco building with a grand portico supported by columns that shot up out of the grass around it, a typical manor home on plantations in Virginia at the time. The plantation fronted on the Rapidan River on the north and consisted of rolling farmland that was adjacent to Morton Hall on the south. There were several large slave cabins, with fireplaces and chimneys (the Halseys usually had twelve slaves of different ages), a cabin for an overseer, a granary, corn house, tobacco house, icehouse, kitchen building, meat house, smokehouse, barn, stable, and a wagon house—a small village. Joseph added a nice touch of his own—a fifteen-by-fifteen-foot law office built in the front yard as a separate building with its own columned porch to match that of the manor house.

Inside, Lessland was just as impressive. Guests entered into a large two-story-high hallway with an elegant winding staircase. To the right was the family library, stacked to the top of the home's fourteen-foot ceilings with books. To the left were a front and back parlor, which were connected by large twelve-foot-high sliding wood doors, kept open when the room was utilized as one large forty-five-foot-long ballroom for parties and dancing. A dining room was at the rear of the home. Upstairs, the Halseys had four large bedrooms. The house had four fireplaces and a large, cool basement for storage. The home had many windows so breezes could circulate through the rooms in the hot summer months.

Morton could be gracious with his son-in-law, helping him set up his plantation business and introducing him to lawyers in Culpeper and adjoining counties who threw him some legal business. He could also be harsh, demanding, and unfair, such as in the winter of 1855–56, when he suddenly called in his son-in-law's "mortgage" and insisted, to Joe's amazement, that the entire mortgage be paid off immediately. This arbitrary act infuriated and greatly depressed Joe and forced him to take out a large loan from a local bank to pay off his father-in-law. He seethed in anger at the man's audacity (as did Millie), even though his own father, Sam Halsey, told him Morton was just trying to make him responsible. "You must not take the world too hard," Sam said, although he, too, told Joe his father-in-law seemed a bit harsh.

The mortgage demand turned Joe against his father-in-law for a time, but it seemed impossible to sever ties with him. Life was too prosperous at Lessland—because of the Morton family. Joe Halsey, like many sons-in-law, found himself in a velvet trap. Lessland provided him with a farming business, and his father-in-law's connections provided him with a successful law practice. His wife, although angry with her father from time to time, did not want to leave the rolling valley of Virginia where she'd grown up and where all her friends and relatives lived, and she certainly did not want to leave the wealthy environs of her youth and marriage. She refused to move.

Joe wrote home several times from 1856 to 1859 that he wanted to relocate to Texas or another Southern state and that he could practice law anywhere. He never said he wanted to cut his ties to Jeremiah Morton, but it was always a whispered hint between the lines of his letters. The family urged him to leave and strike out on his own with his family, but Millie insisted they stay, and in the end he made so much money through the plantation and his Virginia practice that he could not give up everything.

Joe had also lived in the South for a long time. He had arrived there as an impressionable twenty-year-old college graduate in 1843. He married (twice) in Virginia, and both of his wives' families owned slaves. He grew into manhood and fatherhood in a slave society. By the time the Civil War began, Joe had spent eighteen long years in the South, the years when he formed all of his political, social, and cultural opinions. Nearly half his life had been spent in a slave society, and it influenced him.

So did his friends. The social circle in which he traveled was made up almost exclusively of slaveholders. All of his neighbors along the Rapidan River owned slaves, and most of the men he met through his father-in-law were slaveholders. Most of the people he met in his travels as a lawyer were slaveholders or ardent defenders of the system. They shared the same view of slavery as their parents, who had carried that view down from their parents. Most of the Virginia families with whom Joe socialized had been slaveholders for over one hundred years. Slavery was part of their lives and their thinking, and it soon became part of the life of Joe Halsey.

Jeremiah Morton's real effect on his son-in-law was to turn him into an ardent supporter of the slave plantation system. Year by year, Joseph realized, as did all Southern planters, that it was easy to make huge profits with slave labor. And Joe, more than most planters, knew from growing up in New Jersey just how much fair labor salaries cost an employer. So he became a slaveholder and a dedicated one, arguing with everyone that it was a proper and fair system for that area of the country. He also came to embrace, after years of socializing with Morton and his friends, the idea of states' rights, which had become the focus of North-South debates in the 1850s and an idea that led him to defend, as many Southerners did, the expansion of slavery into the territories.

Dear Edward,

As to your evident bitter prejudice against slavery, it is but the manifestation of the feeling all around you, and of which the southern *white man,* who claims to have some rights in this world, has just reason to complain. If his throat is to be cut in order that the North may let loose three or four million negroes to stand and go to nothing, the southern white man will have it honorably done in open war with those who instigate his slaves on his goal to attempt it, and not [have his throat slit] by his servants. You think that New York, Pennsylvania and Ohio could manage the whole South and are actually counting your force, and say the North will set Kansas right whether the government will do it or not? This is *treason,* outright treason, and a pretty commentary upon your law abiding, heavenly philanthropy of higher lawgivers. Now I undertake to say that Virginia and Kentucky alone, in such a contest, would control the three states you name and destroy your men and property faster than you could say farewell to them. You know nothing of the spirit of the South and of the deep feeling of settled hate every day strongly fastening itself upon the minds of the people here towards those who are stealthy, incendiary, lying and hypocritical and with each cowardly forcible means as they dare use, trying to degrade the southern white man and steal his property or incite it to open rebellion and anarchy.

He also believed that the North had gained control of Congress by the late 1850s, through the success of the newly formed Republican Party, and that it would use its newfound political clout to rein in all Southern expansion. He argued with his brother Ed that Congress had no power to control the expansion of slavery into any new territory. Ed seethed at that suggestion, as did many Republicans, because the Southern view was just the opposite in 1820, when Southern politicians forced the Missouri Compromise through Congress, a bill that permitted Missouri to enter the Union as a slave state. Now, Ed argued in a number of heated letters, the Southerners were trying to forbid Northern politicians from doing the exact same thing they had done.

Joe, like so many other Southerners, believed that his state's rights and property rights could not be regulated by Congress and argued that in a prewar letter to his brother Ed.

Dear Edward,

Congress has nothing on earth to do with the domestic institutions of any section of the country, under the Constitution. There are sections which must be worked if at all by slave labor. As to free Negro labors, some of you northerners have seen enough of that. How long do you suppose your white labour would stand in the cotton and sugar fields of the south? The yellow fever which the Negro never has, would sweep them by thousands faster than you could again fill their places. Leave Providence to manage the distribution and avocations of the human race and all will be well. The only curse that comes upon us for holding slaves seems to come from Massachusetts and those who have reaped the greatest benefit from slave labor.

Although never an early secessionist like his father-in-law, Joe came to believe that years of Northern "oppression" of the South might lead to strife and some kind of separation. He even became a bigger supporter of slavery than most because he always felt pressured to support the system to dispel any secret feelings among family or friends that his childhood years in New Jersey made him weak on slavery. The Southern family always wondered about his loyalty to the Southern cause and even generations after his death remembered his spot in the genealogical lineage of the family with this little ditty, sung with gleeful sarcasm by hundreds of Virginia Mortons and Halseys:

> Millie, the daughter of Jerry,
> Married Halsey,
> The damned Yankee from Jersey.

At first, Edmund joked about Joe's sudden turn to slavery and blamed it on his marriage. He wrote: "I was surprised to see a total revolution in your feelings and opinions since you took up your abode in the Sunny South."

But Ed underestimated the depth of his brother's newfound political convictions, and by 1856, Joe Halsey had become a fanatical slave-system supporter. His letters home to his Republican father and brothers were full of hatred for abolitionists, Republicans, and Northerners, and at one point he wrote that he firmly believed that Northerners would soon come south to murder Halsey, his family, and other slaveowners in order to break the slave system. He told them that "the oldest curse of an eternal hell" was being reserved for Northerners.

He seemed to take relish in targeting his brother Edmund for his abuse and in letter after letter argued with Ed, just a college student then, and seemed to see his brother as representative of all he despised in the North. By the mid-1850s, Joe's letters to Ed and other members of the family, even his sisters, had become heated and abusive and their tone seethed with hate and violence. Joe's newfound views disappointed Sam senior, who along with his other sons hated slavery intensely, but Joe's hotheadedness about the issue frightened his father, who had always been concerned about Joe's hair-trigger temper and depressions.

August, 1856
Dear Edward,

It is a matter of cheap mortification and humiliation with me that any of my family should be carried away with the vile notions of the Black Republican Party, a party that I honestly believed would, if they could, while we are quietly sitting at home, be glad to effect the utter destruction by murder of every white slaveowner south of the Mason and Dixon line, the deed to be done by the slaves, incited by their villainous incendiary circulating pamphlets, books, writings. The slaves themselves will be hungry for the murder and the [Republican Party] will seize the spoils. If ever there was a party upon whom one day will descend the eldest curse of an eternal hell, that party is the Black Republican Party of the United States, born in hate, cradled in hypocrisy, lacking in manhood in the second and third generation by fraud and sustaining its existence by feeding upon fear of all factions. It comes like a judgement, cursed by evil.

[Abolitionists] have tried argument, ridicule, abuse the power of speech, of the press and by incessant blowing for so long a time have finally succeeded in overawing a large number of men (unworthy of the name) so that they dare not examine for themselves to see if their creed is respect the rights of the different sections. When she fails to succeed in the Congressional Halls, the Union is at an end, swept in a moment.

Joseph always used the Bible to defend slavery and African Americans as people to be enslaved, as he did in a letter to his brother Ed in November 1856.

Dear Edward,

Begin at Genesis and read carefully and thoughtfully the plain English version, the story of Abraham the father of the faithful and see how it distinguishes between the *slave* and the *hireling*. The slave could be circumcised and admitted to the blessings of the chosen people, the hireling not so. Look at the words of the Almighty in blessing Abraham and see in what the blessing consisted. Follow on through the history of Isaac, Jacob and the Israelites themselves for a time in Egypt and come on to the awful Mount of Sinai and hear the law thundered from its lightening shaken crest and what do you see from the teaching of the Almighty himself in the 21st chapter of Exodus? You see the form of governance proscribed by the Most High himself, with whom there is no variables nor shadow of meaning, and whose principles of morality are eternal.

[Read about] that righteous man, Job, on whether slavery is "per se" and sinful or whether the Almighty did not make a race for that condition. The slaves were from the same people originally, mark that Egypt [Africa], fruitful mother of the race, preserved in records of holy writ on her own hieroglyphics. Then come to the New Testament and read in the various epistles

what is then said and learn whether it is "malicious prohibitionists." Search
for yourself and see.

Sam senior wrote Joe a long letter in 1856 warning him about his
temper and the trouble it might bring: "I advise you to keep very cool in this
matter of politics and not to suffer yourself to be persuaded slavery is a divisive institution."

Sam had worried about Joseph's impulsiveness and hotheaded temper
ever since he was a child. It had become so alarming by his teen years that
Sam even had him taken to a sanitarium when he was eighteen for obser-
vation (the report: nothing more than high-strung behavior).

Angry letters continued through 1859 between the Halseys in Rockaway
and the Halseys at Lessland Plantation. Sam Halsey Sr. tried to balance his
letters to his son with news of the family, but inevitably letters from
Rockaway and Lessland Plantation wound up mired in politics. Sam senior
constantly blunted his son Joseph's attack on Northerners with reminders that
it was the South that kept pushing the slavery issue, not the North, and that
the South had to realize it would not get its way and see slavery extended to
all the new territories. The South, and Joe, Sam senior told his son throughout the late 1850s, had to stop seeing Northerners as mortal enemies:

"The people of the North are constantly excited and outraged by the
mistaken assumptions of superiority and dictation from the South. We are
all treated [on the] slavery question as fanaticals, knavish, low brow race
where opinions are not to be treated with agreement but with contempt."

Joseph always felt he had to defend all of Southern culture, not just
slavery, and resented attacks by his brother Ed that slavery determined and
ruined Southern society: "The Southern States' . . . whole exports do not
amount to the exports of the single state of Massachusetts. Why is it that
they are so miserably deficient in schools, colleges, libraries and in short
everything else? There must be a great reason for so great a contrast. . . .
The North and South started on an equal footing in this country. The South
adopted slavery and the North abolished it." Ed Halsey then added a whole
litany of deficiencies he found in Southern life. In turn, Joe would defend
the Southern way of life against Ed. The bickering went on for years.

July, 1856
Dear Edward,
   It is not therefore for you nor your people to sit in judgement upon the
South and our peculiar institution [slavery], but mind your own business

and keep your own morality and religious peace, not with flashing powd_. without ball from Sharp's rifles, but by cultivating the spirit of him whose kingdom is not of this world, who inculcates love, charity, peace and good will towards *all* men, without being busy bodies, meddling in other men's matters, proud, vain, glorious, full of manner of deceit and hypocrisy and in the South full further of riots, foreign criminals, and paupers, and all the delusions of all the "isms," which believe a lie and yet have the simplicity to think these things do God service.

All the South asks is *let us and our servants alone,* that we may live in quiet and have some security for our lives, our families and not convert our beautiful country into a desert peopled by the cursed children of Ham [slaves] and worse than central Africa, until the whole race thus uncontrolled would be swept from the earth. We do not meddle with you and abuse your class and your private matters and have no wish to dominate over the North, but the South has ever been and still is on the defensive and must succeed so long as there is enough good sense left in the nation to true [illegible]. The prosperity and comfort of this union will be crushed amid the times of a suicidal civil war as the consequence. Republicans now exhibit their class in a form more onerous than the barbarous hordes of Attila (the scourge of God).

Joseph showed nothing but anger in his letters and seemed to take out all his animosity toward the North on his family. He behaved in a sarcastic manner, celebrating various political events that turned out in the South's favor. (He considered the hanging of abolitionist insurrectionist John Brown such an important day that on the morning Brown was hanged, December 2, 1859, Halsey announced to one and all that to honor the occasion he was giving up smoking.)

Joe's letters angered all of the Halseys. Joe's sister Sue sent him a curt note and ordered him to stop writing the family such "horrid" letters. Ed told him his "fanaticism and ranting" about slavery had no effect on anyone and that he should stop writing "raging" letters. Sam senior kept telling him to watch his temper. Sam junior told him that he should stop writing about politics altogether and pay no attention to Virginia politicians, that "scales of prejudice" (meaning Jeremiah Morton) had covered his eyes.

Sam junior told his brother: "It is talk of madness [by you] to talk of our wresting your slaves from you, cutting your throats, etc. . . . madness."

Sometime in early 1859 Joe Halsey stopped his political attacks on his family, and harmony seemed to return. Letters between Sam junior and Joe went so well that year that Sam junior even thought of moving to Virginia to practice law. Sam senior took a train to Virginia in the summer of 1859 and spent several happy weeks visiting with his son and his family.

Even Ed, who had exchanged so many argumentative letters with Joe, felt matters had cooled down. He jokingly wrote him at the end of the year that their letters had gone so well that "I hope before long you will entirely recover from the idea that the North is one great political association formed for the purpose of running off slaves and murdering whites."

Everything changed in the spring of 1861.

4

OFF TO WAR

At 4:30 A.M. on April 12, 1861, Confederate forces in Charleston, South Carolina, fired the first mortar at Fort Sumter, the 300-by-350-foot, brick, pentagonal-shaped federal fort in the center of the city's harbor, which South Carolina officials had demanded Abraham Lincoln surrender to them. The mortar landed in the center of the parade ground of the unfinished fort, which had only 48 of its 140 guns in working order. A hundred more shots were fired in rapid succession, damaging the walls, starting fires, and killing one soldier.

The federals began to return cannon fire two hours later. During the next thirty-six hours, Southern artillery, consisting of thirty cannons and seventeen mortars anchored in Charleston and on nearby small islands, bombarded the fort, firing over four thousand shells into it. Thousands gathered on the harbor front in Charleston, including hundreds of residents as well as Confederate soldiers, and cheered wildly as each shell hit and a burst of fire or smoke could be seen rising out of the fort.

Through a bureaucratic mix-up, federal supply ships and reinforcements never landed. By the end of the second day of the attack, the commandant, Maj. Robert Anderson, realizing continued resistance was useless, agreed to surrender and evacuate the fort.

The American Civil War had begun.

Edmund Halsey was just one of hundreds of thousands of young men from the North and West who went off to war after the Confederate attack on Fort Sumter, a bombardment that shocked and startled Northerners. Lincoln's call for seventy-five thousand volunteer soldiers to put down the rebellion triggered an enlistment stampede that stretched from long green lawns on the campus of Bowdoin College, in Maine, to the broad, dry plains of Kansas and Iowa, from the congested, gritty city neighborhoods of Detroit and Chicago, to the tiny towns that overlooked the Ohio River.

Mayors and governors gave up their posts and formed battlefield regiments in their hometowns. Women formed ladies' auxiliary societies to knit socks, pants, shirts, and uniforms, plus huge, carefully stitched American flags and specially designed company flags. Older men who fought in the Mexican War in 1846 promptly reenlisted, many leaving wives and children behind.

Regiments in Michigan were quickly formed and hustled onto waiting trains in an attempt to be the first to reach Washington, D.C., to protect the capital, its worried residents, and the president, who looked out his window at the White House each day for arriving troops and saw nobody. Soldiers vied for the best-looking regimental flag as their regiments showed off their colors in meeting after meeting and parade after parade in a thousand little villages. Clergymen of every religion soon found themselves busy blessing all of the troops eager to go off to war.

Young men lied about their age to enlist. (A favorite trick was to paint the number 1 inside the sole of one shoe and the number 8 inside the other so when a recruiter asked if the soldier was "over eighteen," he could truthfully answer yes.) Old men grew beards to hide facial lines and lied about their age, too. Into the Union Army tumbled a mixed bag of first-time soldiers— doctors, architects, engineers, clerks, ditchdiggers, stagecoach drivers, train conductors, lawyers, and actors. They all wanted to fight for the Union.

In the North, they went to war for various reasons. Some were hard-core abolitionists who wanted to free the slaves immediately. Many were not abolitionists but believed that if any men were slaves then all men were slaves, and that the slave-labor system would destroy the free-labor system in place throughout the North. Others, who had worked long hours for little pay in Northern factories, saw themselves as "wage slaves" and fought to eradicate the entire idea of slavery by color, certain it would translate into the eradication of slavery by labor. Some signed up just to get away from small towns they had not left in their entire lives. Others were intoxicated with the adventure and glamour of war. Some even did it on dares from their girlfriends.

Most came from states that were completely supportive of the call to arms, states where almost all of the newspapers supported Lincoln (even those opposed to his election) and the war effort. These states had legislatures that passed proclamations praising the war effort, governors who went into battle themselves, and treasuries that spent millions for an overnight army.

And then there was New Jersey.

New Jersey, the Garden State (so named for its flowers and because of its place as one of the country's leading vegetable growers), had flowers of many different colors in its gardens when the Civil War began. Although its soldiers were among the bravest in the Union Army—and proved it repeatedly throughout the Civil War—it quickly became known as the Copperhead State because so many of its politicians and residents were opposed to the war and so many of its newspapers were sharply critical of the Lincoln administration.

While New Jersey was a free state (not a slave state), its geographic relationship to the Mason-Dixon line made it both Northern and Southern in orientation. (The Mason-Dixon line ran along the northern borders of Maryland and Delaware. Thus, while New Jersey was technically north of the line, its southern counties were in fact *south* of the northern parts of a slave state, Delaware.) Throughout most of the war, New Jersey and its residents could not seem to make up their minds whether they were totally committed to the Union cause. The ebb and flow of public opinion about the war was so quixotic that the state had both pro-Lincoln and anti-Lincoln governors during the conflict, and its legislature debated a bill to send all of the state's blacks back to Africa. Many in the state thought the Fugitive Slave Law was an idea of considerable merit, and dozens of legislators and the governor publicly opposed the Emancipation Proclamation.

The deep division of feeling in New Jersey started in 1860, when New Jersey was the only Northern state Abraham Lincoln lost in the presidential election, 62,800 to 58,000 in the popular vote (he did win the electoral vote, 4–3, in a bizarre division), and he would lose it again in 1864 by even more votes (Lincoln did manage to win thin victories in Halsey's home county, Morris).

Politically, New Jersey was a mess. The Democratic Party had ruled the state for decades, but the Republican Party, known simply as the Opposition at first, made enormous gains after its creation in different states in 1854 and 1855. The Republican Party in the state erupted into public view after the controversial Kansas-Nebraska Act of 1854, pushed hard by Illinois senator Stephen Douglas, which permitted new territories to decide whether they wanted to permit slavery. The bill not only brought about the creation of the Republicans, but was the death knell for the Whigs, the old second party of the era, which was torn apart by the slavery issue and ceased to function after the 1854 elections.

Most New Jersey Whigs swung over to the Republicans, but many, mostly conservatives, drifted into the Democratic camp. The Republican Party in New Jersey was so successful so quickly that it won a number of state legislative seats in 1856 and 1858, along with three congressional seats, and then elected Charles Olden as a Republican governor in 1859. The Democrats, however, made a comeback in local offices that same year and managed to capture both houses of the legislature, handcuffing Olden.

In 1860, the Democrats again swept both houses and won big majorities in the state's four largest cities. The Democrats were divided, though, uncertain whether to back Douglas or one of the two Southern Democrats who bolted the party and ran under their own banners—John Breckinridge or John Bell—and at the last minute offered voters a Fusion ticket. The results were a muddle within a muddle.

The state was not only divided among Democrats and Republicans. It was a hotbed of the radical American, or Know-Nothing, Party, whose members were opposed to blacks, Catholics, and immigrants of any kind and which tallied 21 percent of the national vote in 1856. The American Party had such influence in the state that in the 1856 elections it polled a higher percentage of the vote in New Jersey than in any other Northern state except California.

The divisions in the state were dramatically illustrated during the 1860 election. The state's newspapers were almost evenly split between the Democrats and Republicans and spent much of the campaign hurling barbs at all the candidates and each other. Mary Darcy and her sister found themselves in the middle of the wildest political newspaper war in the country in Newark, the state's premier city, which was a thriving manufacturing capital in 1861. There, the *Newark Daily Journal,* a fierce Democratic paper, stood staunchly for Douglas and against Lincoln. The *Newark Mercury* was a solid Republican paper that supported Lincoln. The city's third daily, the *Daily Advertiser,* was conservative but pro-Lincoln for president and then, as soon as the war started, sharply anti-Lincoln.

The highly partisan newspapers were owned or controlled by the political parties. They vented their anger in alarming language, which would today probably bring them in front of a judge in a libel case in one of the state's twenty-one county courthouses. Some newspapers in other states were opposed to the war and some criticized Lincoln, but these were not as vitriolic or numerous as the journals in New Jersey. The *Newark Daily Journal* promised its readers that if Lincoln was elected, thousands of Newark residents would be out of work within weeks. The *Freehold Democrat* told its voters that a vote for Lincoln was a vote for black-and-white marriages. The *Morristown Banner,* one of Halsey's two home-county newspapers, was nominally pro-Douglas but in reality did not like anybody in the election, charging that the Republicans wanted to force freedom throughout the nation and that the Southern Democrats wanted to promote slavery everywhere.

Most Northern papers swung over to a patriotic support of the war once it began, but some New Jersey papers were reluctant to do so. The *Newark Daily Journal,* one of the state's largest and most important, and one Mary Darcy and her friends probably read, was against the war from beginning to end and even labeled one of its April 1861 editorials "The Southern Cause Is Our Cause." The editorial slant throughout the newspaper, an oversize folio publication whose front page, like that of so many other papers of the era, was covered with advertising, was distinctly pro-Southern. Its editorials at first insisted that the war should not be fought and then switched over to a campaign to somehow bring about a peaceful settlement of the war. Its news columns were outrageously pro-South.

Few Union papers actually had correspondents in the field to report on the war and relied instead on reprinting stories from other newspapers that did. The *Daily Journal,* however, ignored Northern newspaper stories and instead published accounts of battles and campaigns from Southern newspapers in an effort to make the Union effort look bad. Defeats on the field were turned into victories by Southern newspapers (including a widely reported and huge Southern victory over the Union Army two days after Gettysburg, a battle that never took place).

These same stories were published daily in the *Newark Daily Journal,* often from the *Richmond Dispatch* and Richmond *Examiner,* the two most important papers in the capital of the Confederacy. All of them often ignored speeches by Abraham Lincoln and Union governors and routinely published speeches by Confederate president Jefferson Davis. The *Journal* adopted New York governor Horatio Seymour, an antiwar leader who vigorously opposed the draft, as one of its heroes and printed many of his speeches. It carefully clipped editorials from other Union papers or public officials who agreed with its antiwar policy and published them together as reaction stories. (Feelings about Lincoln's Emancipation Proclamation were mixed, but a *Journal* compilation of reaction from across the country showed only comments from those opposed.)

The *Journal*'s editors loathed abolitionists and twisted every story or headline to portray them as the cause of the war. They also used the abolitionist label to denounce Union politicians or soldiers. Gen. Ben Butler, as an example, was constantly referred to as "abolitionist hero Ben Butler," and any vile references to blacks or abolitionists were highlighted in sub-heads for stories, including terms such as "nigger abolitionists."

Some of the papers were scathing in their denunciations of Lincoln, such as the *Old Guard*, which called the newly elected president "a deluded and almost delirious fanatic." The *Old Guard* was not alone. President Lincoln was denounced so fervently, and so regularly, that in September 1861 the editors of six New Jersey papers were actually charged with trea-son in a Trenton grand jury presentment and castigated in a report that called them "enemies of the country and more dangerous than open foes." Later, in 1864, after an endless antigovernment editorial barrage, the editors of three more newspapers, the *Newark Daily Journal, Somerset Messenger,* and *Bergen Democrat,* were arrested for "inciting insurrection."

Many New Jerseyans were against Lincoln and the war because they found themselves in a rather odd economic, social, cultural, and political bind. A number of Southerners had gone to school in New Jersey's colleges, particularly the College of New Jersey (Princeton), and were held in high esteem (50 percent of Princeton's students in 1860 were from Southern states), and thousands more vacationed at the beaches at the New Jersey shore and had developed strong friendships with area residents. Many New Jerseyans, particularly in the lower part of the state, had relatives in the Southern states. New Jersey manufacturers and distributors did substantial business with the Southern states, particularly businessmen in Newark, with its busy seaport, where Mary Darcy lived.

Bustling Newark was one of the North's primary suppliers of saddles, shoes, clothing, boots, and jewelry to the Southern states. Manufacturers there were afraid that a civil war would cut off all their customers and ruin them. Distributors of New Jersey–made cereals and cider, popular items in the Southern states, also feared they would suffer and that a civil war would kill off an economic boom that had followed the recession of 1857 that was just starting to benefit New Jersey, according to historian John Cunningham.

Race was another problem that dampened New Jerseyans' enthusiasm for the looming war. Despite a red-hot abolitionist movement in many New England and Middle Atlantic states (the Quakers across the Delaware River had campaigned against slavery since the middle of the eighteenth century), large numbers of residents of the Garden State simply had no great desire to end slavery in the South. New Jerseyans not only did not push for the abo-lition of slavery, but disliked the freed blacks who lived in the state. For generations, slavery had been as much a part of life in New Jersey as it was in Alabama and Georgia.

New Jersey residents had owned slaves for nearly two hundred years. Slaves worked in the different mines and ironworks during the Revolution, many in Morris County. In 1790, more than twelve thousand slaves were in New Jersey (just over 6 percent of the state's population). The number declined as the nineteenth century began and political and religious antislavery movements began in the North, but in 1810 there were still more than ten thousand slaves in New Jersey. That number began to drop sharply after various congressional and state bills to curb slavery and eliminate the slave trade were later passed, and by 1830 the number of slaves in New Jersey had decreased to 2,254.

New Jersey was one of the last Northern states to abolish slavery, in 1846. (Even some of New Jersey's early-nineteenth-century slavery bills were limited and forced slaves to remain in captivity for six years and children to remain as slaves until the age of six. There were still eighteen slaves living in New Jersey when the Civil War began.)

There were never as many slaves in Morris County, where Ed Halsey lived, as there were in seaport areas such as Newark and Elizabeth, but there were always some. At the close of the American Revolution, twenty-four men in Morris County owned a total of sixty-nine slaves. The number of slaves edged upward at the turn of the eighteenth century, to eighty-seven in 1810, ninety in 1820, and eighty-six in 1830. Then, after the passage of the first antislave laws, the number gradually dropped to six by 1850. Col. Joseph Jackson, Halsey's grandfather, owned two women slaves in the 1820s, who each had several children who also worked for him. Benjamin Halsey, another relative, owned two women slaves in 1808. Joseph Hoff, the manager of one of the other ironworks in Rockaway during the Revolution, owned slaves. Several ironworks in southern New Jersey employed slaves before 1800.

The state was hostile toward blacks, and the legislature later entertained a bill to send any newly arrived former slave who remained in the state more than ten days to Liberia. Despite the public outcry in the North over the Dred Scott decision, John Brown's raid on Harpers Ferry, and the Kansas-Nebraska Act, New Jersey was the only Northern state that insisted upon honoring the Fugitive Slave Act and dutifully permitted Southern owners to reclaim slaves they found in New Jersey. White laborers in Newark and other cities were afraid that blacks would work far more cheaply than them and cost them needed jobs. These were among the reasons why slaves seeking freedom via the Underground Railroad found only a few stops in New Jersey and why the state's blacks left the state as soon as they could.

By 1860, there were only 25,318 free blacks in New Jersey, just 4 percent of the population, one of the lowest percentages in Union states. There were few abolitionist groups leading antislavery crusades. In fact, during the 1848 presidential elections, when the antislavery Free Soil Party was very successful in many Northern states, drawing over 33 percent of the vote in most New England states and electing thirteen congressmen, its ticket only drew a paltry 829 votes (.07 percent) in New Jersey.

The deep chasms in support for the war, documented extensively in Rutgers University historian William Gillette's works about New Jersey, and a sense of betrayal at times, annoyed most of the state's soldiers and gave a hard edge to Halsey's wartime papers. The soldiers from New Jersey always felt they had to fight harder than anyone else to prove they were not like many of the residents back home. Still, most of the men in the state responded forcefully to Lincoln's call for troops after the attack on Fort Sumter. (Some were helped by the $100 bonus—slightly less than $3,000 in today's money—the army offered to volunteers.)

Most of the residents of the state were intensely patriotic and fervently believed that the Union had to stay together. Free-labor supporters, and there were millions, feared that a slave-labor system would eventually be reestablished in the Northern states, too, and push them out of jobs. Labor was such an important issue that in 1860 the tariff on imported goods, kept low by Democrats to aid Southern businesses, was a far more important issue than slavery in New Jersey, Pennsylvania, and other Northern states. The Civil War, to many, particularly soldiers and supporters from manufacturing areas, provided the opportunity to crush the despised slave-labor economy once and for all. It was also a chance to preserve the Union, unite the country, a simple but overriding concern to many.

Some were surprised that a war had actually started. Some were startled that politicians, the masters of compromise, had not hammered out yet another political compromise to prevent conflict. Some did not think the men of the South were angry enough over slavery to go to war.

Not Sam Halsey Sr. The patriarch of the Halsey clan, a savvy old politician and veteran of political wars in both New York and New Jersey, saw war on the horizon right after Lincoln's election in 1860 and it frightened him. Three weeks after the election, he wrote his slaveholding son Joseph in Virginia: "North and South are both to blame for this state of things. The remedy no man can confidently prescribe. . . . Everything is jeopardized for the gratification of the worst passions and prejudices of infuriated demagogues and mobs. I do not think there is much to choose between the parties, North and South. All are at fault. When Civil War [starts] insurrections shall drench the land with blood. . . . We are in the hands of God now. May his help be fervently implored by all."

During the last week of December 1860, Halsey begged his son Joseph to leave Virginia and come back to New Jersey. He argued that Joseph had become an accomplished farmer in Virginia and could bring those skills north to begin a prosperous farm in New Jersey. Sam would get him started. But his pleas fell on deaf ears, as the temperamental Joe Halsey, as well as his father-in-law, Jeremiah Morton, a slave trader, prepared for war.

Despite political differences, most New Jerseyans immediately supported the war, despite some newspapers and politicians. Morristown's *Jerseyman,* the home-county newspaper of Ed Halsey, which influenced his views greatly, was behind the war. Its editor, A. A. Vance, wrote: "Rebellion . . . has raised its defiant front—trampling the stars and stripes in the dust, outraging patriotism and bent on disunion . . . the constitution and union must be preserved. Coercion is the last resort, but if the integrity of the government can be maintained in no other way, it must be maintained by force."

War fever swept through the state, overwhelming many antiwar sentiments, and by the time the conflict was over, more than 74,000 New Jersey men had served in the Union Army—one in every ten—and 5,700 of them had lost their lives. That first call-up of troops in 1861 (one of two that year) proved successful. Fourteen infantry companies, a cavalry company, and two artillery batteries were put together, and ten thousand soldiers enlisted. The men were formed into regiments as quickly as possible, and four regiments from New Jersey were among the very first to arrive in Washington, D.C., to protect the capital. Despite the feelings of many of its politicians and newspapers, New Jersey's soldiers were ready to fight.

The outbreak of war thoroughly demoralized Sam Halsey, who slumped back in his chair as he wrote a sad letter to his son Joseph in Virginia, a letter that reflected the feelings of many Northerners that the South had forced the war that should never have been. Sam wrote about the democratic system of government and how it had weathered many storms but was now threatened by the insurrection. The letter exemplified his political beliefs:

"The good of all was paramount to any sectional interest and the majority was supposed to rule among the people. Now particular sections are to be consulted for a policy to govern all and the minority seek to dictate terms to the majority without even asking if they are agreeable or not. The old Constitution of our fathers has heretofore been considered a good bond of Union and now it is treated as a mere rope of sand ill adapted to the wants of those it was made for and wholly powerless to give authority to the government under it."

Ed Halsey, who had just started preparations for the law bar, was talked out of joining the army that spring. Young Halsey, a patriotic young man, just a year out of college, grew more and more heated about the war as it droned on. He, like others, followed events in the *Jerseyman,* which cried out for victory. Wrote *Jerseyman* editor A. A. Vance:

"The dignity of the nation has been insulted and the flag of our country has been trailed in the dust. The period for arguments is past. The war is upon us . . . the country must be purged of these scoundrels. We must fight."

Ed Halsey was one of the most outspoken antislavery young men in Morris County. He had debated the issue with people, North and South, friends and family, for years. Sometimes, dripping with sarcasm, he debated the issue in hot letters to his slaveholding brother, Joe: "You and the southerners say slavery is a blessing? Is it a blessing to the slave, the master or the country?" In biting sarcasm, he told Joseph, "Yes, Negroes are black so they can live in hot climates and have thick lips and degraded looks to make them perfect for domination by whites and they lived far from cities in Africa so they could grow up to be barbaric."

Ed argued against slavery politically and religiously. Politically, he believed that Southern states did not have a right to enforce slave laws because slavery was an affront to man, and that if slavery was legal in states where it existed, it was then illegal in states and territories where it did not exist. Like the lawyer he wanted to become, he used faultless logic in his arguments. He argued at meetings that the South could not believe that it was proper for Congress to legislate slavery in Missouri in 1820 as part of the Missouri Compromise and then believe it was improper for the same Congress to legislate against slavery if territorial residents preferred that in the Kansas-Nebraska Act, ending with a biblical volley about the Southerners that "they gazed with wistful eyes upon the Canaan they were forbidden to enter."

Ed used that same logic to defend the radical views of the Republican Party, telling audiences at political rallies and recruitment sessions that the

Republicans were not formed to "do" anything except defend the rights of Northerners as they started to disappear. If the slave states could ram through the Missouri Compromise and get Missouri into the Union as a slave state, he told recruitment groups, then what was to prevent them from admitting more territories as slave states and then bringing back the African slave trade?

He was rankled about the South. In a letter to his brother Joseph he said the Southern Democrats never compromised about anything concerning slavery. "Give us what we want or we will commit suicide! If you don't give us what we want, we will withdraw from the Union!" he said of the South.

Ed Halsey thought Kansas and Nebraska were perfect examples of the South trying to force something down the throat of the North that was not feasible anyway. Sam and Ed argued with their brother Joe and others that the climate of Kansas and Nebraska was not suitable for growing cotton, tobacco, or sugarcane—slave-produced goods—and that Southerners insisted on the right to bring slaves there just to win a political argument. Ed declared: "If in any state it is found unprofitable to keep them [slaves], then all the democracy between the British Empire and the Gulf of Mexico can't force them there."

His letters show that he felt, too, that the natural political order was changing in America, finally giving the North, and not the South, an upper hand in Congress and that the South had no right to threaten secession just because the political sand had shifted.

A devout Christian, Ed Halsey frequently quoted the Bible in his slavery discussions. "If you believe scriptures, love thy neighbor as thyself, how do you then practice slavery?" he said. "The Bible is full of quotes against oppression of any kind. Slavery is oppression. So if you believe in slavery, how do you believe in the Bible?"

He argued that the agrarian society of the South would not survive the industrial revolution already under way and that Southerners would have to let their slaves go in time anyway, so why not now? He argued that when the nation was populated from coast to coast, immigrants, unable to get work, would move to the South, work cheap, and render slavery useless.

And in one particularly logical and strong letter to his brother Joseph, he railed that "if slavery is such a wonderful institution, why didn't God make us all slaves?"

When Lincoln's second call for troops, three hundred thousand of them, an ocean of blue uniforms, came in August 1862, there was nothing that could stop Ed Halsey, twenty-two, from joining the Army. He had been held down long enough.

That spring, Halsey first tagged along with his brother Sam, twenty-six, who organized meetings in numerous towns to show public support for the war and to raise money to train troops in case of another call-up. These meetings were crowded with intense young men who filled every hall to hear the speakers, young and old, men in and out of office, men who had been in wars and wanted to be in another. Elbow to elbow, hip to hip, men jammed meetings to hear about the army from firebrands determined to make over the country in one tremendous assault on the walls of a Southern Jericho. The meetings were held in churches, schools, or outdoor parks and were usually followed by a public day of support at which a special Union flagpole was raised with great ceremony in a show of support for the Union and its boys in blue.

The Rockaway meeting was one of the largest in the state, attracting over a thousand people to the public square in front of McCarty's Hotel. A local militia group of twenty-four patriotic men fired musket salutes into the air, cheers thundered through the afternoon air, and the American flag was run up the Rockaway flagpole, which was one of the highest in the state at seventy-five feet. Leading the cheers were Sam Halsey Sr., Ed and his brother Sam, and cousins John and Stephen Jackson, who reminded one and all of the vital part the men of Rockaway had played in the American Revolution and would play once again in this revolution for the heart and soul of the nation.

Sam senior, as former speaker of the State Assembly, was always sought out for advice in his hometown and state and was often asked to address crowds. By the summer of 1861, despite his bravado for the Union Army, he was deeply saddened by the war. He declared: "When the history of these times shall be written, many will be immortalized with an everlasting fame that their children will not be proud of. The recklessness with which the southern seceders have sacrificed the peace and prosperity of this once united and happy people will have no parallel in world history."

The meetings had somber religious overtones. Many were preceded or followed by specially called church meetings of different denominations at which ministers and elders leaned far out over the edges of their pulpits, seeking the prayers of the faithful for the boys in uniform. Ministers bestowed generous blessings on any of the men or boys going off to war, and their families were embraced at the end of church services. Religion, politics, and nationalism mixed on the steps of just about every church in the Union.

One of the largest and most ceremonious religious councils in the entire North was at Ed Halsey's church, the Rockaway Presbyterian, where twenty-three ministers from throughout the state, along with dozens of Presbyterian elders from around the metropolitan area, met in special session and approved official, religious resolutions to support the president and the Union Army in its efforts to put down the rebellion. The combination of patriotism and religion, which had been so important in Rockaway during the American Revolution, when most of the men in the Continental Army and militia had held secret meetings in the Presbyterian Church itself, was once again evoked.

Throughout the spring of 1862, Sam Halsey Sr. fretted about his edgy son Ed, who began to spend a considerable amount of time working with local men to put together militia companies and raise money to train them. Sam worried that Ed would insist on going to war if there was another call-up. Ed read the *Jerseyman* and several New York papers every day and talked constantly around the house about the war.

Many others in Ed's position, the sons of the wealthy, did not have to go. So far, in the summer of '62, the Union Army was an all-volunteer army. Despite threats from the War Department about a draft, Sam senior learned from his seemingly endless network of people who knew what was going on in Trenton and Washington that New Jersey would be able to fill its required regiments without one. Even without a draft, his father feared that young Ed, as headstrong as Stephen Jackson in the Revolution and other Halseys in other wars, and a family historian who reveled in telling people about how gallantly the Halsey men had fought in the country's battles, would race off to the army if he had the chance.

Sam had failed miserably in his efforts to talk his older son Joe out of going to war. Right after the attack on Fort Sumter, Sam immediately sent a letter to Joseph at Lessland and begged him to stay out of the Confederate Army. He was terrified that Joe's long-standing hatred of the North and his hotheaded temper would propel him into the first regiments formed in Virginia and that his fury would drive him to rashness in battle that would get him killed.

He also feared the extraordinary influence Jeremiah Morton held over Joe, despite their squabbles. The slave trader was deeply committed to Southern victory in the Civil War because Southern defeat meant the end of his enormously profitable slave trade and the ruin of his plantations. He was such a strident secessionist that he was one of the voting members of the Virginia Secession Convention in the spring of 1861, which voted to pull the state out of the Union. Morton was already a captain in the cavalry and would continue to hold that rank when the Civil War broke out. Sam

Halsey, as a father, knew that Morton would insist that if he was fighting, then his son-in-law had to fight, too. Sam also knew that Joseph would embrace the same attitude, and that his wife, Millie, raised in the traditions of Southern family life, would urge her husband to fight for the South.

"I feel very anxious about you," Sam wrote his son Joe on April 29, 1861, two weeks after the attack on Fort Sumter. "[Sumter will force] a universal uprising of the people of the north and west. [I believe] that an awful waste of life must attend . . . war. Virginia will become a battleground and must be desolated. Your state, being the camping ground, must suffer dreadfully. We tremble for your safety and wish you were safely among your friends and family. Here you would be safe from danger. . . . Where you are, [you are] exposed to destruction. Virginia is doomed. We are entering a fratricidal contest that will not end without rivers of blood."

Sam begged Joseph to leave Virginia and come to Rockaway with his entire family for the duration of the war. He felt that if Joe, Sam junior, and Ed all lived with him, or near him, he could continue to persuade them to stay out of the army. (Sam was aghast much later when he learned that in June 1861 Joseph's young son, Morton, nine years old, had joined a local ceremonial kids' corps, the Culpeper Yellow Jackets, and was proudly showing off his junior-size Confederate uniform to friends and family.)

Sam also had nightmares about his worst fear, that Joe and Ed would one day be firing bullets at each other on a faraway, bloodied battlefield. Sam was appalled at the heated letters his sons had exchanged during the last few years and feared that, as often happens, politics would tear them apart.

In those letters, Ed constantly chided Joe for his beliefs and offered myriad and complex reasons why the South should not secede and why it could never survive as an independent nation. In one letter he mailed just before Christmas in 1860, after Lincoln's election, he told Joseph that the Republicans only wanted to preserve the Union, help people get new land via the Homestead Bill, pass a protective tariff to help American businesses, and let Congress decide on any expansion of slavery. He told Joe the slave states would be committing "political suicide" if they seceded.

Ed wrote his brother: "The cotton states do not produce the grain they consume let along the manufacture they [need]. They must have New England take all the cotton she wants and your surplus must go North, too, or your producers of it will starve." Ed added that the North made everything it needed except cotton, and that if the South seceded, the North could always buy cotton from England. He constantly tweaked Joe about the ability of any collection of Southern states to fight a war, too, and concluded many of his letters arguing that the South was forcing a war that would ruin it:

"Disunion would be followed by the most awful insurrections you ever heard of and no power on earth could stop them, either. War will not make it any better for then ALL will be abolitionists and the South cannot reduce the North to the state of a subjugated province."

Ed also often quoted Scripture in letters to Joseph: "Can any impartial person take these facts and say that slavery is a blessing, a divine institution, state over and over again its advantages? Back it by scripture and think it strange the north does not fall down and worship it?"

Joseph answered all of Ed's letters with angry charges that Northerners would start a war just to punish the South for having its slaves and that any war would always hang on the North's conscience, not the South's. He saved his most vile attack on his brother's logical arguments for discussions of the Declaration of Independence, which Abraham Lincoln, the Republicans, and the Halseys used as their prime attack on slavery, that it declared all men equal.

Joe said men are not equal because some are better looking, richer, shrewder, more talented, more educated, and more religious than others. He concluded with a dart to the heart of his brother. "The Declaration of Independence," he said, "is a damned lie."

The debate never seemed to end.

Sam wanted all such talk to stop, although he knew it could not, and even ended one letter to his son Joe with a promise, a promise he would not be able to keep. "None in my family will fire a shot at the South!"

Sam's worst fears were realized when Lincoln's second call-up came in August. The federal government, now convinced that the war was going to drag on for at least another year, needed fresh troops at once.

Sam senior once again talked Sam junior out of going to war, citing his responsibilities to his new wife, planned family, and his law practice, but it was impossible to dissuade his young son Ed from joining. Ed explained carefully that he had to fight for himself, for his town, his state, and his country. He reminded his father that the men of the Halsey and Jackson families had served their country in every American war back through the Revolution. He was from a long line of patriots, and he not only wanted to go to war, he *had* to volunteer.

The day after Lincoln's August call, Ed heard that a new regiment, the Twenty-seventh New Jersey Volunteers, would be formed and that H

Willis, a friend and neighbor from Rockaway, would lead it. Willis asked Ed if he wanted to help him recruit soldiers for the regiment and, when it was formed, serve as his lieutenant. Ed was thrilled. On most nights in August he finished dinner with his family and walked across the back lawn, eyeing the river as he went, and opened the doors to the long stables to find a horse. He galloped out of the stable, across several acres of Halsey property to the main road, and then galloped off into the night to Denville, Boonton, Parsippany, Butler, and other nearby towns to recruit troops for the new regiment.

Throughout August he also went with Willis to a newly created army camp in Newark where the Twenty-seventh would be trained and housed before going to Washington, D.C., and then the war. Halsey went to Newark again on August 22 as the keynote speaker for a large recruiting meeting. He was good at recruiting, and his patriotic speeches grew better and better as he delivered more of them. At that meeting, eight men signed up for the Twenty-seventh, adding to more than twenty he had already recruited from his hometown of Rockaway and some nearby villages.

Sam senior, worried about his son's energetic activities on behalf of the Twenty-seventh, was afraid that the regiment, sent off from the state's largest city, might be targeted for dangerous combat duty. He did not want his son in combat. Sam reasoned that if he could not stop his son, he could at least get him a job behind the lines in a regiment that might not see any action.

Sam Halsey had one or two regiments in mind that, politicians who knew told him, would stay far from the fighting. (He was also hopeful he could pull strings to land Ed a job as an adjutant, or clerk, a man who did paperwork and never saw battle.) He managed to talk Edmund out of enlisting in the Twenty-seventh right away, to give it some time, and then began his campaign, using every friendship he had cemented over thirty years of New Jersey politics, to find a safe slot for his son in a safe regiment.

At the same time, a Halsey cousin, Alanson Haines, thirty-six, a minister, joined the Fifteenth New Jersey Volunteers, a regiment housed at Flemington that included men from several northwest New Jersey counties, including Morris. The Halseys were very close with the Haineses. Alanson's father, Daniel Haines, was a former governor of New Jersey. Alanson told Edmund that several of Ed's former classmates from Princeton were in the regiment. Sam senior learned that Ed could join it as an assistant adjutant, or clerk, and keep safely away from the fighting and began to push him toward it, using cousin Haines and Halsey's Princeton friends as his major trading card.

Sam senior spent more than a week trying to convince Ed to choose the Fifteenth instead of the Twenty-seventh. For Ed, the advantages of the Twenty-seventh were numerous. (1) It was mostly Rockaway men, boys with whom Ed had grown up; (2) it was clearly bound for the war zones; (3) Ed would be an officer; (4) it was a regiment he had personally helped recruit. Sam argued that Ed's skill as a writer would make him a better adjutant than a soldier in the infantry. He told him that as a college graduate, he would become an officer soon anyway. Sam, the sly old politician, now also put Ed's two sisters to work on getting him to choose the Fifteenth. Finally, Sam orchestrated a family dinner on Friday, August 22, to discuss the regiments. He could now work on Ed in tandem with Cornelia and Anne. By 10 P.M. on August 22, Edmund Halsey decided. It was the Fifteenth. In return for choosing the Fifteenth, though, he had one demand—he had to join right away. He did not want to miss one more day of the war.

Halsey's correspondence and diary indicate that Sam senior made one last, gallant attempt to persuade his son, twenty-two, from joining the army the next morning, but failed. That Saturday morning after breakfast Ed hugged his sisters and bade them goodbye and then walked slowly with his father to the Morris and Essex rail depot in the middle of Rockaway Village, hard against the banks of the river. It was hot. The father accompanied his son to Morristown, trying hard to keep up his own spirits despite his fears, delaying the farewell as long as possible. Before they left, Sam and Ed telegraphed Sam junior, who worked in Morristown, to meet them at the Morristown train depot to say goodbye.

Sam junior was thrilled that Ed was going to war and insisted that if he was going to join the army, he had to buy a brand-new, specially made army uniform at Perry's, the upscale men's department store in Newark. (Perry's specialized in fashionable menswear, such as gauze merino shirts. It was one of the most expensive stores in the country. Their best coats cost $16, more than a soldier's monthly pay, or over $500 in modern currency.)

Sam senior hugged Ed and bade him a tearful goodbye, which Ed said later was one of the most difficult moments of his life. Sam senior was sad, and angry, too, that his youngest son was defying him. Ed pulled away from Sam senior slowly and, with Sam junior, boarded the train. He looked back, his head stuck out of the window, to get one last look at Sam Halsey Sr., the powerful former speaker of the New Jersey Assembly, friend of William Seward, one of the richest men in the state, the courtroom conqueror of the mighty Morris Canal, now just a father, standing all alone, tears in his eyes, desperately fearful for his son's life.

Sam and Ed arrived in Newark in late morning and went to Perry's, where Ed was custom-fitted for the handsomest soldier's uniform either man had ever seen. Sam and Ed went to the train station in Newark and said their goodbyes. Sam embraced his brother warmly and wished him well, then boarded the Morris and Essex train back to Morristown while Ed boarded the New Jersey Railroad for Flemington and the camp of the Fifteenth. He shoved his bag under his seat and stared out the window as the train rumbled through the rolling hills of northern New Jersey, past its many streams and ponds, to White House Station, eleven miles from Flemington, where he got off.

There, Ed found himself in the middle of a chaotic riot of men from every part of the state on their way to join the army. Dozens climbed aboard the few stages leaving the train station, jamming into the tiny compartments, sitting on the roof and on each other. Some walked alongside the stage and every few miles exchanged seats or rooftop perches with the men on it. Halsey was one of them, alternately walking and scrambling onto the top of the stage, which was designed for six people but now carried fifteen men.

Halsey saw many familiar faces at the hastily built recruitment camp, Fair Oaks, at the Flemington Fairgrounds just outside the town. He looked for and found his cousin, Alanson Haines. One of the men who gave him directions was John Emery, another Princeton classmate. He met several other Princeton men and boys he knew from Rockaway and Morristown and nearby Boonton. Later that night, he and others officially took the oath, and he was immediately mustered into the U.S. Army as a private. He was to be paid $13 a month plus a $100 bonus. He also had his first look at army corruption when an officer scribbled Halsey's name on Halsey's pay slip but pocketed the money himself.

Halsey was a welcome addition to Company K, where he was assigned. As a college graduate and veteran writer, he was a natural for the assistant adjutant's job, which was to do all the company paperwork, write all the orders, and keep records of men in and out of the company, men in the hospital, and the payroll lists. He was quick and efficient and well organized. They put him to work the following morning. He also went to town to supervise others in loading incoming baggage and the first day's mail for the troops. He later helped some officers having trouble with their own paperwork. Company K had its assistant clerk.

Rockaway's Edmund Halsey was just one of several Halsey cousins to fight for the Union. Cousin Thomas J. Halsey raised his own regiment, the Eleventh New Jersey, and became its captain. Henry W. Halsey, of the New

York branch of the family, enlisted in the 165th New York Volunteers, Duryea's Zouaves. Gaius Halsey, who was one of several Halseys to race to California in 1849 during the gold rush, returned in 1862 and became a surgeon in the Union Army. Dr. Luther Foster Halsey enlisted as a doctor in 1862 and wound up running a hospital for black troops as well as one of the army's only smallpox hospitals.

There were Halseys on the Southern side of the war, too, in addition to Ed's older brother Joseph. Capt. Edwin Lindsey Halsey was head of a Confederate Army artillery battery and claimed to be the man who fired the first shot of the Civil War, at a Union supply ship headed for Fort Sumter before the actual bombardment started. Robert Seymour Halsey, who went to North Carolina with his brother Ben to be a doctor in 1853, became a surgeon in the Confederate Army. Young Joseph Halsey, just fifteen, a cousin, joined the Confederate Army and was killed when he charged an artillery battery. Some Halseys worked for the Confederate government and state governments, such as Edmund J. Halsey, who was the editor of a newspaper in Alabama before the war and from 1860 to 1865 served as the secretary to the war governor of Alabama.

Ed Halsey had his first chance to see or meet the men of the Fifteenth that first morning. They were an unusual group, an odd mix of young and old men, college graduates and grade school dropouts, lawyers and mechanics, rich and poor, farmers and doctors. Some had served in the Mexican War and some had never fired a gun. Most were at Fair Oaks and some joined the regiment later: Capt. Lambert Boeman, a partner in a Flemington store and the father of two, formed an entire company on his own and brought them to Camp Fair Oaks. Ellis Hamilton, sixteen, was the regiment's youngest soldier. Josiah Grimes was an abolitionist and the assistant head of the Underground Railroad in Morristown. George Libby was an unemployed carpenter. Sam Stahler, sixteen, was the second-youngest recruit. Col. Sam Fowler was a local politician and mining engineer. John Brink left a wife and six children.

Chaplain Alanson Haines, Colonel Fowler's cousin and a cousin to Ed Halsey, was a Princeton theology graduate and minister. His brother joined the First New Jersey cavalry. Enos Budd had traveled with the army in the 1859 campaign against the Mormons in Utah. John De Resmer had fought in the Mexican War. George Justice, thirty-four, was a professional actor. William Cornish joined as a lieutenant. Ira Lindsley was a thirty-four-year-old carpenter. William Monks was a forty-year-old blacksmith.

Joseph Moser, a thirty-six-year-old Tennessee carpenter, was drafted, against his will, by the Confederate Army. He deserted, moved to Philadelphia, and joined the Fifteenth New Jersey to fight against Tennessee. James Whitten was another deserter from the Confederate States of America. Charles Paul dropped out of Princeton to fight. John Clift was from England.

Dr. Charles Hall, one of the surgeons, was Halsey's classmate at Princeton. Dr. Emil Ohlenschlager, another surgeon, one of the first doctors to volunteer for the Union, had served sixteen months already. Col. William Penrose, who would lead the regiment throughout most of the war, was the son of an army major and, officers said, a natural soldier. August Rust was a thirty-year-old German sailor. John Williams was from Dublin, Ireland. Canadian-born Sam Rubadeau was the father of three. The men were as diverse as the country for which they would risk their lives.

Two days later, after he wrote his first letter home, to his girlfriend Mary Darcy, Ed Halsey was issued his soldier's uniform, which he donned proudly (the special uniform from Perry's was delayed in the mails), and on August 29 the Fifteenth New Jersey Volunteers rose at 4 A.M., while it was still dark, and began the long journey that would bring them to some of the greatest battles and slaughter in the Civil War.

At exactly 6 A.M., as the sun came up, the Fifteenth struck its tents and began the march to the town of Flemington with the drum corps of recently recruited musicians briskly playing "The Girl I Left Behind Me" and local residents cheering loudly as the regiment of raw recruits passed by. Later, in Lambertville, Trenton, and Philadelphia, the scene was the same for the Fifteenth, as it was for all the fine young men going off to war. They were cheered in Lambertville, then passed through thousands of strenuously waved American flags in Trenton, before being feted with a scrumptious supper in Philadelphia.

Then, in the middle of the night, they marched through the city of Philadelphia, flags flying and bands playing, as thousands of city dwellers stayed up to cheer them on, some waving flags out of fourth- and fifth-story windows and others showering the soldiers with flowers. Bright torches lit the night sky. Little boys ran after the soldiers as they moved on, eyes ahead and rifles resting smartly on their shoulders. Block by block, yard by yard, they moved out of the city, away from the marvelous music and into the warm summer night and off into the darkness toward the war.

The patriotic music rolled through Edmund Halsey's mind as he marched, smiling at the pretty girls who pelted him and his fellow soldier boys with flowers. Also rolling through his mind was his father's last instruction: somehow, someway, amid the battles and the cannons and the charges and the retreats, he was to find his brother Joseph in the Confederate Army and make sure he was all right.

The call from Abraham Lincoln to the men of the Fifteenth came at a critical time. The Union Army went into the spring of 1862 with a real chance for victory over a Southern army without a solid leader and inferior in arms, supplies, and numbers of men (the North's advantage was better than three to two, as it remained throughout the war). It was a bad spring for the North, however, and things got worse in summer.

The spring was supposed to bring the destruction of Stonewall Jackson's army in the Shenandoah Valley and the capture of Richmond by Gen. George McClellan, thirty-five, the boy wonder of the Union Army. The collapse of the Southern capital might have ended the war. However, the South had promoted Robert E. Lee, who turned out to be one of the greatest and most admired generals in American history, to head the Army of Northern Virginia, and brilliant tactics by him, and hesitation by McClellan, turned the war around.

Lee ordered Jackson to race as swiftly as he could through the Shenandoah to make it safe for the Confederacy, and he did, with lightning-quick movements that resulted in five impressive victories over Union forces in just forty-six days. The valley safe, Jackson then moved to join Lee near Richmond in June. McClellan had ninety thousand men poised in front of Richmond to Lee's eighty thousand, and the Federals had another fifty thousand men under Gen. John Pope moving slowly toward Richmond from the Blue Ridge Mountains.

Lee, seeing himself caught, divided his army in half and sent twenty-four thousand troops under Stonewall Jackson and J.E.B Stuart to stop Pope, which they did (on the very day Edmund Halsey enlisted). Lee then moved on McClellan. Over the course of seven days, Lee drove McClellan away from Richmond. In late August, Jackson and Longstreet, despite miscues at Cedar Mountain that almost cost them victory, defeated Pope again at Second Bull Run and drove his entire army, weary and beaten, back to Washington. In just several months, the rebels had cleansed the Shenandoah of Yankees, united under a popular leader, saved their capital, and driven all Union forces out of Virginia. They were in charge of the Eastern Theater.

The news that clattered into the telegraph office at the War Department, where Abe Lincoln spent many nights, was not much better anywhere else in that spring and summer. In June, the Confederates repulsed a federal assault at Secessionville, just south of Charleston, keeping the vital seaport safe. Confederate ships prowling the seas were sinking Union vessels. Grant's early victories at Fort Henry and Fort Donelson did not make up for his fight with the rebels at Shiloh, where a Union victory cost a staggering thirteen thousand men killed and wounded. Union forces arrived in other areas, such as on islands off the coast of the Carolinas, and just sat and waited.

The inability of the North to win had an ominous ripple effect in Europe, where the leading politicians of several nations entertained the idea of recognizing the Confederate States of America as a separate nation, a diplomatic blow that would have severely hurt the Union. Public support in the North waned, too, as the army was unable to produce a victory, and Lincoln's popularity plummeted.

The Fifteenth New Jersey arrived in Washington on August 30 and found the war easily enough. It was gloomier than the flag-raising ceremonies, church meetings, picnics, parades, and twenty-four-gun salutes back in Rockaway. Halsey's diary picks up in the nation's capital, where he first saw the long lines of wounded and sick staggering back from the second battle of Bull Run in Virginia.

EDMUND HALSEY'S DIARY

September 1864.

September 24th Saturday
Hot.

Advanced about 8 am for a time saw nothing of the enemy. At Mt. Jackson when we came upon their hospitals they were little in force. From the high ground on which Mt. Jackson is located we could look across a level flat, "around which circles the Shenandoah, and see the rebels on the hill beyond. Our artillery practiced on them with some little effect but their right was turned by our cavalry and we were soon in motion across this plain — halting once or twice in line of battle at right angles to the pike.

(Artillery we heard was superseded by order of Gen Sheridan for not attacking sooner or at all on the enemy's right.)

Once across this plain we fell in with the rebels in full retreat and we pursued them till dark through New Market and Sparta — in all twenty miles.

This advance was one of the magnificent sights of the war. From the top of the hills we could see their long lines of battle stretching across the valley and moving away from us. Passing over cleared or plowed fields their lines could hardly be distinguished from the ground save by the flashes of their musket barrels in the sun

This entry of Ed Halsey's diary concerns the Shenandoah Valley Campaign, famous for "Sheridan's Ride," which resulted in the Confederate Army's being pushed out of the valley it had used as a highway throughout the war. (Rockaway Borough Library)

5

A SOLDIER IS BORN

August 30–November 27, 1862

August 30

Started from Baltimore about 2 P.M. and reached Washington at 7 P.M. Cavalry regiments at relay house about to start for Harper's Ferry. We passed sick trains in the way. The regiment lodged at Soldiers Rest. Went with adjutant, two lieutenants and Dr. Sullivan to a house and stayed. City filled with rumors. Heard firing when ten miles from Washington of a battle going on at Centerville.

The trains of sick coming from Washington were not pleasant to see and the low booming of artillery . . . were the first sounds of war.

🖎 [LESSLAND PLANTATION: Sam Halsey Sr. had some relief when he learned that Jeremiah Morton was just as eager to look after his son as he was and won Joseph Halsey a commission as a captain in the commissary unit of Virginia's Orange Rangers and then in the Sixth Virginia Cavalry, where he was responsible for finding food and drink for the army and stayed well out of the line of fire. Morton had probably been under intense pressure from his daughter Millie, Joe's wife, to protect him. Millie Halsey was extremely upset when Virginia seceded and joined the war. She was never a secessionist diehard and feared for the safety of her husband and father, in the cavalry himself, even though in his sixties. Joseph, along with Jeremiah Morton, joined the army just two months after the bombardment of Fort Sumter, within days of Virginia's secession. Sam Halsey Sr., of course, had managed to get Ed a similarly safe job, as a clerk, but Ed wound up in the line of fire anyway.]

September 1

🖎 [Rumors flew through Washington daily that the Confederates, massed
on the other side of the Potomac in Virginia, would attack at any
moment. Halsey and the men of the Fifteenth were constantly prepared
for an invasion that never came.]

September 2

The regiment got our orders to march at a moment's notice. Drew a
new Enfield rifle, cartridge box and equipment, 50 rounds of ammunition
and determined to go along [there is no record that Halsey had ever fired a
gun before the war, even hunting]. Got lunch at a farm house and supper at
a hotel. I wrote to Captain Willis in the evening, put papers together and
packed up, ready to start if ordered. Heard news that General Pope had been
driven back and we would be attacked . . . all the camp lay on their arms.

September 3

[Camp Kearny, in a Washington, D.C., suburb]

Immediate danger passed. In the afternoon, several whole army corps
came up and encamped near us. They were a distressed lot. [They] had not
changed their clothes since leaving Harrison's Landing, four weeks before,
dirty and ragged, officers and men lost all but what they had on them.

The contact between these troops and our men was striking. Our men
looked at them with amazement, little thinking they could soon look and be
exactly like them—browned by the sun about to blackness, no baggage, but
a blanket each and not appearing to need any, a black cup or tin plate their
only cooking utensil. They were just the size of one of our companies, with
muskets bright as silver and maneuvering their whole corps with less fuss
and less time than our regiment would require.

🖎 [The Fifteenth then began to move to camps that they would inhabit
until the wobbly leadership of the army was solidified and some kind of
campaign planned.]

September 5

I rigged up the tent with hay for a bed for the first time. Got dinner at
a farm house before moving.

We started for Camp Kearny about ten. [Heard] that we are to build a
fort here and stay a month. From where we were, we could hear the cannonading over the river sounding like distant thunder. I like this place. First

rate. It is off from the travelled roads. At Camp Kearny we got our meals at private houses (at our expense) and lived well till the old troops came in. Then it was not easy to get anything to eat.

I occupy a wall tent (like Alanson's) with the adjutant. We sleep in the same break (which is under with four stakes with poles across and boards across them). Up till today we had only a blanket over the board but tonight I secured some hay and anticipate a pleasant night.

As to my first [paycheck] . . . the money has been drawn by Captain Hamilton as the signature is "Edward Halsey" and I neither signed it or received the money.

September 7

At 9 A.M. . . . cleaned up, putting on my [new] government pants. Alanson preached at 4 P.M. at the edge of the parade ground. Said: "I know he who hath begun the good work in us is able to [continue]." His congregation was about 300. We had 200 men at work on the fort all day.

Reports that the railroad was torn up between Baltimore and Washington and that the enemy was four miles beyond Rockville, Md.

✍ [These were the first rumors of a massive invasion of the North by Robert E. Lee and the Army of Northern Virginia.]

September 8

Carried night color guard [men who carried the flags of the United States and New Jersey] for first time in our dress parade.

Bad news. Rebels all around us . . . four miles from Rockville . . . 8 miles from here. They crossed the Potomac in three places. Received papers and bundle from Perry's [department store]—two blankets, pants, fatigue coat, three woolen shirts, three undershirts, 12 paper collars.

They say over 100,000 men have passed through Tennallytown and Harper's Ferry. We are about 1½ miles to the northeast of there and can hear the rumbling of the wagons, the bugle calls of the cavalry and in some cases the cheers of the men.

September 10

✍ [Halsey wrote another letter to his father. Sam senior had written him a harsh letter right after he left home for the army and at first refused to correspond with his son. Sam senior was still angry about Ed's decision to join the army. Ed then received a second, softer letter, in which his father asked Ed to search for his older brother Joseph if the army ever moved into Virginia. Sam was extremely worried about both sons. At home, whether in business or state politics, Sam was able to control everybody and everything. In a war, he controlled nothing. The uncertainty of the war, and his inability to get much information, bothered him. He felt that if Ed could just find Joseph, or find out how he was, that knowledge would calm his fears. Sam always worried about his son Joseph because Sam feared his thirty-eighty-year-old son's temper would get him killed. He believed that if Ed, who was even tempered, could find him, he could calm down his brother. In his letter, Ed talked about camp life in general but dropped an ominous line about the movements of Stonewall Jackson.

LESSLAND PLANTATION: Millie Halsey continued to worry about her husband, Joe, who found himself in some of the heaviest early fighting of the war. He rode with Stonewall Jackson's army during the spring of 1862 in its highly successful campaign up and down the Shenandoah Valley in the western part of Virginia, a campaign that booted the Federals out of the valley and made it a safe highway for the movement of troops for the next two years. Joe was with Jackson's army when it destroyed Union forces under Gen. John Pope in the second battle of Bull Run in the summer. The Sixth Virginia Cavalry was detached from Jackson's army when it moved with Lee into Maryland, towards Antietam, and sent to Manassas for special duty.

Even though Joe Halsey was a commissary officer and out of the line of fire, Millie fretted. History, she knew, was full of dead men who were out of the line of fire.

Ed Halsey wrote his father.]

Dear Father,

I have been getting two or three meals a day at a farm house nearby but 75 cents a day is too expensive for a man on $13 a month. I dined today (with the regiment) on a cup of coffee, fresh meat with brown sugar with beans and a piece of fresh beef. Tonight I could have had good beef and coffee. There isn't much style about it but I have come to a very philosophical contempt for food. I have of the $20 given me by you and the $25 [other]—$32 left. I have a good deal of writing to do but it is in the way of learning. All the orders pass through my hands. [Stonewall] Jackson, they say, has gone up through

Maryland to the west of us. Burnside and McClellan are close behind him and he won't come back. You may depend on it.

Sunday night, we could hear troops passing all night. The rebellion is on its last legs and nothing but starvation drove the rebs into Pennsylvania. The way the timber is falling about here is a caution to all concerned. Thousands of axes are at work. It is impossible for an enemy to get through. The tents are as big as a house and the bottoms can be opened up to give air.

Banjos and fiddlers abound and all goes merry as a marriage bell. The men who sold the guards whiskey and got caught have been standing on barrels with knapsacks slung [over shoulders] in the company street today.

September 14

[Halsey had the first of nine brushes with death.]

Had an escape in the afternoon. A colt pistol accidentally went off in the hands of a private. The ball struck the ground to my left, throwing the dirt in my face. It glanced past me and into Major Brown's tent and struck him in the leg of his boot, making a black and blue spot. Its force was stopped by the ground under the tent.

There has been heavy firing all day in the direction of Harper's Ferry and a cavalry now reports a great cannonading that way.

🖋 [That night, Halsey wrote the first of many letters to the *Jerseyman,* a Morris County, New Jersey, newspaper, which kept residents of Rockaway informed about the Fifteenth.]

September 18

Rumors of a great battle during the last two days in western Maryland of which we heard the firing. Papers report a great success.

In the night, about 11 o'clock, a guard of six men were sent out to a farm house where some men of the 113th New York were raising cain.

🖋 [The "great battle" was the bloody encounter at Antietam, fought on Ed's twenty-second birthday. Lee invaded Maryland, after splitting his army in half, seeking a public relations as well as military victory. He felt that a movement into Maryland would not only result in some victories, but convince the people of Maryland, which surrounded Washington, D.C., to swing over to the Confederate side. Lee also thought the invasion of Maryland would scare Northerners into believing that his army could later swing deep into the North and, at the same time, draw off federal forces from assaults in Virginia to meet him. McClellan, even though accidentally discovering Lee's plans, and knowing of the army split, failed to pursue the Confederate Army vigorously and did not encounter Lee until the Southern general surprisingly decided to make a stand behind Antietam Creek, near Sharpsburg, with just nineteen thousand men (and twenty-one thousand on their way), against a force of over seventy thousand Federals.

Brutal fighting took place all day, with charges and countercharges through cornfields and over dangerously exposed stone bridges. So many sheets of bullets cut the morning Maryland air that thousands of stalks of corn were cut evenly in half by them. The creek ran red with the blood of men from both sides. Despite superiority in numbers, McClellan could not defeat Lee. In late afternoon it appeared that the Federals would crush Lee's flank, but the arrival of Confederate general A. P. Hill, wearing his familiar bright red shirt, and his men, after a forced march from Harpers Ferry, routed the Federals.

It was one of the single bloodiest days in American history, with dead and wounded from both sides totaling over twenty-six thousand. Lee planned a counterattack against the much stronger federal army the next day, but was dissuaded from doing so by Stonewall Jackson and James Longstreet and withdrew. McClellan, with twenty-four thousand troops still in reserve and twelve thousand newly arrived troops, had an opportunity to crush Lee on the second day, but chose not to engage.

Technically, the mutual slaughter at Antietam was a draw, but the fact that the seemingly invincible Lee had been stopped, and that the Army of Northern Virginia was repulsed and driven out of Maryland, signaled a dramatic turn in the momentum of the war, at last giving hope to the Union Army and the public.

Meanwhile, in Camp Morris, outside Washington, the Fifteenth was held back in anticipation of an attack on the nation's capital. Halsey's diary and letters from that week, and for many weeks, reflect the rather casual, almost summer-camp atmosphere in the Fifteenth, an atmosphere that would soon change.]

September 20

🖋 [LESSLAND PLANTATION: There was no summer-camp atmosphere at Lessland, the home of Ed's older brother Joe, a captain in the Confederate Army who had been with the rebels for over six months. Captain Halsey, slumped over the neck of his horse, sweating profusely, arms and legs weak, arrived home at his plantation, extremely ill from typhoid fever. He had been sent home on furlough after becoming sick at Centreville, where the Sixth Virginia Cavalry was ordered following its long and successful campaigns with Stonewall Jackson. Doctors in the army camp believed he could get better treatment and rest at home on his plantation than he could in the middle of a makeshift army hospital tent.

The typhoid fever that knocked Joe Halsey out of the service was his second major illness. In December 1861, he was sent home with pneumonia, barely making it back to Lessland alive. Halsey spent several months recuperating and then, against doctor's orders and still feeling weak, returned to the Army of Northern Virginia. His wife argued long into the night in an effort to make him stay home, but he insisted on returning to the army. This second time, bedridden for several months with the fever and at one point near death, no one who knew him thought he would ever go back to the Army.]

September 21
    [Letter to Ed's girlfriend]

Dear Cousins (Mary),
    My health is perfect. The colonel and Major have just told me I am growing fat and I feel so myself. I turn in about ten or eleven P.M. and sleep like a log with the sounding of reveille or "peas upon the trenches" [when I] turn out and go to the company and get a cup of coffee and whatever they claim to have—if I want it. By that time it is 6:30 and the reports come in which I have to consolidate and take the regimental report to brigade headquarters. I generally get through with them by nine and after that I have so far had enough writing to do to keep myself busy all day. This is pretty well [routine]. At dress parade at sundown I act as right guard at guidon after which I distribute my details—little slips with the numbers of men each company is to furnish for guard or fatigue duty the next day and get my supper. We have had good bread and good coffee, fresh meat once a day and with money to get potatoes, catsup, ginger cake I get along first rate. Tell father the [weather] changes here do not affect me. I do not even have a cold.

September 23
    Received photographs. [These were the photos Halsey sat for when he first arrived in Washington, D.C. Most men in the service, North and South, had their pictures taken and sent home to family and loved ones.]

Dear Father,

The proclamation issued by the President [the Emancipation Proclamation, first released on September 22, 1862] is either the best or the worst thing which could be done—best if it does not irritate the border states or divide us.

My health remains very good. I will give you a sample of a day's fare: for breakfast a cup of tea, fresh bread and beefsteak cooked in a spit. I also invested in a ginger cake. For dinner, fried beefsteak (cooked by the company cook), potatoes, bread and an onion. For supper, splendid soup thickened with good bread and a slice of bread and molasses. Our private cook (John P. Forbison, of Franklin) being on guard and representing the stock of potatoes low. I will indulge tomorrow morning in a breakfast of hot biscuits and pancakes outside the lines where some of the line officers board.

The month I have spent in service has passed so rapidly I cannot realize it has been so long but I have learned to distinguish between essentials and non essentials.

The fort we will have done in two or three weeks and an extra detail of 200 men has been made to build a road between it and Fort DeRussy about a mile off.

✒ [Lincoln had wanted to issue the Emancipation Proclamation, which freed all the slaves in the Southern states at war with the Union, for months, but he was convinced that its issuance while the North was losing the war would appear to be a desperate act. He needed a victory of some kind and decided Antietam, even though a draw, was it. The president hailed the Antietam engagement as a great Northern victory and then issued the proclamation. The document signaled a new political factor in the war. It was no longer being fought only to preserve the Union, but to free the slaves and change the entire political and cultural life of the nation.

The proclamation, which would become effective January 1, 1863, raised the issues of the American Civil War into something more than an effort by soldiers in the North to put down a rebellion by soldiers in the South. It turned the war into a moral and cultural crusade, an almost religious war of the righteous with the elimination of slavery and the slave system, and a whole new American political and social system, as its goal. It would not only add a second wave of support to the war, but generate the enlistment of nearly 180,000 black soldiers, who would, in the future, give the Union Army much needed help, playing an important role in the North's ultimate victory.]

October 1

The regiment embarked on the cars about 3 A.M. I slept til six and when I woke we were a good ways from Washington. Reached the relay house at 7:30 and Frederick, Maryland, at 6 P.M. passing 12 or 14 regiments. Stops were frequent. Slept at night in the baggage car.

Some of the people of Frederick showed themselves very generous to us. Some of our men went to private houses and were hospitably entertained by those who refused to take anything in return and who fed as many as they possibly could. The people were very pleasant spoken and good looking. [John] Hilt and the hospital Steward and I obtained a nice supper at some private home.

October 2

Left Frederick at 3 P.M. with light marching order. I carried a blanket, canteen and extra shirt. Bill Jackson (a colored servant to another officer) carried three days rations in my haversack (a knapsack)—one blanket, overcoat, morning report book were fastened in the adjutant's horse which Lt. Col. Campbell (who had just joined us from the 3rd Regiment) rode. Left adjutant sick at Frederick. We crossed the first range of hills and camped for the night in an open field to the left of a road about seven miles from Frederick. We left the city with flags flying from every other horse.

October 3

We marched 16 miles over South Mountain through Boonesborough, came to Antietam and through to Bakersville. We passed trees marked by balls, ambulances, hospitals, dead horses, fresh graves and some of the men saw dead rebels yet unburied. The roadway was very dirty indeed and the day very warm. Got a good supper at a farm house and camped in the open air as before. We passed through the "corn field" noted in the Antietam battle.

October 8

[Letter to brother Sam]

Dear Sam,

The probability is sure that we will move into Virginia in a few days when we will probably be the reserve corps. The other regiments are pretty thin. Col. Ryerson has recovered entirely and looks a little more flinty than he did. [Col. Henry Ryerson, of the Tenth New Jersey, was one of the most popular officers in the state].

I am dirty as a pig. I weighed yesterday—135 lbs, as much as I ever weighed.

🖎 [THE WAR: Confederates under Gen. Braxton Bragg invaded Union territory in Kentucky, the second invasion of the North in a month. They were turned back by Federals under Gen. Donald Buell in a brutal battle that saw one-quarter of the rebel army killed or wounded. This second halt of Southern forces, added to Antietam, earned more support on the home front for the war.]

October 9

Went over with Lt. Emery to see (cousin Alfred) Jackson and had a long talk with him. I like the officers of the 4th very much.

There are a number of negroes, servants, in the brigade, and they with the men have open air concerts and dancing abounds every evening if [there is] moonlight.

🖎 [Many freed blacks in New Jersey, mostly cooks and servants, followed men for whom they worked into the army. They were not soldiers and were not allowed to fight, but helped with mess and worked as valets for the officers. Blacks did not come into the army as soldiers until 1863.]

October 13

[Letter to the *Jerseyman*]

Mr. Editor,

Since the last army correspondence from this regiment a great change has taken place in our situation and condition. Then we were "playing soldier" with large and comfortable tents to live in, and everything which could be reasonably expected. Within the lines of the defenses of Washington, and all fear of invasion from the northwest secured by the victory of Antietam, we felt as secure as we would at home.

Now we are a fighting brigade, which is a part of a fighting corps, and posted in the front only a mile from the Potomac, whose opposite bank is lined with rebel pickets, while the news of the raid into Pennsylvania, and an occasional boom of a cannon to the west of us tells us that any hour our courage may be put to the test. Our "Sibley's" (tents) are exchanged for the frail shelter tents which the men brought with them on their backs, and the officers are crowded into the few wall tents which slender transportation and new regulations have left us. The knapsacks of the regiment are in Washington and in all probability we will have to do with what we have on til active operations for the season are over. The men . . . are in excellent spirits.

The final orders for our departure came to camp late in the night and at six o'clock the next morning the regiment, with three days rations in their haversacks, and in light marching order, were filing down through the woods towards the capitol, where they expected to embark for Frederick immediately, but so many troops were before us bound for the same place that it was three o'clock the next morning before our train slowly moved out of Washington. After a tedious ride, at a rate which Artemas would characterize as that of a well conducted funeral procession, we arrived at our destination at nightfall and encamped with thousands of others in the open fields. Here some fondly hoped our travels would end—for awhile at least.

The next afternoon with three days rations of hard crackers and smoked pork in our haversacks, the regiment left Frederick for "the front" leaving our adjutant, who ill health would have made any other man ask for a furlough, behind us to recruit. Our road lay through a beautiful section of country in a high state of cultivation and as we looked from the top of a high hill at the city we had left lying in the center of a wide and fertile valley, it seemed not so strange that the rebels should have risked so much to gain it. We camped for the night after a seven mile march on the ground.

[The next day we marched 16 miles through Antietam] and when you consider that it was done on a broiling hot day, with the trees so thick that a captain could scarcely see the rear of his company and without losing a man, you will acknowledge it was something to be proud of.

The vestiges of the great struggle which had taken place were thickly strewn along the whole route. Long trains of ambulances passed us bearing the wounded to Frederick. Every large building seemed filled with those of both armies. Trees mangled by balls, newly made graves and half burned carcasses of horses showed how desperate and destructive had been the struggle whose event had secured the safety of Maryland. Some of the rebel dead were not discovered and buried until two weeks after they had fallen.

We have been placed in the 1st N.J. brigade [Sixth Corps]. The day before yesterday, the 23rd N.J. (enlisted for nine months) came up to join the Brigade, making it about three times as large as it was before we reinforced it, so much had the Peninsula service and recent battles reduced its number.

Our camp is on a high hill, commanding a view of a dozen camps, whose fires at night resemble those of a large city. It has the great disadvantage of being without any shade which would have been a luxury, since the first week were here the weather resembled August more than October. The old regiments are in a pleasant grove about 200 yards south. Among them are a few still left who went from Morristown seventeen months ago, whose faces are always welcome with us and their adventure are well worth listening to.

The brigade is hourly expecting marching orders, but when we will move, and where to, no one can tell.

🖋 [THE WAR: In a long and heated letter, Lincoln accused General McClellan of being overly cautious in his conduct of the war. Lincoln was already furious with McClellan for not chasing and destroying Lee's army after Antietam. He urged McClellan to continue pursuit of Lee and to attack Richmond.]

October 16
Dear Father,

You have no idea what effect it has to think, to know, that one has friends who are thinking of him and willing and to do what they can for him if he needs assistance. Perhaps this is the reason I have never felt discouraged or downhearted since I entered the service. The nearest I ever came to it was when I received your first letter in which you seemed to feel as though I had deserted you. This now is the only reflection which causes me to think I may have mistaken my duty. I surely did not intend to do it. This is a time when every one is expected to make sacrifices and I cheerfully do what is required. The danger is not so very great as one may suppose.

The first New Jersey Brigade now numbers only one fourth the number it had at the beginning ... many die in hospitals from diseases caused by their own imprudence or from diseases which would have caused their death any-where. Not a few deserted and not a few are killed in action. Ogden Ryerson's company never had a man killed. Of the 17,000 killed, wounded, missing and captured in the seven days fight, only 825 were killed, less than one twentieth. There are only 350 left of the 1st N.J. Cavalry but an officer tells me they never lost in action but 20 or 30 men and but two officers, Tom Haines and Austin. [Tom Haines was the younger brother of Halsey's best friend, Alanson Haines, and the two later searched for Tom's grave.]

A soldier soon learns to make the best of everything. A day has not passed in which I have not had "my liver turned over" by something.

October 17
    Read Casey's tactics through School of the Soldier (20 copies of the book were issued). [This activity was part of the ad hoc officers' school Colonel Penrose set up, with himself as teacher, because he felt his officers were trained so badly.]

October 18
    [Letter to Sue]

My Dear Sister,
    We have been in this place now two weeks and begin to feel quite at home. How long we are to stay here is very uncertain, probably not more than a day or two as it is supposed that there will soon be a grand advance crossing the river at Harpers Ferry, Dam No. 4 (where we are) and Williamsport and marching down the Shenandoah Valley. All the troops around our division have moved off somewhere and we expect orders every hour. As one of the old soldiers told me the other day, a man can't go off to wash himself without risk of his regiment leaving him. Thursday there was a continual cannonading going on to the South and Southwest of us which you will find accounted for in Friday's *Times* either as the crossing at Shepherd's or the advance to Charlestown.
    The soldiers of the old regiments say the accounts given of the terrible slaughter of the rebels at Antietam and the destitution are not at all exaggerated. Many were so run down that the least wound killed them. Their raid into Pennsylvania was a matter of necessity with them. All a great many of them had to eat before there was corn taken from the fields where it was growing. They fight well though, considering the differences and quality in their supplies.
    The knapsacks of the men came in last night and a good many of them not being marked there was a good deal of "smouching" and a good many things were lost. I was lucky enough to get my valise and all the blankets which I did not bring with me in the box of adjutant's things and they all came on together. I hope to continue the dodge but it may be my luck as it has been that of others to lose everything which I have not on at the time or at least make a selection of what I want to carry and let the rest go by default in some of our hasty marchings. The first thing to look after is one's

blanket and overcoat, haversack and canteen. With these, he can get along for two or three weeks without much trouble—at least I did—if he can get an extra set of underclothes that comes next. Extra pants [and] boots are handy but not so very essential. I do not know what I would do without the colored woolen shirts I have. They do not get dirty in two or three weeks and they do not show it and are easily washed.

I have a good many necessaries stored in my pockets and in the drawers of the adjutant's desk which since the adjutant stopped at Frederick sick I have the charge of and MUST go with the regiment if anything goes.

I breakfasted on fried pork, fresh beef and gravy and coffee, which is worse than usual for us. My appetite is good and I feel good and better than I did at Camp Morris or at home. The life seems to agree with me as I am heavier by considerable than when I left.

The "church call" has just sounded but as the meeting house is the big tent and it is sprinkling preparatory to a thunder shower, I think I will stay where I am. This morning there was a Brigade inspection which in strictness requires the attendance of every man not in the hospital but I was left to receive orders which might come in and seized the chance to take a good wash and put on some clean clothes for the first time in ten days and feel like a new man. Do not think by this that I am at all slovenly in my habits more than the rest. The fact is we do not often have a chance to exhibit our fondness for water and I feel what a luxury it is.

I have been interrupted. There is a report that one Morris Hammond, a citizen, was in custody for selling brandy to the soldiers of the 15th and was told to have him fed and safely kept and his case was attended to. I am now writing for Company supplies and will then finish it and have it signed or take or send it over. This is a fair sample of my duties on Sundays spent in camp.

The weather is quite cool, nights especially, and sometimes it looks like fall but except mornings have not felt like having a fire. I sleep on a bed full of straw, one blanket under and one blanket and overcoat over me.

I am glad to hear from Sill [the family's nickname for his sister Cornelia] that a picture has been made of the glen and hope you will keep it. I have often wished I could paint for that very purpose.

Don't wait to write. I wish I could write two or three a week. Send me all the news and believe me ever. Give my love to all your family and enquiring friends.

October 21

I heard firing more or less in the night and through the day, a [sign] that we will not stay here long.

🖋 [He was right. Lincoln wrote an angry letter to McClellan on October 25 after the general told him the army was unable to move because its horses were fatigued. "Will you pardon me for asking what the horses of your army have done since the battle of Antietam that fatigue anything?" Under extreme pressure to do something, McClellan ordered the Army of the Potomac to begin crossing the Potomac into Virginia the next day.]

October 28

🖋 [LESSLAND PLANTATION: Tragedy struck at Lessland when Joseph and Millie's seventeen-month-old babe Jane died of pneumonia. It was the second child the couple had lost. Another baby, Samuel Beach, named after Joe's father, had died in 1857.

Halsey received letters from his family, friends, and girlfriend, Mary, frequently, but had had none since his enlistment from his older brother Abe, living in California where he sought to make his fortune in the gold fields following his marriage to an Indian woman. Halsey wrote Abe at his last known address, Toulamange Chinese Camp, outside San Francisco, and complained that he had not heard from him. He told his brother that he did not think the war would end soon.]

My Dear Brother,

Whether the war will be finished in a year or two years or ever no one can tell. My own impression is this: that in that time the rebels will be too much reduced to put a large army in the field and the war will be confined to guerrilla warfare. The Army of the Potomac is now an immense one composed, to be sure, of a great many unreliable recruits but with a seasoning of the best troops the world ever saw together. The rebels are hungry and half clothed but . . . they fight well, better, perhaps, than ours would under similar circumstances.

I could tell you long stories about our provision supplies and how we live generally but it would be nothing new to you, who have gone through the same mills. I once detested pork but have learned to like it from having to go without that or anything. . . . At Camp Morris (our old camp) we had enough to eat of pretty good quality. Still, it was only playing soldier. [The food has changed] to hard tack [and the tents] from Sibleys to shelter tents. There, we had plenty of water and used to keep neat as pins. Now we are content to wash occasionally and dress as warm as possible without any great regard to features. I drew a dress coat with the rest yesterday and put it on right over the other. I think I can wear all the clothes I have on my back and may do it yet.

I was interrupted in the above by an order from Brigade Headquarters. We are to hold ourselves in readiness to move tomorrow morning if such orders should arrive from Division headquarters. This may be only a flash in the pan but still it is expedient to be ready.

🖋 [In a postscript, Halsey told Abe that his boyhood friend Aldus Neff had died from typhoid fever in the Peninsula campaign, suffering badly and soaring up to two hundred pounds in weight just before the end.

October passed slowly for Halsey and the men of the Fifteenth New Jersey. They constantly heard battles in the far distance, were constantly told they were going to move to the front, and constantly got ready for action. Halsey wrote that the officers were frequently told orders would arrive any minute for a move—and never did. Nothing ever happened.]

November 4

[The Fifteenth moved into Virginia and headed into the Shenandoah area.]

Cannonading in the evening to the west of us. Four of our men were arrested for marauding.

🖋 [November 4 was election day and the results severely depressed Abe Lincoln, who received them from the War Department's telegraph office. The president, a masterful politician who managed to get elected with only 39 percent of the popular vote in a four-way race in 1860, feared defeat in many districts in the off-year elections, and he was right. The people were tired of the war that would not end and, in November of 1862, did not think the Emancipation Proclamation had the power they would later come to believe it did.

The announcement of the Proclamation had, in fact, angered just as many Northerners as it pleased. In New Jersey, split over the war as always, the 1862 political campaign became a nasty, race-baiting election in which speaker after speaker warned voters that hundreds of thousands of freed slaves would move to New Jersey, taking jobs away from whites. "The present contest is a contest between the white and black races for supremacy. President Lincoln and the abolitionists have made it so," editorialized the *Belvidere Journal*.

The Democrats swept to victory in many pro-Republican areas in New Jersey and the Union, winning thirty-four additional congressional seats nationally and cutting the huge Republican majority in the House of Representatives in half. Democrats won up and down the Hudson River in New York, the state whose electoral votes had made Abe Lincoln president in 1860, and elected Horatio Seymour governor. The worst blow of all for Lincoln occurred when the Democrats were victorious in his own home congressional district, in Sangamon County, Illinois, where his longtime friend Leonard Swett, one of the men whose hard work had made Lincoln president, was defeated.

Halsey's home state of New Jersey turned on Lincoln, too. Democratic gubernatorial nominee Joel Parker won election in a landslide. The Democrats won four of the five contested congressional seats and swept into a majority in the state legislature, guaranteeing the election of a Democratic U.S. senator (state legislatures elected senators in that era). The voters in Halsey's home congressional district, whom he counted on for support of the soldiers in the field, turned on Lincoln, too. Democratic congressional nominee Andrew Rogers, a Newton lawyer who conducted a highly charged campaign of race baiting and Lincoln bashing, defeated Republican nominee Ed Linn.]

November 5

[The Fifteenth camped near Berryville, Virginia.]

We had fine view of Ashby's Gap, but our way was through a country made desolate. Now the season would naturally make it [pretty]. Houses had planted little or nothing. On coming to a halt, I secured a rail before fences were broken and when camp was formed we had a grateful fire and a cup of coffee [with it]. Supper was of hard tack, a ginger cake and the remnants of pork.

✒ [THE WAR: A frustrated Lincoln fired the slow-moving McClellan on November 7, 1862, and replaced him with Ambrose Burnside, a move that stunned and upset the army.]

November 6

[A local farmer] had a friend in Confederate Army General James "Pete" Longstreet's division that he heard from lately. He and his friend were well, the latter in Richmond. [The farmer] had heard about us. He evidently sympathized with the rebels and knew all about them. He said his whole stock of sheep were taken from under his eyes the night before, that coffee and sugar were unknown and the last whiskey he saw sold was not two weeks ago and brought $10 per gallon.

We marched about 12 miles and camped after dark on the Manassas Railroad near White Plains. The fires of the division camp at night looked like the lights of a great city. The day was raw and cold and an overcoat not uncomfortable on the march. My cold was getting better. The view of Manassas Gap was beautiful as were several views of the mountains. We saw a few fine houses but the country generally seemed desolate and barren.

The rebels had swept all the single men and most of the married ones into the army and seized all the horses and wagons and made off with the pigs, sheep, poultry and fences.

November 8

We are waiting for supply trains. The snow is quite thick upon the ground but the air is clear and warmer. I had my desk put up and acted as clerk for the major, who tried to [conduct] a court martial for the men who were absent with leave a few mights since. [The ad hoc court-martial was called by Colonel Campbell to punish men for "marauding" and to stop others from doing so in the future.]

Heard that the railroad is open to Washington again.

November 10

General McClellan accompanied by General Burnside (who is said to have superseded him) with a troop of other officers, aides and orderlies, passed rapidly through the camps where the troops were drawn up to receive him and was enthusiastically cheered. He rode with his hat off, bowing to the troops as he passed them.

🖋 [The roars of approval that went up from each regiment as the swashbuckling McClellan rode past could be heard for miles. The personal popularity of McClellan among the troops was impressive, despite his long list of defeats and general ineffectiveness. Time and again, as the army engaged in battles in the future, troops would fondly remember the "little general" and wish that he were back in charge.]

November 11

In the afternoon, I took a walk with Alanson to the top of what I suppose is the end of our campsite. From the top we could see 15 or 20 miles to the East over a flat, desolate looking country. The Blue Ridge far to the west and the smoke of camp fires to the south towards Warrenton. Nothing living could be seen but soldiers and army trains which seemed innumerable. One train going towards Warrenton had a mile and a half of its length in sight. New Baltimore was as mean and intense a place as ever I saw. The houses were dilapidated with windows broken and occupied by soldiers. Occasionally an old woman showed herself who corresponded with her surroundings.

November 21

[Letter to the *Jerseyman*]

Dear Editor,

Having marched over 125 miles on the "sacred soil," we are now stationed near Stafford Court House, Virginia [about twenty miles south of Washington and about ten miles north of Fredericksburg, Virginia] and wait for supplies, or dry weather, or for some other good reason, before continuing our march in the rebel stronghold. The regiment crossed the Potomac at Berlin, Md., on November 2d at 7 o'clock in the morning and I could not but think how many of us who trod the pontoon that Sunday full of hope and enthusiasm would never recross that Rubicon, and wonder if the advance was destined to meet with no better success than those of the last campaign.

Nevertheless, remembering scriptures, "It is the third time that wins," that with an army largely re-enforced, and with the experience gained in former efforts, we felt as though success must attend us.

Our march down the eastern side of the Blue Ridge . . . was over country which, in times of peace, must have been beautiful, but the war had swept away the young men into the army and the few tilled fields and lonely scattering of houses so different from what we see in Jersey gave it, to me at least, the appearance of desolation. But if I call that desolate, how can I describe the region between the Bull Run mountains and this place? Pine thickets and barren clay wastes with here and there a wretched looking house, were the main features of what might well be called a wilderness. The few half way respectable farm houses we passed were visited by stragglers, which are more or less numerous in every army, and everything in the line of eatables which the rogues could lay hands on carried off. No one who accompanied us in this march can deny that the fruits of this rebellion are bitter, though it is to be feared that it is tested by the innocent as well as by the guilty.

Day before yesterday the regiment was sent out two miles to the east on picket, and is still on that duty, having full benefit of the rain which has not been so very violent, but most providing STEADY ever since they left camp. On the road out we pass directly by the Court House, Tollbooth and Clerk's Office. The Court House and Clerk's Office are completely gutted—sashes and doors broken, book cases torn down and the records of the County strewn over the floors and yards, kicked about by the soldiers who pick out some of the oldest as curiosities to send home.

It is a sad sight, for a federal even, to look at papers which age and association has made almost sacred, and which are of inestimable value, trampled in the mud and scattered to the four winds of heaven. Still they follow the fortunes of war and are but a small loss to the treasure . . . which this country has lost in this rebellion.

The Morris County boys, sent to Harper's Ferry sick, are all well and in good spirits. Lieut. Connent has been acting for the past month as adjutant of the regiment in the absence of our old adjutant. The major is well and continues as a great favorite as ever with the boys.

[We hope] that you will have some more showy achievements of the regiment to publish than mere marches. . . .

November 23 (New Stafford Court House)
The brigade was drawn up for church at 11, the band playing. Alanson preached from text.

At noon, Pvt. Peter Cartwright died of typhoid fever (the second death in the regiment). There was quite a lot of difficulty in getting boards for a coffin for him but we at last made one from boxes and he was buried just after dress parade with the customary three volleys and band returning, playing Yankee Doodle.

November 27 Thanksgiving Day
A clear, beautiful day, Thanksgiving Day. I rode a horse to Aquia Creek for the captain to come home and had a ginger cake for dinner. At

camp I [was happy] to find three letters. We were able to see steamers in the Potomac.

Bread sells at about 25 cents a loaf and other things in proportion. I do not wonder at delays and halts since I have been here. Railroads are torn up and a regiment ten miles from its supplies with only two or three teams to haul them would starve to death.

6

FREDERICKSBURG

December 5–31, 1862

[The Union Army's new commander, General Burnside, was a colorful figure to his men. Adorned with a thick mustache and wide muttonchops on his cheeks (linguists soon turned Burnside's chops into "sideburns"), he walked about camp boldly with a large floppy hat. He had had some success in South Carolina and was popular with the men, mainly because, a prodigious eater himself, he paid special attention to food supplies. He had a well-organized plan to capture Fredericksburg, Virginia, a key transportation center between Richmond and Washington, and then, from there, sweep Robert E. Lee's army off the field and end the war—on paper. The Army of the Potomac was to move down the Rappahannock River on the north side, moving in the tidal basins along the riverbanks for easier traffic, and, somewhere in the vicinity of Fredericksburg, cross the river on pontoon bridges and storm the city.

Reports were that only a few regiments, less than two thousand men, were guarding Fredericksburg and that Lee's army was a good week's march from the town. Stonewall Jackson's army was farther away still, somewhere amid the winding creeks and deep forest glens of the Shenandoah Valley. All Burnside needed were 120,000 soldiers and the pontoon bridges. He had the soldiers. He did not have the bridges.

The delay of the bridges at Fredericksburg was symbolic of the incessant bungling that went on behind the Union lines, bungling that Halsey chronicled again and again in his diary. This time no one thought to tell the men responsible for the delivery of the bridges that they had to move quickly to beat Lee's men to the city. Unaware of how critical time was, they moved slowly. Finally, when ordered to hurry, the officers in charge of the bridges sent messages back and forth to Washington about them.

Instead of using the newly installed and highly effective military telegraph lines, hanging right above them, which could send messages in minutes, they decided to send messages and orders by mail. The mail took a week. That delay alone set the date of the attack back nearly ten days. Then it rained and construction on the bridges was halted and delivery became impossible because of muddy roads. The rain was followed by misunderstandings and botched orders. The bridges were scheduled to reach Burnside at Fredericksburg on November 14. They finally arrived near the end of the month. During that time the Fifteenth New Jersey and other regiments repeatedly prepared to move and did not. In early December, as rumors flew that they were going to Fredericksburg, the Fifteenth New Jersey finally moved out.

The men of the Fifteenth, especially Halsey, were eager to attack Fredericksburg. They had been in the U.S. Army for over three months and had not been directly involved in a single battle. They wanted a piece of the war, and they would soon get it.]

December 5
  [Letter to Sue]

My Dear Sister,

Yesterday, we marched from our old camp ground near Stafford Court House about 16 miles to this place which they tell me is two miles from the county seat of King George—the object of the movement of our corps was to cross the Rappahannock below Fredericksburg and make an attack on it from the flank. We passed the boats for the pontoon bridge a mile or two back and there was a report that the crossing was to be effected today. This morning about 9 it commenced raining and it has rained steadily ever since (it is now 3 P.M.), what effect this will have on our future movements remains to be seen. The few weeks dry weather we had dried up the roads very much so that with the exception of some holes and gullies it was tolerable—good enough for us to bring along most of our baggage. One of our teams, though, got fast and had to leave part of its baggage to be sent for this morning with the commissary stores of the Brigade which were also left behind.

From appearances, the present will be a long tedious storm, the beginning of winter, and any great movement by land will be impossible though it may be attempted. We have been to work all this morning trying to get settled and have our tents planted on the top of a hill ridged with old tobacco rows and covered with a dense growth of pines which have sprung up since it ceased to be cultivated. The regiment lays immediately at its foot and across the little valley is Brigade headquarters. I have not my desk out yet but am writing on a piece of paper on a pass book I carried for such an emergency in my pocket.

I cannot express how much I was delighted to get your "family letter" and hope you will often repeat it. Tell Fred whenever we get to a place where I have better opportunities for writing I will suitably acknowledge his favor as well as his father's. If I could get such a letter once or twice a week it would do me good. [Fred was Fred Beach, son of Ed's older sister Susan. Fred was in grade school and moving along rather slowly. His parents fretted about his academic progress and urged Ed, a stellar student, to encourage their son. He tried through letters, often not answered. Later, as the war continued, young Fred began to write his uncle more often.]

We had a mail last Tuesday but there were no letters for me. Three Observors from the Doctor relieved me somewhat from the idea that I was the only one whose friends did not remember him. Perhaps I expect too much in hoping to hear from home every mail, though the feeling is natural. You have all done a great deal for me in this line.

If we march in [this rain] it will be beyond description—horrible—it may cause us to go into winter quarters and then we can soon put up log houses and live as comfortable as you please. I am very fortunate in having a good wall tent to sleep under and in having plenty of blankets and clothes. I drew a knit coat and blouse before marching which I wear under my common coat. Then I have an adjutant's rubber coat and a slouched hat which will keep me dry any way.

December 9

[Halsey amused himself reading the novel *Rory O'More*.]

Orders were received for the corps to march tomorrow. Extra ammunition was given out.

🖎 [But, once again, the Fifteenth did not move. The men shrugged and remained in camp . . . again. Finally, on the morning of December 12, the Fifteenth New Jersey finally went to war at Fredericksburg. They took part in one of the most ill-planned assaults of the war, an assault riddled with miscues, misinterpreted orders, bungling, and, even Burnside admitted later, plain stupidity. The chaos started early in the morning on the twelfth when 120,000 soldiers massed on the riverbank could not cross over on the pontoons because a small regiment of 1,500 fierce Mississippi soldiers were holed up in residential and business buildings in Fredericksburg, laying a steady fire on the bridges. Unable to weed them out of their secure positions behind town-house windowsills and riverside roofs with sharpshooters, Burnside ordered his artillery batteries to open up on the civilian homes and began to bombard the city in one of the first outright attacks on civilians in the war. The artillery barrage battered hundreds of buildings and started fires that swept through entire neighborhoods. Even that did not work because the Confederates, still alive, continued to fire from the rubble. They were finally stopped by several thousand Union soldiers, braving a storm of bullets, who ferried across and attacked the neighborhoods along the river where they were trapped.

Burnside's nearly four-week delay enabled Lee to move his entire army, plus the newly arrived army of Jackson—a total of 78,000 men—into an impregnable hilltop position on a low plateau, Marye's Heights, behind the town. From that perch, they were unbeatable and Lee knew it. Union forces would have to cross a four-hundred-yard, wide-open plain to reach the bottom of the hill, where a sunken road protected by a stone wall afforded Longstreet a chance to hide thousands of riflemen. Not only did Lee have 78,000 men, but he had one of the largest collections of artillery batteries of the war and unlimited ammunition. He had so much firepower that when Longstreet asked one of his artillerists if he feared a battle against 120,000 Federals, the artillerist assured him that he had "enough ammunition to kill every man in the Union Army this morning." Later, Longstreet confidently told Lee that "a chicken could not live on that field when we open up on it."

Burnside's delays and bungling were costly. Most of his men, after crossing the river, massed in and around the business district and residential neighborhoods of the city of Fredericksburg itself, some looting stores. To shell the federals, Confederate artillery batteries had to bombard the city itself, leveling many buildings and setting fire to homes and warehouses. Fredericksburg was left in rubble by both armies, a victim of the war.

Halsey and others began moving across the river on the pontoons early in the morning and over two days the largest army in the nation's history made the crossing—only to be trapped.]

December 12

We crossed the Rappahannock at Franklin's Crossing on a pontoon bridge, about a mile below Fredericksburg, at about nine o'clock, our band playing Dixie. We were formed in a line of battle on the south bank while other troops crossed behind us. We lay during the morning in a small orchard, behind a slight raise in the ground a few yards from the high bluffs south of the river. While here our cavalry made a reconnaissance in front and did not seem to draw the fire of the enemy, who were in the hills.

Later in the afternoon, the brigade was formed, 15th on the right and 23rd on the left, in the front line and the four old regiments, one, two and three and four in the rear line (their limited strength being the same as that of the two new regiments) and moved forward [towards Marye's Heights]. (Alanson and I walked together behind the 15th.) The 2d brigade was on our right.

The brigade had not moved far before the enemy opened on us, the first shells exploding high over our heads. They soon got their range and would have hurt us considerably had it not been for Deep Run Ravine, which we reached and down which the line moved. The first line ascended the south bank and commenced to form again when we were ordered back into the ravine. One man of the 23rd was wounded in the cheek with a piece of shell and one of the 2d also. We remained in this spot til dark when we moved down the ravine, through the brush, towards Fredericksburg.

December 13

The regiment went out on picket in early morning along and in front of the Bowling Green Road and railroad. . . . I went back to the rear to get provisions for the staff, taking [men] with me. Here at the crossing I saw troops crossing the bridge and going down to the left. Prisoners and unneeded men from where the battle began about nine. Shells flew and cavalrymen and horses were killed. The cannonading and fighting about Fredericksburg and the heights above was continuous all day. The chaplain was in the town where shells were bursting in the streets. Went out to the skirmish line to the right of our regiment and witnessed a part of the battle on the heights. After nightfall the scene was terrific, the cheers of the men, flashes of muskets, and the roaring of the guns.

🖌 [That final, nighttime assault he saw against the Heights, lit up like a Fourth of July picnic by bombardment and rifle fire from both sides, was the heroic and fruitless assault of Rush Hawkins's IX Corps Brigade. The men were cut to ribbons in the assault, and then, as they retreated, they wandered into the plain in front of the Union's II Corps line and were shot at by pickets who feared they were Confederates. Hundreds fled down the hill in the dark, including twelve-year-old drummer boys howling and trying to carry their huge drums with both hands amid the shells exploding around them, screaming at the top of their lungs. Dozens of soldiers fell and were trampled to death by their own men, who could not see them in the dark.

Halsey and the Fifteenth joined the Fourth New Jersey in a 3 P.M. assault ordered by General Torbert on the rebel Sixteenth North Carolina, panicking the rebels, who fled. The Fifteenth, Halsey in the middle, dug in for two hours, but then became the target of a huge counterattack along the line by rebels charging while screeching out the terrifying rebel yell, which could be heard throughout the battlefield, its awful and ominous high-sounding, shrill notes raising the hair on the backs of the Federals. One Union soldier said after the war that "if a man claimed he heard the rebel yell and said he wasn't scared, then he didn't hear it."]

The rebels charged our pickets on the left and a [counter] charge was made by our 4th and 23rd in which Col. Hatch was mortally wounded. The Rebels wounded about 100 of our men. We captured many of the Rebels. Our reports tonight is three killed, 17 wounded and three missing, our losses chiefly in the left company. [Halsey did not know it, but Sergeant Major Fowler, one of his friends, was shot through the thigh and quickly bled to death just yards away from him.]

Alanson and I slept that night at the Ben Ward mansion (the large house just east of the crossing and which was filled with our wounded) along with Major Brown who was slightly wounded in the leg. Colonel Hatch lay at our feet all night.

🖘 [This was the first of several nights that Halsey would find himself sleeping next to the corpses of dead men, something that quickly became common practice in the war.

The Fifteenth's troubles were mirrored just about everywhere. Burnside sent wave after wave of Union regiments toward Marye's Heights. They came out of their lines in perfectly symmetrical formations, grouped in rectangles or long, thin lines of battle, and then slowly began to move up the extended, unprotected slope. As soon as they started to trot, over four hundred yards of deadly acreage, they were targets for the thousands of sharpshooters Longstreet had lined up, as well as for the nonstop fire from the rebel artillery. Shells burst among them for hours and soldiers fell every few yards, one man shot dead in mid-yell as he was exhorting his men to charge. One line of blue after the other was turned back, with enormous and terrible losses, as low-rolling clouds of cannon smoke drifted across the fatal fields in front of the heights. One Confederate general said later that toward the end of the day there were so many Union dead and wounded—over twelve thousand casualties, 10 percent of the army—that the field in front of the dug-in Confederate hilltop line looked like an unbroken sea of blue. Later, nearly a thousand dead Union soldiers were found just in front of the sunken road alone, which is as far as the suicidal assaults ever got.

Halsey sent this short article to the *Hunterdon Gazette* about the death of one of his friends in the carnage at Fredericksburg. The short column is a fine example of Halsey's sensitivity and writing style and reflects the rather heroic view he took of the war in general.]

A NEW JERSEY SHARPSHOOTER—In the late battle near Fredericksburg, Va., private Michael Mulvey, of the 15th NJ Volunteers, a fine marksman, had been doing good service with his Enfield rifle, when he was cautioned by an officer against exposing himself to the fire of the enemy's skirmishers. With a patriotic answer, he sprang forward to a pile of railroad ties. A rebel sharpshooter was posted on the opposite bank of a stream, behind a tree, and would load and fire when he could get a fair shot. Mulvey soon discovered him, and watched for his opportunity. The rebel put his head and rifle out from the tree; Mulvey did the same above the pile of ties. There was a double explosion. Mulvey fell back, pierced through the brain with a minié ball. The rebel marksman tumbled over, his body in full view, also pierced to the brain through his eye, from the unerring aim of poor Mulvey.

At sundown the regiment held the ground in that part of the field and his comrades buried him, wrapped in his blanket (the soldier's shroud) in the field nearby, where the grass looked greener and the soil less disturbed. There was no monument to mark his grave—not even a board could be had—and the place and circumstances will soon fade from remembrance; and perhaps even the name of this young patriot and gallant Jerseyman will be forgotten.

[That night men on both sides had trouble sleeping because of the eerie series of moans and cries for help or water coming from the still-living wounded stranded somewhere in the middle of the vast landscape of the dead and dying. In the night skies, the "northern lights" were seen, some said, for the first time over the heartland of Virginia, and the rebels took it as a sign from Providence that God favored them.]

December 14

I went out to the Ravine from the hospital with Alanson in early morning and then out to the picket line where the regiment was being relieved. A colonel was killed while being relieved. Colonel Lindsley had a bullet taken from the back of his dress coat which made nine holes in his clothes without doing him harm.

The regiment was relieved about 7 A.M. and remained in the ravine all day. Alanson had service at ten. There was only occasional firing during the day except on the picket line.

December 15

🖋 [As adjutant, Halsey's job was to ride from place to place to deliver orders. He was not supposed to be directly in combat, but, like so many adjutants, wound up in the thick of things at Fredericksburg, fighting for his life with the men, as he would in many other battles.]

All quiet in front. In the afternoon, I went with Alanson to visit the wounded at Brevard Mansion.

We went to the bridge. Col. Fowler, who had come up during the day, obtained the body of the sergeant major, John P. Fowler (his cousin), and was returning with it to Salem. Alanson went with him and I went on to the regiment, where reports had been called for which no one seemed able to make out in my absence.

A man had been looking for the colonel's horse and Colonel Campbell gave him an awful blowing up. I made out the reports and got some flour cakes made up for my supper when Captain Willis came along and, being hungry and I modest, I saw them disappear. I consoled myself that I would have one warm sleep in the Chaplain's wolf robe and was fairly disposed for the night when around midnight orders came to get up. . . .

December 16

Rose at midnight and to get men up I walked over the left wing where they were sleeping in their blankets, without tents, while Cornish got the right side up. As quietly as possible, we moved out of the ravine and stood in line on the North Side. There were many troops over the river behind us. It was cold and dark. In my hurry, and sleepy condition I had put my right boot on my left foot and could not tell what made my feet hurt so. About an hour or two we ran to the bridge and over it, our brigade being the last to cross. We marched to the hills then. Each along their foot for half a mile and then by a road up the hill. It was then just becoming daylight. As it grew light we moved west of the road and made camp.

We could see the rebs advancing continuously over the ground we had left and advancing a battery there, firing some shells at us. The last of the whole army had crossed in the night, the last of a move about which had been going on since the attempt to turn the rebel flank on Saturday had proved unsuccessful.

Our loss in this battle: four killed, 20 wounded and five missing. Killed: Sgt. John P. Fowler, Randolph Earles, Sergeant and Mulvey. Wounded: Major James Brown.

December 21

Rumors that the rebels are crossing the river. I wish they would for I hate the idea of falling into another such a trap as Fredericksburg.

December 22

[Posted letter from President Lincoln to the Army in a newspaper clipped by Halsey for his diary. He often clipped letters from Lincoln to the troops and clipped stories from newspapers, usually dailies from New York, and sent them home to his girlfriend, Mary. He was disgusted with the anti-Lincoln coverage of the newspapers in Newark and wanted her to see the war the way the New York writers saw it, the way he witnessed it.]

"The courage with which you in open field maintained the contest against an entrenched foe and the consummate skill and success with which you crossed and re-crossed the river in the face of the enemy show that you possess all the qualities of a great army, which will yet bring victory to the cause of the country, of popular government. . . . I tender to you . . . the thanks of the nation."

December 23

I never saw so many discouraged and discontented men in the regiment before.

🖋 [Lincoln was exasperated with Burnside and began looking for another general to lead the Army of the Potomac.]

December 25 (Christmas Day)

Received a visit from Smith, Freeman, Morgan and Lt. Joe Bowers of the 27th. I had reason to regard my want of rank in entertaining them. We made a Christmas dinner of wheat cakes with butter and sugar and a piece of steak.

December 26

Storm. Passed an awful night. I have severe pain in right breast and painful cough which prevented sleep. Could only sleep on left side and in one position. I used liniment during the day and felt easier. I had no appetite.

Reading the book *The Temptations.*

The staff tents were put together. The doors are made of cracker boxes.

December 27 (White Oaks)

🖋 [Halsey's level of cheer or despondency was often in direct proportion to the number of letters he received from home. It was heightened during his first Christmas away from home. He had no letters for weeks, and then, suddenly, the day after Christmas he received two, from his cousins Anne and Sill and from his sister. They were the best Christmas gifts anyone could have given him. Still, his relations with his father remained strained. He wrote to complain that his father had sent him only two letters during his entire four-month enlistment. This letter shows his obsession with his lines of communication to home, and to civilization. It also recounts in sad detail the ill treatment of soldiers by their own army in the days after Fredericksburg and, along with other letters written after December 13, shows how shaken Halsey was by his first major battle.]

My Dear Father,

I had almost despaired hearing from home again, it having been I do not know how many weeks since any of you had written when yesterday's mail brought Anne and Sills combined letter and one from Sue. I don't think I exaggerate when I say I write three letters home for every one I receive. From you, I think I have received just two letters during four months and begin to believe I am slipping from your mind. However, I will charitably conclude it is not forgetfulness but your business which keeps you all silent.

I wrote Sue a long letter the first of the week and to Sam night before last giving all the particulars. I could recollect the recent fight and the small part I took in it and our skedadle and march back here.

The day after we returned to (White Oaks), the 28 sick we had left behind at a camp were sent for and they had a hard story to tell of the way they had been attended in that camp which the boys have christened by various undesirable names. Two had died (John Hall was not one as was reported. He is doing well now), one of them I am convinced from sheer exposure. One died on the way here. These things united with the memory of our defeat threw a gloom over the camp.

Since then, things have been cleared up a little. We are getting more comfortably settled, the sick are doing well with a few exceptions and the weather has been moderate. Lt. Foster of Chester is still sick of typhoid fever and two others in the hospital are quite sick.

Including the loss in action (four killed and five missing) we have lost at least 15 in the last two or three weeks. I suppose now the only movement they will make with us, if any, is back to the Potomac until the political magnates shall have mystified themselves and the country as to the cause of the recent disaster. One thing is certain—the army should have crossed three days before it did or never have crossed at all. The [decision to cross early] is said to have been owing to [Montgomery] Meigs [quartermaster general in charge of supplies], that they did cross is due to the peremptory orders of Burnside. After all I begin to believe that McClellan is the man and they will have to fall back on him again. He used to take good care of his men anyway and if he had been ordered over the river as Burnside was he would have refused to act against his better judgement. If they do put him in command, his first move will be for the Peninsula where he can get close to Richmond at once without having his army destroyed by 60 miles of fighting.

Perhaps at no time did the prospects of our cause appear more gloomy but still we ought not to be discouraged. As the men of Israel went thrice up to Gilead before they were victorious, so Providence after testing our faith may give us also the victory at last.

🖋 [As he would often do, Halsey made a quick transition from the horrors of the war to his personal life in camp and how much items from home meant to him, thus, as always, creating a parallel universe of home and hearth that helped save his sanity over the many years he was at the front.]

I received with the girls' letter a pair of mittens from Newark with a note for cousin Eliza saying they had not heard from R. in a long time. Sill, it seems, is at fault all around. The mittens I consider my Christmas [gift] and you cannot imagine how much pleasure the receipt of all the letters or things of yesterday gave me after so long a silence. You would be surprised to see the things which come in the mail—gloves, shirts, boots, tobacco, etc.—and day before yesterday one man got some chestnuts, a piece of turkey and a dozen other things with a little bag wrapped up in a paper. Sometime the postage amounts to $3 or $4. I hope we will soon be where packages can reach us by express. At present there is too much risk.

As for my health, with the exception of a heavy cold, which I never have passed winter yet without, I am very well indeed and very well situated.

I trust I have written enough to relieve your uneasiness concerning me and to cause you to break your long silence. As I have four correspondents at home—yourself, Anne, Sill and Greenwood—can't you manage to write me regularly at least twice a week? Alanson wishes to be kindly remember to all.

Your affectionate son,

🖎 [The cold and cough Halsey picked up in the winter of 1862 would nag him throughout the war.]

December 28
[Note to his girlfriend, Mary]
The fight in the hills back of Fredericksburg of which I had a good view was terrific, especially after sundown when the flashes of artillery or musketry could be plainly seen. This and the smoke were accompanied by the roar of the pieces. The screaming of shell and the shouts of the men was the most sublime I ever witnessed or ever wish to again, especially if the sacrifice is made for so little.

What will be done with the army now I cannot conjecture. As I wrote to father, it won't do to be discouraged. We will hope that equal good fortune will attend our cause and that the coming year will see this infernal rebellion crushed and the nation at peace again.

PS: The doctor has just come in saying another man is dead in the hospital, the seventh we have lost in nine days.

🖊 [Later, in his diary, he noted that the men buried yet another man later in the day. Many of Halsey's letters ended like this, with a last-minute tragedy. The letters, written almost every day, gave his family and girl-friend, Mary, an almost live, episodic story of the war.

THE WAR: On December 29, Union general William Sherman failed to take Vicksburg via a battle at Chickasaw Bayou that was reminiscent of Burnside's suicidal charges at Fredericksburg. Sherman sent his men across an open plain, uphill, toward a dug-in Confederate line of men. The Federals were driven back repeatedly, losing 1,776 killed, wounded, or missing, and retreated. Grant's supply depot in Holly Springs, Mississippi, was attacked and destroyed the week before by Earl Van Dorn's Confederates. They captured 1,500 Union soldiers and destroyed over $1.5 million in supplies. The combined Mississippi defeats, added to Fredericksburg, made for a grim holiday week throughout the North.]

December 31

Read note from Emery at Baltimore, offering me a detail in another regiment. I declined.

🖊 [A cruel irony of the war was the order sent to all the troops of the Army of the Potomac that day, just a week after twelve thousand of them were killed or wounded in a hail of thousands of cannonballs and millions of bullets at Fredericksburg. Orders: Brigade commanders will take par-ticular pains to prevent any discharge of firearms during the night of the thirty-first and on January 1. The order effectively prevented any cele-bration of New Year's Eve, 1862, which passed quietly in North and South.]

7

A WEARY WINTER,
A SAD SPRING

January 1–April 25, 1863

[The Army of the Potomac, safely across the Rappahannock River and away from the cemetery of Fredericksburg, trudged wearily back to its old camp at White Oak in Falmouth, northern Virginia, on what were becoming too familiar roads, and settled in for the winter. The men were demoralized and the weather was freezing cold in one of the bleakest and blustery winters in Virginia history. It was a season of bitter winds that plunged the windchill to below freezing on most days, and the Blue Ridge Mountains all looked gray.

The camp at White Oak was a haphazard little city of shacks and tents, tossed together by men who had never built a camp before. There wasn't enough food or the right food, and what was prepared had little to do with nutrition or diet. The huts were not ventilated properly and the bad air stayed inside. Tents were large and bulky and semicomfortable for people like Halsey who built chimneys or had several blankets for cover, but for most, tents were cold and the harsh winds of the Virginia winter buffeted them all night long.

Soldiers began to die from the cold and rampant diseases that swept through the camp. Hundreds died of pneumonia, diphtheria, and other ailments, often treated with nothing more than daily doses of tea and comforted by little more than a thin blanket wrapped tightly about their bodies as they listened to tent poles and canvas creak from the winds outside. Others, who had arms and legs amputated after the fatal fighting at Fredericksburg, died from surgery complications. Surgeons, trying their best, could not keep up with the long line of patients and made do with insufficient anesthetics and scantily equipped hospitals. Some soldiers died of starvation amid bitter complaints that while warehouses in Washington, D.C., were stuffed with food supplies for the various Union armies, little of it was being delivered to the troops in White Oak. Thousands of soldiers came down with what became known simply as "soldier's cough," a nagging, annoying, and persistent cough that they picked up in camp in December of 1862 and could not get rid of until the spring—and sometimes never. Generals said that when the brigades were in formation for inspection, orders could hardly be heard over the incessant coughing of the men. It rolled across parade grounds like a grim hack.

Halsey was one of the soldiers who picked up the cough early and could not lose it. He referred to the cough often, although deliberately downplaying it, in his diary and letters. He also referred frequently to the death and dying all around him in winter camp at White Oak. Like most soldiers who wrote home, he did not describe the death and disease in camp in graphic fashion because he did not want to alarm his family, but there was so much death and dying that a simple obituary line in his diary or letters, day after day after day, was more powerful than a thousand words. Conditions in the camp became so bad so quickly that some later called the White Oak Camp in Falmouth "the Valley Forge of the Civil War."]

January 1. New Year's Day

Writing as winter rolls on. The cold is piercing. My cough is very troublesome. Read the newspapers from home. I have to make out all the company rolls and the field and staff rolls and monthly returns, quarterly returns and all in triplicate.

January 2

Cornelius Nevius, of Company A, died. I slept little at night, being quite sick.

A large number of the sick were sent to the general hospital. Since moving to the present camp and with consequences of exposure at Devil's Hole, we have lost a good many men. Since December 1, twelve men have died at camp or in the hospital. We had four killed and five missing for a total loss of 21. Virgil Howell froze to death and we have others whose feet were frozen in the hospital. Things looked blue here for a time.

The note from John Emery was to ask if I would like the position of chief clerk to the musical director in Baltimore.

Have been reading [books].

🖎 [John Emery was one of a number of friends trying to get Halsey out of the Fifteenth because its fatality rate was so high. Halsey entertained each suggestion but turned them all down, determined to stay with the Fifteenth through the end.]

January 3

I wrote my sister Sue that I was sorry to have caused her so much pain by my last complaining letter [after Fredericksburg]. The fact is I was terribly down just at that time. As an army we had been beaten and were on the retreat. Many men I knew and liked were killed and wounded. Men were dying about one a day and personally I was more than half sick.

January 5

Pvt. Hopler of Co. F died this morning.

January 8

[Letter to brother Sam]

Dear Sam,

My cough is better . . . my appetite and strength have been restored. At one time I thought I was going to go under for certain.

I had an opportunity to send to Washington for a couple of sticks of licorice via Nicholas Vanderveer's brother in law from Chester (whom I wish you would thank for me).

We are located just as when I last wrote. I have three days rations on hand and must be ready to march at 12 hours notice. The weather keeps good though I am in hopes if it is going to rain it will do so before we are ordered to march for I am afraid of being stuck somewhere.

We had splendid doughnuts last night and for the first time drew flour and potatoes from the commissary.

The chances of the paymaster arriving by the 15th are getting slim. I have 75 cents on hand.

I await your opinion about the Baltimore position.

🖊 [The Vanderveer father and brother visit to bring Lieutenant Vanderveer home was common. Fathers and siblings often traveled to Union Army camps to take home very ill soldiers. Unfortunately, some died just as fathers arrived or on the way home. These visits were always sad.

THE WAR: One of the reasons President Lincoln signed the Emancipation Proclamation was to give free blacks and newly freed slaves the opportunity to enlist in the army. In early January 1863, he asked for enough blacks to fill four regiments. The response was an avalanche, and by the time the war was over more than 180,000 African-American soldiers fought for the Union Army. Their courage and bravery, sometimes in the most difficult situations, such as the near suicidal assault on Fort Wagner, outside of Charleston, in the summer of 1863, impressed the officers and men of the Union Army and the people of the nation.]

January 10
[Halsey's satire could be biting.]
A barrel of apples sent to the regiment by the sanitary commission were ruled unfit for the sick and placed in my quarters for the field and staff.

January 16
We are expecting orders to move any hour and have been for over [weeks].
I was appointed Sergeant Major by regimental order number 6 today.

January 18
James Dayton, of Co. A, died during the night.

🖊 [Winter camp was harsh and bitter, but the soldiers and officers of both sides knew they could not avoid it. The armies of the Civil War did not move in the winters because rain, cold, bitter winds, and snow made any traveling or fighting impossible. It simply wasn't done. Gen. Ambrose Burnside, still smarting from his humiliating defeat at Fredericksburg, had a brainstorm in late January, though. The Confederates would never expect another attack in the middle of a freezing January. Why not launch a secret surprise attack and crush them? Lee was in winter camp outside of Fredericksburg and would never expect it. The Union could not only destroy Lee's army, but take Fredericksburg, removing that blemish from Burnside's record, at the same time. With Lee's army crushed and Fredericksburg his, Burnside could then move on Richmond and end the war by the end of February. The January offensive would have the same striking morale effect on the public that Washington's Christmas attack at Trenton had in 1776. President Lincoln had already vetoed the idea of any winter attack, but Burnside went ahead with one anyway, ordering the assault on January 20.

Burnside surprised nobody with his oafish expedition. It started in a maze of confusion when different regiments left camp at the same time and the roads became hopelessly snarled with Union troops. Confederate pickets followed every single movement of Burnside's army and reported its every turn to Lee. The Southern commander had nothing to worry about, however, because on the first night of the march the reason why armies did not fight in winter arrived. Cold, driving rains came down hard on the night of January 20 and became worse the next day. The army could not move through narrow dirt roads flooded with torrents of water, and wagon wheels could not navigate the deepening slush and mud. In the middle of the second day of the march, the Union Army immobile, some Confederate soldiers put up a large sign that the Union soldiers could see that read: "Burnside Stuck in the Mud."

It became an instant joke. Burnside's ill-planned "mud march" went nowhere, and after a few days, with an entire army stuck in a miles-long sea of mud and sheets of rain, he gave up and ordered everyone back to camp. The soldiers, glad to be out of the mud, arrived back in White Oak in much worse shape than when they'd left. Burnside, convinced he could not fail in his brilliant idea, had ordered the men to destroy all tables, chairs, and other accessories in camp because they would not be returning to White Oak. They had little left when they did return. Many found that while they were gone a newly arrived cavalry regiment had taken axes to many of their huts and used them for firewood to keep warm. The only regiment that found its tables, chairs, and tents in the same condition as before was the Ninth Massachusetts, whose colonel had such great faith in Burnside that he told his men they would probably be back in camp in a few days and not to destroy anything. Halsey's account of the "mud march" was a dreary one.]

January 20

We received orders about 9 to be in line at noon. We marched about ten miles during the afternoon in a circuitous direction (to avoid being seen by the enemy) to about three miles northwest of Falmouth and about 2½ miles

from the river where we camped at dark in a wood. Col. Campbell, Sharp
and Sullivan under two rubber blankets made into a tent!

A letter from Sam says that Adj. Seymore and Major Brown are in
Morristown expecting to return to the regiment this afternoon.

January 21

We marched in a drizzly rain (it had rained all night), halting every
100 yards or so in the road towards the river. I went down the line and
found a sleeping place with privates Fields and Osborne of Company F.

January 22

It has rained all night and we understand the movement has failed. It
cleared in the afternoon and a whiskey ration was given out. It was a dreary day,
wet and with nothing to eat but fried pork. Slept with Dr. Sharpe and Alanson.

January 23

Companies D and I were detailed for duty at work hauling pontoons
back from the river through seas of mud. Col. Forbes and Dr. Sullivan went
off to a farm house and Alanson and I had a tent to ourselves.

January 24

[LESSLAND PLANTATION: Ed's search for his older brother Joe began
here when by accident he met a woman who was a good friend of the
Jeremiah Morton and Joseph Halsey families and had visited Joseph at
Lessland Plantation. It was the start of a search for which his father had
pleaded. The search would continue through just about any town in
Virginia where Ed believed residents might know his brother. In time,
his hunt for his brother became a mission.]

Alanson, Dr. Sullivan and I went to the house of Mrs. Sweetmen, who
has a son in the rebel army and another in the Union. She knows [brother]
Joseph and remembered his wedding. We had a good dinner of bacon and
hot cakes. I went to a neighbor's to get some soda for her and she was going
to use it to make biscuits for supper. The regiment, with Colonel Campbell
at the head of it, waded by and I was called in without my supper.

January 25

The regiment got marching orders about noon and marched back to
the old camp at White Oak Church by night.

🖋 [The "mud march" was the last straw in Lincoln's tolerance of General Burnside. He was replaced the next day.]

January 26
[Fighting Joe] Hooker commands now.

🖋 [Hooker's elevation was no surprise. A veteran of the Mexican War, he left his farm to rejoin the army when the Civil War broke out. The hot-tempered Hooker came back as a brigadier general and served with distinction in the defense of Washington and the battles of Malvern Hill, Yorktown, Williamsburg, Fair Oaks, and Second Bull Run. He was named commander of the III Corps, I Corps, and V Corps. He did not pick up his nickname for fighting. A reporter titled a spring 1861 story "Fighting" and wrote the name of the subject of the story underneath it, "Joe Hooker." An editor ran them together and "Fighting Joe Hooker" was born.

Hooker's cultural claim to distinction, of course, was that he permitted prostitutes to follow the army and they were quickly nicknamed "hookers."]

January 28
My heavy losses in the move away from the secesh were one pair of pants, the knees of which were burned out by a camp fire.

January 29
🖋 [Halsey wrote his cousin Eliza and spent the first part of his letter urging her to assure her sister, his girlfriend, Mary, that he truly loved the slippers she had sent him and that his quick dismissal of the slippers in a previous letter was not intended. He felt, like all boyfriends, that he was never quite able to say or do the right thing with Mary. Then he went on in a typical letter that mixes the world of war and the world of literature, which always gave him an escape from the grimness of the conflict.]

Last night I was invited to attend a meeting of the Adelphi Literary Society, composed of the enlisted men of the regiment entirely (with the exception of its worthy President, the chaplain), who strive for distinction in the arms of the muses while the chariot of mars is stuck in Virginia's mud. The meeting was held in the chapel which had just been fitted out with the luxury of benches which as Alanson told me were built in the woods that morning. After calling the roll and dispatching a large amount of unfinished business, the society listened to quite a witty essay on Yankee Notions. Then came the debate on the important and very vexed question (slavery), and never worse vexed. I think that too much for me but I withstood the temptation to speak. An oration followed on the state of the union and then came tattoo and I adjourned.

But debating societies are not the only refining influence at work. For the past month, headquarters has been astir with preparations for the reception of Mrs. Penrose and the young Penroses. Yesterday the Colonel went to Washington for her and tomorrow is the day on which the family gathering will take place. Won't we have to stand around then! To use the dialect of soil, I reckon right smart we will! I have some anxiety to see her and it seems so have the boys who spied a [fine-looking] lady with horse and equipment Petruchio would have envied, coming towards the camp.

All gave voice "here comes Mrs. Penrose," indefinitely prolonged and repeated. Now, I hope you don't think that they wished to insult a lady which they are incapable of, for she was as yet a great ways off.

I received a letter from Anne tonight in which she says the old place [Rockaway] has become quite lively again. The young ladies are all present and with fine skating the ponds are full of pleasure parties every night. I believe I wrote you how they had me out the night I arrived and the tenor music of skate irons dignified by the occasional bass of a fall. They kept us till near the wee end hours.

Sam P. [his cousin, the new Presbyterian minister] had a surprise party which passed off very pleasantly excepting in a balk of a speech from the "School Superintendent" that afforded amusement to some showing that evils are not universal.

Dr. Sullivan brought back from furlough quite a library of novels among which I found one which is splendid—*Very Hard Cash,* by Read. It is a sequel to *David Dodd or Love Me Little.* I can't remember a novel I became that interested in. Have you read it? *Kate O'Donahue, Hinton the Guardsman, Bleak House* and *At Odds* have also passed inspection here. They are all good books of very different styles. You will wonder how one can find time to read so many, but then recollect a novel carried in the pocket can be read any time wherever one happens to be and when it may be impossible to write [letters] for several days.

But I must close this fair proportion of an epistle. Thank Mary again for her present and with regrets* that I was not somehow able to acknowledge it [in letter to her] . . . believe me.

*the cup of thanksgiving mingled with the persistent tear . . . you observe.

✎ [The "real adjutant" was William Seymore, who was constantly sick. Halsey had become the "real adjutant," of course, to Colonel Penrose, who kept telling him that Seymore, gone for months already, would solve all of the regiment's problems upon his return. Waiting for Seymore was like waiting for Godot.]

January 31
I am reading James Fenimore Cooper's *Redskins*.

February 2
Dear Sue,
The army seems since the recent move [mud march] thoroughly demoralized, officers and men cursing the administration and the war. The disasters of Vicksburg, Fredericksburg, Galveston, Stono River, the *Monitor-Merrimac,* all cast a gloom over the army, which [reminds one] of the dark days of 1776. The men in their shelter tents are but barely supplied with shoes and have been disheartened and begin to think they can never succeed.

February 7
A little after dark, an ambulance came in from Belle Plain bringing Major Brown (absent wounded since Dec. 13), and Adj. Seymore (absent sick since Oct. 31) with Mrs. Bentley [to visit her sick husband, Lt. James Bentley]. The accommodation of the latter caused some little embarrassment but she was finally settled in the wall tent of Co. H.

February 11
Mrs. Bentley found her husband quite sick and efforts were made to get him off to General Hospital which proved successful. They left for Washington today.

February 15
Dear Sister Sue,
I had hardly commenced this Sunday letter before I was interrupted by visitors who prevented any further writing for the night.
Yesterday, I was fully improved by a Brigade dress parade and drill in the morning. It is a fine sight to see two thousand or more men maneuver especially if closed in mass, the bayonets glistening in the sun like silver or

moving from column into line, ploying and deploying. Our General, A.T.A. Torbert, appears in a suit of blue velvet, handsomely mounted in his Mexican saddle and everything to match, aides all in their finery. To those who had only some forty or fifty men parade on a Fourth of July, it would be a sight worth seeing.

I have now a very good man in my place as clerk who does all the heavy writing and although I have still the general supervision of the office, I have now a chance to go about. I appeared on guard mounting at half past eight in the morning, dress parade and battalion drills whenever the weather approves of them. I like it rather better.

Last week, I had a chimney built in the back of the tent which makes it right comfortable. On one side of the tent is the table at which I am writing and on the other my bed made of poles raised on crutches and covered with pine boughs—the regulation bed. The chimney is built of poles set up in the ground in a semi circle and pitched with clay, the side towards the tent above the fireplace covered with cross pieces. It draws well and you would be surprised to see how comfortable it makes the tent.

I received a joint letter from father and [sister] Sill enclosing college circular last Friday night. It is strange that it is so hard to get a girl. I thought it was the men who were scarce since the army was raised. I should think that while their husbands are away and they complain of not receiving pay, the wives of some of the soldiers would "work out." By the way, father thinks it strange that John Hall did not send any money home. He was sent off to General Hospital just before the last march and therefore was not here to be paid. John has been sick ever since the march to King George early in December. He has the peculiarity of his family—continually complaining and easy discouraged—which with better treatment than he could get here would make his recovery doubtful. The very worst thing for any man is to get discouraged. I have noticed it in a good many cases—men without any elasticity if they get sick.

The 27th [the Rockaway regiment] has, I hear, shipped to Belle Plain, probably for North Carolina. The 9th and 12th corps, too, have gone somewhere. I think it is likely a movement will be made there to draw off from the army in our front and give us a better chance.

I hope you will succeed in getting a good picture of Susy [his sister Susan's daughter]. Couldn't you persuade [sister] Anne to have hers taken? I should like very much to have one.

We expect Alanson back tomorrow or the next day and also the two captains who went with him. If Alanson had time to call at my house, he could give a better account of me than I could myself. He has been a very good friend of mine.

But I hear [bugle call] "peas upon the trenches" and must go. Write regularly!

🖋 ["Peas upon the trenches" was a soldiers' nickname for the bugle call for breakfast. "The General" was the nickname for the call to move out. "Tommy Totten" was the call to go into battle.

LESSLAND PLANTATION: On February 18, Joseph Halsey returned to the Sixth Virginia Cavalry after four months at Lessland battling typhoid fever. He was attended by an Orange County doctor and cared for by his wife and gradually recovered from the typhoid, which he was certain would kill him when he came down with it in camp. Friends asked him to reconsider going back to the army because of his weak condition, and the chance that he would come down with the fever, a frequent killer in camps, once again. He shrugged and told them that nothing could keep him away from the Confederate Army. As soon as he felt reasonably well, he kissed Millie Halsey and his children goodbye, took his horse out of the stables at Lessland, walked it past the house, trotted through the gate, and then galloped down the winding road that leads from Lessland to the Rapidan River. His wife and children watched him as he rode past the lower reaches of the plantation, past the cornfields, and along the road that hugged the river. They could see him getting smaller and smaller until he was finally too far out to follow. As always, Millie wondered if it was the last time she would ever see her husband, whom she loved so much.

Joe Halsey's return to the army was turbulent. As always, his temper got the best of him and he wound up in a heated dispute over regulations requiring a doctor's note for his absence on the very first day he came back. He was still weak and felt he should have received thanks, not disdain, for coming back to the army. "I do what I can for the regiment, but don't intend to risk my life again," he angrily told the doctor.

Another dispute arose over his status. Urged to resign when he left in September because of his deteriorating condition, Halsey had sent in papers of resignation. He then asked to have them rescinded. Colonel Morton saw some people in the army who promised to take care of the matter. Somewhere, all the papers were lost and Captain Halsey, risking his health to return, was listed as AWOL and brought up on desertion charges within days after his return to camp. It took weeks of legal wrangling and meetings with different officers to convince the army that he had been on approved furlough because of illness. He was angry that the army would question his word and hurt that anyone would charge him with desertion after he had worked so hard for the army.

It took a long time to clear up the matter because Halsey, temperamental as always, got into countless arguments over his status. Back at Lessland, wife Millie, who had seen him bedridden twice now with serious illnesses, worried constantly about his health. Joe had always had health problems. In the winter of 1855–56 he had nearly died with pneumonia, and during the last few years his health had been marginal. He seemed vulnerable to any fever or sickness that was in the air. She knew all too well that death rates from disease were just as high as from battles in the Confederate Army.]

February 24

The effect of the severe weather has been an alarming increase in the mortality of the regiment—seven died in less than two weeks and there are a great many more quite low of fever.

February 28

Colonel Fowler returned to camp and Mrs. Seymore also arrived. To accommodate her, I gave up the office to her and her husband and turned in with Marcus Duvall.

✍ [By March, the productive Halsey had been put in charge of all paperwork for the regiment and assigned two clerks to help him. He was given a furlough home in reward for his hard work, but in a strange last-minute request, was asked to take Mrs. Seymore as far as Washington for protection in what turned out to be an intriguing little melodrama.]

March 3

I started for Belle Plain with Mrs. Seymore in an old two horse ambulance. Got passed in the road and broke down. I ran about a mile only to see our boat leaving the place. The mud was at its worst. I stepped on a dead mule in a pile of dead grass. Found quarters for the night at the (boat) *Frazier* till evening and then upon the *Ewold Dean* till morning. Mrs. Seymore found Mrs. Harriet Stimson, a volunteer nurse, for company.

✍ [THE WAR: Unable to raise necessary additional troops by enlistment, Congress, at the request of President Lincoln, passed the Enrollment Act on March 3, 1863. It authorized the president to draft as many troops as he needed to continue the war effort.]

March 4

We steamed up the Potomac at Acquia Creek, taking a larger boat. The adjutant [Seymore] joined us unexpectedly at Acquia. The sail up the river was a beautiful one. At Washington, I left Seymore and his wife at the door of their hotel, he saying he would be back in the regiment in a few days. Took train at 6:30 for New York.

✍ [The Seymores dropped off the face of the earth the next morning. The "real adjutant," rumored to have left the country to fight for the Mexican Army, was never seen or heard from again. His disappearance turned out to be one of the great mysteries of the war, and each month more and more information, and rumor, floated through camp about him.]

March 5

✍ [Halsey was home in Rockaway on furlough for a week. He spent all day March 11 with Mary Darcy and returned to the regiment on March 13.]

March 16

Hilton, our hospital steward just commissioned as an assistant surgeon, was taken sick quite suddenly. It was a reaction from taking a wrong dose of needed medicine. Another man died suddenly at the spring. Capt. Wright, Co. H., had his resignation accepted.

March 17

Hilton died. His death caused a deep sensation in the regiment where all loved and respected him.

✍ [LESSLAND PLANTATION: Millie Halsey had to work harder than ever to keep the plantation running after her husband returned to the army. Each day, she and the children, and the few slaves that remained, went to the cornfields to work and spent many mornings starting potato fields.

Joseph Halsey, back with the Sixth Virginia Cavalry for over a month, found himself in yet another argument with officers when he complained bitterly about Gen. William "Grumble" Jones. The general, who rarely had praise for anyone, issued a proclamation complimenting the Sixth Virginia for its efficiency. Most officers, startled, relished the rare compliment, but Halsey said of the general that "if we had to depend on anything efficient about him, the regiment would starve to death."]

March 24

A rigid inspection was made by Colonel Duffy. After the usual examinations the men were ordered to take off their shoes and stockings. Their underclothing was also examined. The result was fearful to behold.

✍ [The condition of the Fifteenth New Jersey, and the Army of the Potomac in general, was pathetic. Soldiers wrote home that illness, disease, battlefield deaths, incapacity, and desertions made the actual fighting strength of every regimental grouping of one hundred men only about that of thirty men.]

March 25

My Dear Sister,

We are now rather scant for officers and somewhat anxious as to who will be our new ones. Lt. Col. Campbell is all there is left of the three field officers. The adjutant [Seymore] is still unheard from. Many of our officers are away sick and some are present sick or on special duty. This afternoon from half past two we had battalion drill which is under the senior captain and there were only one commissioned officer to a company and the acting adjutant being sick I performed my own and most of his duties. It was the best exercise I have had in a long time.

Since I began this, two leaves of absence have come in approved for five days instead of ten and it is understood there are to be no more furloughs granted. I was just in time with mine. We have been dreading all day the order to turn in our tents, an order expected for several days past. General Torbert after inspection yesterday invited the officers of the regiment to his quarters to call on him. He informed them that baggage must be reduced to the lowest possible figure and he would not be surprised if orders should come to have all their baggage except what they carried boxed and sent to Washington. I am in doubt what to do with my overcoat and extra blankets of which I have three.

There were hardly a dozen in a company that had feet which would pass muster and many a "greyback" was discovered. It has had a good effect and men were shamed to cleanliness who could be forced no other way. [The inspection, however, drove home to the army brass the poor condition of the men's shoes, which caused such problems with their feet.]

March 29

That Seymore was once a peculiar devil. He was an editor of one of the principal Philadelphia newspapers and on the state committee for the Bell-Everett ticket in 1860. He became a Lt. Col. of the 99th Pa., raised largely by him, and when he resigned he left destitute.

✒ [THE WAR: The entire Confederacy was shocked on April 2 when hundreds of men and women surrounded a bread wagon, overturned and pillaged it, and then ransacked food stores in downtown Richmond in a "bread riot," which underlined that food supplies were dwindling throughout the South. The riot was halted by Confederate president Jefferson Davis himself.]

April 3

[Halsey to Cousin Eliza]

Your very interesting letter, with the "lines," which I hereby acknowledge duly to have received this time, reached this knighted region last Thursday and my humble self shortly after. [Halsey always referred to Virginia as the "knighted region" with sarcasm or wrote that he was on "sacred soil" to poke fun at the haughtiness of the "cavalier" attitude he felt most Virginians carried.] Do you see that I am prompt to answer and only wish I had one like it to answer every day.

As yet our wall tent have not been taken from us as was expected and with the exception of the smoke which a perverse wind drives down the chimney, we are comfortable notwithstanding the weather. Those who know say the season is unprecedented in this country. For the past week, it has been generally clear overhead but quite cool. This morning, we found it snowing and blowing very much in a northern style. The snow is an inch or two deep and will probably not last very long. Those who are waiting their turn to visit the scenes of their early life and are fearful that the order to march will defeat their plans see in it a favorable omen.

The great event of the past week has been the review of the 1st division by General Hooker. The order came just as I was about to bid farewell to cause and trouble for a few hours, about 12 Thursday night. Of course, this gave us little time for preparation as we were to be in position the next morning at ten. Everyone was busy cleaning up. Boots and shoes were blackened which had not been blackened for weeks. White gloves were put on. Those without gloves were put in the rear rank and everything done to make the appearance of the regiment the best possible. At a little after nine, the procession moved.

First we marched about a mile and halted for the brigade to form. Then we marched much farther and halted for the division to form. The line was nearly if not quite a half mile long, in close column by division (that is, not to be guilty of military pedantry, five double ranks deep) with short intervals between the regiments. After standing there till the place was getting familiar, we were ordered to pass in review which consists in wheeling to the left and marching down the front of the line, which was then moving the other way, following us around—and back again to the same old spot. General Brooks standing opposite with his staff.

There we waited again for an hour I suppose. Suddenly, old Joe Hooker appeared on our right with a cloud of generals, aides and witnesses, who rode at a gallop up in front of the line and then back in the rear of the line and up to his place in front. We then went again in review and after passing the general broke up by regiments and marched back to camp. The troops looked very well advancing in columns, two companies abreast with ten or fifteen paces between. I liked the appearance of Hooker very much (although he looked older and less dashing than I had heard . . .). He looks determined but there is something about him which belies the idea of rashness one would gather from his reputation.

The papers made a mistake about Colonel Ryerson. He is to be Colonel of the 10th N.J. regiment which has been doing provost duty in Washington. As for my own promotion, I must say blessed are they who expect nothing for they shall not be disappointed. I have never allowed myself to consider promotion as sure or speedy so when it does not come I can say I am as well off as before. I have had promises, to be sure, but there are these two things to look at: the "promisor" may change his mind or he may be unable to fulfill his promise. I have seen a good many make themselves ridiculous by calculating on commission. All the places in the line are now full. The colonelcy and majority are vacant. The adjutant has not been heard from in over a month. As for myself, it makes little difference where I serve provided my friends are equally content. They seem so, and I was glad to hear you are of the same mind. Therefore, I am tranquil. I am philosophic (I have been reading *Les Misérables* and the ardor may appear in my style).

As for the war prospects, like yourself we are one moment lifted to the seventh heaven in our hopes and the next cast down, but I may add not disheartened. Our attempts at Vicksburg seem to have been a failure and so will the expedition to Charlestown if they do not do something pretty soon. It will be Fredericksburg all over again, I am afraid. What Hooker's ideas are is a mystery to every one. Some say another corps is to be taken from this army, others that it is to be broken up entirely. One day we hear the heights opposite have been evacuated; the next that they are reinforced and perhaps the next that Richmond is evacuated. In this also there is need of philosophy and cooly to wait for events. We ought to whip them, therefore I think we will.

🖋 [The rest of Halsey's letter was a reaction to the raging debates in the New Jersey legislature over the war and the "peace resolutions" passed by the legislature calling for a negotiated truce. One of the peace resolution sponsors, Will Wright, was a longtime family friend of the Darcys' and Halseys'. Ed Halsey was livid about the legislative action.]

Will's speech seems to have gained a great deal of favor in many quarters, from what I hear from home and which is equally on his side, a good deal of criticism from others. Tell Mary I consider her decision final and as she pronounces it fine I will at the first opportunity to congratulate him on his success. Nevertheless I am afraid the eloquence of Demosthenes would prove unequal to the task of changing the opinions of our copperheaded representatives. [At this point Mary may have been hoping for a negotiated peace as her father's business crumbled. It was the only moment of weakness about the war she entertained.]

I never was so supremely disgusted with them as in reading their address or rather joint resolutions passed March 24 and read at the head of every regiment in this brigade [the peace resolutions]. Its smooth noncommittal unminded sleek style with its sly reference to the ballot box for redress (as if granting that there were grievances requiring redress) and after all agreeing to support what they consider constitutional measures made the thing a party slur unworthy to issue from the state which furnished the heroes of Gaines Hill, Crampton's Pass, or Williamsburg. I can see now Cromwell's excuse for his hasty or too often condensed style of timing and the long parliament.

I can imagine you having a good "read" in Trenton and wish very much I could be present. How do you like *Les Misérables?* I think you said you had been reading it. Tell Mary I am VERY much obliged for the "lines" and regret quite as much that my time was so short in Newark. It corresponded with my other visits, five minutes in a place.

🖊 [Halsey remained bitter about the "peace resolutions" passed by the Democratic-controlled state legislature back home in New Jersey. The resolutions not only criticized the Emancipation Proclamation, but protested the proposed creation of a pro-Union state of West Virginia and criticized the Lincoln administration. The most controversial of the resolutions was a demand that the New Jersey legislature circumvent the president, Congress, cabinet, and entire federal government and appoint its own commission to strike a settlement to end the war with the Confederate government. (Lincoln had insisted from the first day of the war that the conflict was a rebellion and not a war against another country, and therefore the government of the United States could not, legally, have any peace negotiations with the South.) The highly irregular, and extralegal, idea was presented by Democratic legislator Will Wright, a longtime friend of the Darcys', in a fiery speech on the floor of the legislature. He was attacked by many but supported by many others, including, it seems, Mary Darcy. Republicans and soldiers were furious. Pro-Union newspapers throughout New Jersey condemned the resolutions. One Union Army officer read them to his assembled regiment and then barked as loud as he could that anyone who voted for them was a "traitor." Other regiments gathered signatures on petitions to protest the peace resolutions.

The peace resolutions were, as far as just about every resident of every other Union state felt, the final nail in New Jersey's coffin. The opposition to the war by so many New Jersey politicians and newspapers had annoyed people throughout the North for over two years. People had referred to Northerners opposed to the war as copperheads and now, in the spring of 1863, people throughout the country began to refer to New Jersey as the Copperhead State. It infuriated Halsey and the New Jersey men risking their lives for their country.

The swing against the war by some of the most important newspapers in the state started in January 1863 with the signing of the Emancipation Proclamation. The *Newark Daily Journal,* antiwar from the start of the conflict, was very critical of it and warned its readers that President Lincoln was now giving the slaves complete equality with Northern whites. The *Journal* and other antiadministration newspapers savaged the March 3, 1863, Enrollment Act, which authorized a nationwide draft if enough recruits would not continue to join the army. The editor of the

Journal, Edward Fuller, wrote that the Enrollment Act was not only unconstitutional, but was needed because no one wanted to fight the war anymore. "They will steadily refuse to be offered up as victims to the infernal destructive policy of the abolitionists," he wrote. He was not alone in his condemnation of the government and the president. Lincoln was savaged almost daily in the partisan New Jersey copperhead press. The *Hackensack Democrat* called him "a backwoods buffoon . . . the father of all iniquity" and said that he was "the death knell of the Union." The *Somerville Messenger* called him "a Presidential pygmy."

Hundreds of large broadsides denouncing Lincoln and the war effort were nailed to the walls of buildings throughout Newark by anonymous dissidents. Unsigned letters denouncing Lincoln and the army tumbled into the editorial offices of the state's leading newspapers, and antiwar speakers could be found just about anywhere in the state in the spring of 1863, but particularly in Newark.

The war surrounded Newarkers, too, and in a more fearful way than it did people in most Northern cities. Newark had a camp where soldiers were trained, and those soldiers could be found anywhere in Newark, particularly on Pink Row, where the houses of prostitution, given new birth by the war and the influx of soldiers, were located. Newark was a manufacturing city, and much of the cannons and ammunition, caissons and carriages, for the army were made there.

The most fearful sign of the war, though, could be seen in a small Soldiers' Hospital started by politician Marcus Ward, later elected governor, in Newark's downtown area. Within just a few months, the hospital grew to over 2,800 beds for returning soldiers. All of them were full. The lists of maimed and badly wounded infantrymen and officers grew daily, and soon the entire building had to be expanded and then nearby warehouses appropriated. The hospital used open floors as wards, and doctors stacked the beds as close to each other as they could to accommodate the army of the wounded arriving each morning.

Doctors not only had to do bloody amputations and treat potentially fatal diseases, but they had to operate on men who were little more than stitched up in quick battlefield surgery before being sent to Newark. In many cases, doctors in Newark had to undo hasty and uncertain surgery performed on the front lines. Windows had to be kept open because of the stench in the wards. The scene of the dead and dying in the middle of the city was a daily reminder of the grimness of the war the people of Newark thought the North was losing in 1863.

The leader of the copperhead movement in the North, Ohio congressman Clement Vallandigham, a newspaper editor, was soon arrested and deported for what Abraham Lincoln considered treasonous views. He was even invited to Newark by leading Democrats on February 14, 1863, to speak at Concert Hall. A capacity crowd, including many legislators and newspaper editors, listened to him blast the president and the war, which he called "this miserable crusade against African slavery."

The visit of the controversial Vallandigham to Newark and the daily sniping of the *Journal* rather quickly made Newark the Copperhead Capital of the Copperhead State. Not everyone was a copperhead, though, and the pro-administration *Newark Advertiser* routinely blasted legislators who voted for the peace resolutions: "While our soldiers in the field have added lustre to our name, politicians at home—the tools of demagogues of other states, have robbed us of our hard earned laurels and for the time caused the very name of New Jersey to stink in the nostrils of patriotism."

Newark in the spring of 1863 was not only New Jersey's largest city, but a thriving community of more than seventy thousand people, including a large German and Irish population. It was growing by 5 percent per year and had become a major Northern seaport and transportation center and, with three daily newspapers, a national media center. It had a large and contentious school board that oversaw dozens of schools whose teachers educated 10,700 pupils and debated bilingual instruction in English and German. It was a relatively crime-free city. The distribution of counterfeit money there was a major problem throughout the 1860s, as it was in most of the state, and it had its petty criminals, black and white. The police department's official crime report for 1862, however, showed 269 assaults, 344 cases of public drunkenness, 576 cases of public disturbances, but just three cases of shoplifting, one rape, and one murder, quite a moderate crime rate for a seaport city its size.

Some of its businesses maintained prewar profits, but many suffered. Employment remained the same in some industries, but slumped in others. The growing copperhead movement in Newark, and the daily dosages of venom spewed forth in the pages of the *Journal,* made the feelings about the war there dramatically different from what they were in sleepy little Rockaway. Halsey's hometown was never split on the war. Its residents were fiercely patriotic. Rockaway had no local newspaper, and the two county newspapers, printed twice a week, were pro-Union. People did not read about dissension, unless they read editorials critical of it.

Halsey's family viewed the war one way, but Mary Darcy had to view it quite another. She and her sister heard talk of the antiwar movement constantly and read about it daily in the *Newark Daily Journal*. Mary and her sister never wavered in their support of the Union, even though Mary apparently supported the peace resolutions. The two girls joined one of the area's ladies' auxiliaries and from time to time worked in the Soldiers' Hospital in Newark or took a train to Trenton to work with other women taking care of soldiers in a hospital there.

The support of the war by Mary and her family came at an exceedingly high price. The war crippled the Darcys financially. Mary's father and his brother-in-law owned a large clothing store whose main business was the exporting of thousands of shirts, pants, coats, and other apparel to stores throughout the South, with large accounts in Galveston, Texas, and New Orleans, Louisiana. That business died within a year after the bombardment of Fort Sumter as just about every Southern market refused to buy Northern goods. Henry Darcy's business practically collapsed. He was apparently saved from bankruptcy by loans from his father, whose railroad business grew during the war, and the slow retooling of his company into the production of other goods that he could sell throughout the North and to Europe. Still, despite the collapse, Henry Darcy and his family remained loyal supporters of the Union Army and the war.

It was difficult for anyone in Newark to be loyal without questions because of events in the city, such as the huge crowd for Vallandigham's speech and the pelting of abolitionist leader Henry Ward Beecher with eggs when he got off his train at Newark for a speech in 1863. The *Newark Daily Journal* was full of antiwar editorials and stories and highlighted any problems of the Union soldiers stationed in town. Any story about a Union soldier in a bar fight became headline news in Newark, and any antiwar letters from soldiers at the front were published and showcased.

Stories from Southern newspapers that charged any Union general or regiment with abuses were printed word for word, such as stories from New Orleans papers alleging that the army of William T. Sherman was looting villages in its way in the spring of 1863. Ben Butler suffered the same fate, castigated by Southern editors whose stories would quickly resurface in Newark papers. Even the mass enlistments of free black residents and recently freed Southern slaves into the Union Army was greeted with jeers in the *Newark Journal*. Its headline for one such enlistment effort was "Negro Soldiers: The Degradation of Our Race and

Country." Pro-Union residents had to ignore the *Journal* and the public speakers in town, which many of them did. It was difficult, however, and much of Newark remained antiwar.

From time to time Mary Darcy's fervor did waver, as it did over the peace resolutions, because she was fearful for her boyfriend's safety and her father's business. Mary wanted the war to end, like so many others, and in the spring of 1863 felt that some kind of peace commission might do it. Since her letters were not preserved, it is uncertain what she said to Halsey about Will Wright's speech and the peace resolution uproar, but it appears from Halsey's correspondence to her—then and later—that she was still determined, no matter what happened to her father's business or what she heard or read, to convince her boyfriend that everyone he knew on the home front, especially her, was solidly behind the war—and behind him.]

April 4

🖋 [Halsey wrote in his diary that he had finished reading Victor Hugo's novel *Les Misérables,* keeping up his novel-a-week pace. The religious Halsey complained that no one had preached to the men since January.]

April 8

Grand review for President Lincoln of four Corps—Sedgwick's, Meade's, Reynolds' and Sickles'. We left camp at 8 and marched about three miles to near the Fitzhugh house when we (6th corps) were drawn up in three lines of regiments. Over a hill could be seen the black masses of another corps, their bayonets giving them the appearance of being frosted with silver. President Lincoln, whom I had a good opportunity to see, appeared very pale and [sickly]. He rode up and down the line with General Hooker and a crowd of staff officers and then the command was given to march right and we passed in review, in division columns [in front of the president].

🖋 [The president, riding a huge bay horse with his energetic son riding right behind him, enjoyed the review and cracked a small smile when, spontaneously, a throaty cheer for him went up from the army of sixty thousand men. He was also impressed with the choreographed symphony of boat and locomotive whistles that went off to greet him when his boat landed at Acquia Creek, a tributary of the Potomac west of Washington, D.C. He was not there only to review the troops. Lincoln had nagging doubts about Fighting Joe Hooker. He was impressed by the way Hooker had reorganized the Army of the Potomac in the three months he had been in charge, but thought his new commander was overconfident and did not see the war as he did. Hooker kept telling Lincoln that if he could take Richmond, he could win the war, and Lincoln kept telling Hooker that the enemy was not a city, but Robert E. Lee's army. Lincoln also urged Hooker, again and again, to throw everything he had at Lee and not to send troops in bit by bit, as Burnside and McClellan did, holding thousands back in reserve.

Hooker, his colonels surrounding him like a flotilla of ribbons and swords, promised that he would hurl the entire army at Lee as soon as he found him and win the war. Lincoln was pleased, for the moment, but as he boarded his boat to go back to Washington, taking one last look at his army, he still worried about Joe Hooker.]

April 14

Marching orders came last night after I had gone to bed and the day has been a busy one, packing, drawing and issuing arms and ammunition. I issued 21,500 rounds to make each man (60 per). Each man is to carry eight days rations!

Alanson divided his delicacies from home—chocolates. The box ordered from Major Brown two months ago suddenly arrived, with a diary, stationery.

The cavalry, 15,000, started yesterday.

🖋 [By now, the men of the Fifteenth—and of the entire brigade—were certain that the Army of the Potomac was going to strike at the Confederacy soon.]

April 19

There were reports of an accident to Hooker. Reports, too, that President Lincoln was back in camp.

Dr. Charles Hall, Princeton '60, joined us as assistant surgeon.

🖋 [Lincoln was in camp, and he left unhappy. Hooker, whom friends said drank and talked too much, again gave Lincoln a long speech about how he would take Richmond to end the war. An exasperated Lincoln, who had heard the same speech from Irvin McDowell, McClellan, Pope, and Burnside, insisted that the way to end the war was to find Lee's army and crush it, not to simply attack Richmond. He left hoping that Hooker had listened.]

April 20

In the afternoon, all the haircutters were at work cropping the men close to the skull.

April 21

🖋 [The regiment's new colonel, William Penrose, arrived in camp and assumed command. Halsey immediately disliked Penrose. He complained that within twenty-four hours of his arrival, Penrose began to admonish his officers for the slightest infraction of army rules.]

April 25

Fixed up the roll book for Paul Kuhl, to whom I have taken a great liking.

8

CHANCELLORSVILLE

April 29–June 30, 1863

[Hooker, taking Lincoln's advice, decided to cross the Rappahannock River in late April 1863, in a campaign to destroy Lee and the Army of Northern Virginia. His plan was simple: he would send a wing of the Army, including the VI Corp and Halsey's Fifteenth New Jersey, led by Gen. John Sedgwick, as a decoy to attack Fredericksburg. At the same time, his main force, nearly seventy thousand men, would cross the Rappahannock and Rapidan and move through a wilderness to the tiny junction of Chancellorsville, to the left of Lee and between him and Fredericksburg.

The army would then move out of Chancellorsville, through the thick wilderness around it, and lie in wait for Lee. At the same time, Gen. George Stoneman's cavalry would ride fifteen miles west and around Lee's army. Hooker believed that Lee would rush his entire army to Fredericksburg when the VI Corps attacked there. When Lee started to move, Stoneman's cavalry would attack his rear and drive the rebels directly in front of Hooker's main force, waiting on the other side of the wilderness, which would crush them. "May God have mercy on Lee, because I will not," said the bold Hooker.

On paper, the plan was perfect. It did not work well, however, because Lee received early reports from J.E.B. Stuart's fast-moving cavalry scouts that although a Union army was on its way to Fredericksburg along the Rappahannock, a much larger Union force was moving across the Rapidan and moving toward Fredericksburg from the west, apparently going through the wilderness and past the tiny junction of Chancellorsville. Lee, sensing that the attack on Fredericksburg was a feint to deceive him, split up his army, sending just ten thousand men under Gen. Jubal Early to Fredericksburg and keeping the main army, close to forty thousand men, with him.

Sedgwick's men and the VI Corps met strong resistance when they reached Fredericksburg. Early's men arrived in time to defend the city and were dug in behind the stone wall that ran along the crest of Marye's Heights, where so many Federals had died in the December battle there.

Halsey and the Fifteenth moved out with Sedgwick.]

April 29

We were aroused at midnight but did not move till about 5 A.M. when a volley was heard from the direction of the river. This was the reception the rebel pickets gave the 95th Pa. who made the crossing. We moved double quick time down the hill and over the plateau and jumped in the boats and were rowed over. Russels' Brigade (3rd) was deployed as skirmishers a little way out from the bluff bank of the river and we lay along under the bluff, the 2d brigade behind us.

April 30

I was on picket watch. Relieved about 5 A.M. Only one division has crossed the river as yet. We could see the enemy on the hills indirectly watching us and then saw their artillery batteries to the right. The order of General Hooker that the 3rd, 5th and 11th Corps had made a brilliant move and that "the enemy must either come out and fight us on our own ground or ignominiously flee . . ." was read to us.

When relieved, I fell back to the little rifle pit which had been occupied by the rebs on the bluff bank of river and which had been buried during the day (south bank).

*[The next day brought one of the strangest events of the war.]

May 1

At Franklin's Crossing . . . warmer.

We lay in the rifle pit near the landing all day, the only excitement being occasional picket firing and once in a while a rebel shell going over our heads and bursting behind us. At sunset, the pickets of our division were relieved by Piatt's Brigade.

All the other troops of our corps and as we think the 5th corps were paraded on the Stafford side of the river in full view of the rebs. Bands were playing and there was a general cessation of firing. We heard the rebel bands playing "Yankee Doodle." Our brigade band was directed by Capt. Cooke from the river bank and responded with "Dixie." The rebels could be seen in the flats and on the hillsides. Both armies cheered. It was a strange sight and the sun going down at the moment made a deep impression on everyone.

May 2

We remained at the same place and were disturbed by occasional shells and picket firing which kept us on the alert.

In the afternoon, heaving firing—cannonading and musketry—could be heard in the direction of Chancellorsville. On the hills we thought we could see the rebel regiments on the march, but their uniforms made them hard to distinguish from the gray side hills.

Toward evening the pickets were arranged to the edge of the road or to the Bowling Green road, a very spirited affair which seemed not at all like fighting. The men of the Corps moved quickly to the river, crossed and passed us marching towards the ravine where we lost sight of them in the darkness.

We thought the enemy had left our front and we had only to move in and occupy their places.

✒ [Sedgwick ordered his men into battle at Fredericksburg on the morning of May 3. The Confederates pinned them down at first and thwarted several assaults on Marye's Heights, but their much thinner forces were unable to withstand the Union Army throughout the morning, and by noon the rebel lines had been broken and Early's men retreated. Some of the men speculated that they could have destroyed Early's entire army then if they had pursued them, but they had other goals. Sedgwick, under orders from Hooker to get his men to Chancellorsville as soon as possible, began moving his soldiers down a road away from Fredericksburg. On the road to Chancellorsville, the Fifteenth stumbled into one of the fiercest fights of the war, and Ed Halsey had his second brush with death.]

May 3

At daylight, we moved out by the flank, inclining to the left to the Bowling Green Road in front of the Brevards Mansion. Marching along this road, we were suddenly quieted by half a dozen shells from the edge of the wood. Instructively, the men ducked their heads but General Brooks, riding along the side of the regiment, noticed it and his "test . . . test . . . test" order stopped the involuntary movement. The road had ditches on either side. The dirt from them made ridges on either side. McCartney's Battery was brought up behind us and opened up on the rebels.

At first, we lay along the south side of the road but when our battery opened up we were moved over to the north side where we had to stop behind the low mounds to prevent our own guns from hurting us. The rebel picket lines crossed the road to the east and kept up a fire at us from that bank. Co. B, with which I was in, was in the extreme left flank and the ditch was full of water so that we had little room.

Suddenly the rebs advanced their line and the regiment was rushed over to the south side to meet them. Something struck me in the leg of my boot and I tumbled into the water. I was getting out of [the ditch] and fell when the regiment rushed past me and back of the battery so that it [artillery] could play on the advancing line.

Supposing myself to be wounded and hearing the voices and steps of the rebs, I lay perfectly still in the road for what seemed an age. The batteries used our very best pieces. A shell struck the ground within an inch or two and a bullet passed between my face and the ground. I heard the groan of one of our men growing less and less audible in the ditch south of the road till they stopped altogether. Finally, Col. Campbell appeared up the road coming along the ditch and the chaplain came up to carry me in.

I found I was not hurt and went in alone, but I was a sorry looking spectacle, the wet clothes having collected the dirt of the road. I started that morning with two big haversacks. Fairclo's and my own. Fairclo wanted to be unencumbered to manage his company and [I took his haversack]. It broken down [and slid off me], pulling me back down into the ditch.

The firing gradually slackened and from our position back of the battery we had a fine view of the Fredericksburg hills and saw our second division carry them in fine style. It was a great sight to see the long blue lines advance steadily up the sides of the hill, not checked by the fire of the rebel pits in front of them. After their success, our line was withdrawn and we moved by the flank along the road towards the city. We had lost several men in this affair. One man was killed by the accidental discharge of one of our own muskets, which the colonel then ordered broken.

At a house on the outskirts of the city we halted n hour or two. There was quite a number of prisoners there.

About the middle of the afternoon we men put in motion to join the rest of the brigade which we had not seen since morning. We passed through Fredericksburg meeting here and there one of our dead in the streets. Over the hill, down a hill and up another hill and then along a pike towards Salem Heights we walked. Troops were laying on either side of the road making way for us to pass. As we neared Salem church the picket firing seemed to become heavier. We filed to the right into a field, formed and moved towards a wood in the line of battle. Capt. Cooke saw us coming from the wood with his hand on his shoulder, where he had been struck by minié ball [bullet].

"They nipped me," he said to the colonel.

[The Fifteenth had stumbled into the core of the larger battle that raged around Salem Church. The Third New Jersey, Cooke's group, had been driven into the field near the church, using rails for defense, by a group of Georgians and were pinned down. They yelled to the men of the Fifteenth to protect themselves.]

A handful of men apparently lay along an old rail fence which separated the woods from the field. They sang out "Throw off your knapsacks. You don't want them here."

Col. Penrose took the hint and the knapsacks were laid on the ground. The regiment then advanced towards the fence. As I was coming a miniball struck the fence right between my legs. I don't think we had advanced twenty yards before we caught a terrific volley. The command "fire by file, commence firing" was shouted but the regiment really fired by volley. The line staggered for a minute but only a minute. It again advanced a few yards to where the rebs could be seen and here continued for an hour or an hour and a half, until their ammunition was exhausted and we were relieved by the 95th Pa.

[Halsey did not know it, but the Fifteenth came within a few minutes of being completely wiped out within the fences. They were practically surrounded by rebels. The Ninety-fifth tried to save them, but their lines were quickly cut down by a horrendous volley from the rebels, and they suffered 130 casualties in just five minutes. All around them, thousands of Union troops were in full retreat, an endless run of blue soldiers, under the assault of Lee's men. Hundreds charged past the Fifteenth in a general skedaddle as it struggled to stay alive.]

The 3rd N.J. was relieved and came in to our aid, too. In a short time they moved back and I went back with them to the edge of the woods supposing the whole line was coming back afterward seeing they were alone. One man of Co. G. was shot in the body close to me and turning to leave the field his blood [gushed out] all over my boots. The woods was full of smoke and the firing was continuous. Seeing and hearing battle was difficult.

At dusk, the regiment came out of the woods, picked up their knapsacks and moved to the east of the pike. The relieving regiment followed the 15th and the rebs came to the edge of the field. Bishop (I think) was killed picking up his knapsack there.

🖎 [Halsey and his men managed to slip out to safety because a New Jersey artillery battery opened up on the Georgians who had them pinned down. Firing with extraordinary precision, the battery badly damaged the rebels. The Fifteenth also benefited from volleys of bullets from the rebs that flew over their heads as they backed out of the field. The Fifteenth was able to retreat in a generally organized fashion and pulled back to near the river.]

I went out with Fairclo to gather what news we could of our wounded and of the battle. It was bad enough, all right. Capt. Snidely and Lt. Fowler were left dead in the woods with many others and our advance had been checked.

Our regiment loss during the day was 25 killed and 125 wounded and four missing. We number that morning about 450 men and of these one of every three was either killed or wounded. Many of the wounded died afterward.

🖎 [The Fifteenth had arrived in Chancellorsville a day after the battle began and in the middle of what was developing as not only one of the great defeats of the war, but one of the greatest military defeats in American history, as well as a textbook example of on-the-field tactical brilliance by Robert E. Lee.

On May 1, Lee, sensing Hooker's strategy of creating a ruse, did not advance toward Fredericksburg, but instead attacked Hooker's army as it started to move through the wilderness and away from Chancellorsville. The Union Army moved out in an orderly fashion, but once it made it to a series of low ridges around Chancellorsville, it encountered heavy resistance by what were at first thought to be rebel pickets. The Federals met stronger resistance within the hour, but were certain they could defeat the rebel force. Hooker, however, panicked and ordered all his men back to Chancellorsville (he later admitted that "Joe Hooker just lost his nerve").

Lee then took a major gamble in an effort to turn the tables on Hooker and deceive him. On May 2, Lee split his army in half again, keeping seventeen thousand men under his command and, with a wilderness guide, sent Stonewall Jackson with an army of twenty-six thousand men on a circuitous, sixteen-mile march in a broad semicircle around the Union Army to put themselves in position for a charge on the Union right flank. Jackson and his men would emerge from a thick forest, an area guarded by only a thin line of troops from the XI Corps. Lee foolhardily hoped that Jackson's bulky army could make its march without being seen. Dozens of Union pickets saw the army, though, and its ammunition wagons, moving through the thick forests of trees, thickets, vines, pricker bushes, and small, rock-filled streams, and they reported it to Hooker, who incredulously decided it was not an attack, but a retreat, and paid no attention to it.

Just before 6 P.M. Union pickets noticed hundreds of frightened deer, their eyes wide, racing toward them out of the woods. There was a pause, and then came the familiar spine-tingling, bloodcurdling sound of the rebel yell as Stonewall Jackson's entire army of twenty-six thousand men attacked through the trees, vines, prickers, and bushes, some men with the shirts torn from their backs by the sharp underbrush. Their attack, Union sentries said, sounded like a loud crash. They pounced on the XI Corps on the right flank and drove them back like a mass of jelly. The attack nearly destroyed the entire Union Army, pushing much of it back in toward Hooker's headquarters. Only the arrival of darkness stopped it. (Jackson pleaded for permission for an unprecedented night attack, certain he could roll up the entire federal army, but Lee turned him down. An hour later, Jackson was riding through the forest and by accident was shot by his own men and later died.)

The next day, reeling from Jackson's attack the night before, Hooker leaned against a pillar on the porch of the house he had commandeered as his headquarters. A rebel shell hit the pillar, splitting it in two, and knocked Hooker down. He remained groggy all day. Hooker, uncertain how large Lee's army was, decided to dig in for a defensive fight even though he actually outnumbered the rebels three to one. His last hope was that Sedgwick's army, with the Fifteenth New Jersey, was on its way, which the rebels knew. Lee, realizing that Hooker thought he was out- numbered, saw a sterling opportunity. He left half his men in place to attack Hooker and then himself led a force of some twenty thousand men against Sedgwick, and the Fifteenth, which caught the Federals on the road to Chancellorsville near Salem Church on May 3. The Fifteenth, surrounded on three sides by the Confederates and with their back to the river, were hit again by Lee on May 4 and seemed doomed unless they could somehow get to the pontoon bridges on the river. Lee had in- credibly surrounded the Union Army on three sides, a textbook near- impossibility, and appeared on the verge of squeezing and then annihilating it.]

May 4 (Salem Heights)

In the morning we were filed to one side and then to another as an attack seemed imminent. Most of the morning we were on the south side of the pike, in line parallel to it, supporting a battery near a small house. From where we were we could see very little but heard a great deal. Heavy musketry was heard believed to the right of us. Then [we heard it] next in front and then to our left. We [suffered from] great anxiety. We watched the latter area [hidden men moved]. As it moved more and more to our left until it was between us and Fredericksburg, we knew we were cut off.

The last position was in one of the lines of battle massed behind the church and here we lay till near dark. Then commenced the retreat to Banks Ford. Skirmish lines were formed one behind another, the first line holding their area until the last minute and then taking the line in the rear. Our artillery mowed down the advancing rebs with great slaughter appar- ently, but darkness seemed our best defense.

As we marched along we could hear the rebels yelling in our rear. We arrived near the ford and we lay for a time in an old rifle pit probably dug by the rebels. Afterwards, we moved to the woody back of the ravine where most of us fell asleep. A bullet went whistling over our heads occasionally and shells hit around us at random. We were to be rear guard it seemed but just before daylight we were aroused and moving upstream to the pon- toon bridge. We crossed simultaneously with a New York regiment, the two bridges fusing and forming one bridge. Shells struck the water on either side of us but we were too sleepy and tired to notice them. As we went up the road to the north side it became daylight and the rebels saw us and shelled us as we gained the top of the hill.

🖋 [The Fifteenth faced the same plight as all the other regiments at Chancellorsville. They outnumbered the enemy yet did not know it. Their enemy was an aggressive army bent on destroying them. It did not retreat and kept coming and coming and coming, its battle flags waving majestically in the smoke drifting over the thick forest glades surrounding the tiny Chancellorsville junction. The Southerners had completely outfoxed the Federals with Jackson's charge, and then, in a brilliant reflex, Lee had kept the pressure on Hooker on May 3 and 4 while attacking Sedgwick and preventing him from helping Hooker and then covering the entire army's left flank.

General Hooker had dug in to battle defensively, pulling his troops back into a semicircle to defend the few buildings in Chancellorsville and his path back to the river. As his men fought bravely, urged on by gallant generals and colonels, the Confederates turned to their artillery. Lee had artillery batteries placed in strategic places to hammer the Federals from three sides. Heavy, and accurate, artillery fire kept the Union forces pinned down. Lee moved his men and artillery in closer and closer until his cannons were within five hundred yards. They fired every shell they had at the Federals, and when they ran out of shells, they used twelve-inch-long pieces of steel railroad ties and pieces of chain and fired that.

Hooker, unable to make any headway and fearful that he would be encircled and wiped out, ordered a retreat back to the river. Despite the pressure from Lee's army, federal artillerists kept up a heavy fire themselves, protecting the men as they crossed the pontoons and fled to safety after the disastrous defeat. The Union suffered seventeen thousand casualties and the South twelve thousand.

The resounding defeat at Chancellorsville created havoc in the halls of the federal government in Washington. One senator charged into Secretary of War Edwin Stanton's office when he heard the news and screamed, "All is lost! All is lost!" Lincoln, hurt badly by the defeat, turned to one of his secretaries when he got the news, his lanky frame shaking with emotion, and blurted out, "My God! My God! What will the country say?"

Back in northern Virginia, the Union Army retreated methodically.]

May 5
Moved back a mile or so from the river near our camp of January 22. The camp was filled with the carcasses of horses and mules who had died in January and [had been left]. The enemy occasionally fired shells at us.

May 7

Alanson and I visited "Willow Grove." I gave Mrs. Durchuan a little package of green tea which she said was the first she had seen for a year. They reported that the mass of musketry from the battle on Sunday sounded like a thunderstorm.

[Willow Grove was one of the plantations in the area, and Mrs. Durchuan was a friend of Joseph Halsey's whom Edmund knew from prewar visits to his brother's Lessland Plantation. He asked her for information about his brother, but she had little.

The heroism of the men from Morris County in Company A of the Fifteenth Regiment quickly became myth back home in New Jersey. Lt. George Justice wrote a poem about the company, and about slain Cpl. Warren Dunham, which was published in the *Beacon,* in Lambertville, and reprinted widely.]

POEM

There's a cap that was lost,
Not tatter'd, but blue,
Of very slight value,
It may be, 'tis true,
But crowns, jewel studded,
Can't surpass it today
With its letter of honor,
Brave Company "A"!

Bright eyes have looked calmly,
its visor beneath,
O'er the work of the reaper,
Grim harvester—Death
Let the muster roll meager
So mournfully say,
How foremost in battle,
Went Company "A"!

Whose footsteps unbroken
Came up to the wood,
Where Rebels in masses,
There threateningly stood,

Who, closing up breaches,
Still kept on their way,
till guns downward pointed
Faced Company "A"!

Like cameras awful,
Stood cannons aloof,
Till signal was given,
To strike off a proof
Of the soul of the soldier,
To send up to him
Pray God That He Knew It,
Though bloody and dim.

Though our hero is sleeping
today with the dead,
And daisy and clover
Bloom over his head,
I would smile through tears
As I lay it way,
That battle worn cap,
Lettered Company "A"!

May 10

[Halsey read the novel *Miriam*.]

Preparations are afoot for another assault on the enemy's stronghold. [I am] full of anxiety having seen the report in the *Tribune* that I was wounded.

Benjamin Wear died at two o'clock this morning. Sent the $11.15 found on him home by Alanson.

May 12

🖋 [Halsey wrote an emotional set of resolutions for the men of the Fifteenth following the deaths of popular Captain Lindsley and Lieutenant Fowler. The resolutions were printed in his letter for the Jerseyman.]

RESOLVED: That in the loss of Captain Lindsley and Lieutenant Fowler, the regiment has been deprived of two of its most worthy and efficient officers. Always at their posts like true soldiers, whether in the discharge of their duties in the camp, or in the presence of a wily and dangerous enemy, their attention to duty, their steeliness and bravery in the perilous hour of battle, proves them to have been undoubted patriots, and true representatives of their gallant native state.

RESOLVED: That though we deplore their loss as officers, and greatly miss them as comrades in the interchange of those courtesies and civilities incident to the soldier's life, yet we do not view their death as a useless sacrifice, but as an offering to perpetuate to their country and posterity that civil and religious liberty that traitors would wrest from them.

RESOLVED: That we deeply sympathize with the families of the fallen, by whom their loss will be more severely felt. But there is consolation in the reflection that they fell in honorable warfare in defense of the dearest rights of a freedman.

RESOLVED: That our warmest sympathies are extended to the families and immediate friends of those heroic men, who fell in that conflict in defense of our common cause, and in aiding the regiment to earn that glorious name it now wears, and though their forms may never more be seen in our ranks, we are proud to have the privilege of recording that they were once there, and sustained to the last the character of the true Jerseymen, falling face to the foe.

🖎 [Halsey was despondent over his friend Lieutenant Boeman's death, too, but just as upset at the news that his cousin Thomas J. Halsey, who had led the Eleventh New Jersey into battle at Chancellorsville, had been wounded, captured by the enemy, and sent off to Richmond's notorious Libby Prison, where he remained for eight months.]

May 17
   We [Dr. Hall and Halsey] walked out about a mile to the East, where we found a nice stream in which we took a good bath.

May 22
🖎 [Halsey was in high spirits despite the defeat at Chancellorsville, his attitude buoyed by a visit from his brother Sam, who took trains to Washington and then a boat to the Fredericksburg area. He told Halsey that his cousins Eliza and Mary were having a short vacation in Trenton. Halsey wrote Eliza.]

Dear Cousin,
   Your letters are always so patriotic and so hopeful that they would raise the spirits of the most discouraged. To know that you have friends who think of you and to whom your well being and success are of some interest is indeed something to be grateful for. After all, men are more influenced by the good opinions of others than they are aware of and I cannot consider myself an exception to the rule.
   It is hardly necessary after my last long letter and the accounts you have seen in the papers to say anything about the battle. The official reports will give you the best idea of the whole thing when they are published. Newspaper correspondents sometimes get things strangely confused. For example, in the clip you sent me [the story was] for the most part true yet in it there were some things wrong—Col. Brown was wounded in the wood and the command devolved (Col. Caleb having been killed) on Col. Buck who had command until Monday night when his horse fell in a rifle pit at Banks Ford. And THERE Col. Penrose took command. Col. P., I understand, is not a graduate of West Point, though brought up in the army, having been born in a garrison, and deserves all that has been said of him.
   Our regiment on its return went into their old camp but it is considered unhealthy for troops to live in huts "mudded up" in the summer and so the day before yesterday we were moved to a hill opposite and have been busy since policing and cleaning it up, somewhat of a task as it is full of stumps

and bushes. I will send . . . Mary a sketch of a tent which you can no doubt certify to be [a] correct [sketch].

Sam's visit was a great treat. The weather was pleasant and [on] the second day, in company with two officers, I went with him to Falmouth and to the camp of the 11th N.J., where he stopped. From the hills near Falmouth, we could point out the whole scene of the first battle and of our last operations on the noon of the 3rd, when we passed over the heights. I am in hopes he has had time to stop and see you. He can give you so much better description of the present condition and situation of the army than I can. My faith still clings to Hooker.

🖋 [Halsey's rather unemotional notes in his diary and letters, and belief in Hooker and the army, reflected the general feeling of the troops in the Army of the Potomac. They felt demoralized and doomed after Fredericksburg, but now, after another huge defeat, their attitude was considerably better. No one was sure what gave the army its upbeat demeanor. Some said it was the realization that the newly passed draft bill and the first enlistments of black troops would bring in thousands of fresh troops. Some said it was the recognition that despite the defeat the army was still huge (133,000 men) and still strong. Some said it was the feeling that despite some copperheads back home, the general feeling in the North had started to swing toward continuing the war. The men of the Army of the Potomac, and Halsey, did not look at Chancellorsville as the end of anything. It might even have been the beginning of something, the feeling that even if they did not defeat Robert E. Lee at Fredericksburg or Chancellorsville, they would defeat him somewhere . . . and soon. The Army of the Potomac had its second wind.

LESSLAND PLANTATION: The battle of Chancellorsville created pandemonium throughout Orange County, Virginia. Until the Union crossing of the river and the battle of Chancellorsville, residents in the Orange and Culpeper County areas felt reasonably safe. Their slaves did not feel there was much chance of the Federals intruding on the life of the residents, either. However, Chancellorsville changed the way local slaves viewed the war.

The Confederate Army won the battle, but the closeness of the Union Army gave slaves throughout Orange the courage to escape from their plantations in the middle of the night and risk their lives in a bold dash to the camps of the nearby Union Army. The Federals were within ten or fifteen miles of thousands of plantation slaves in the two counties and welcomed any runaways. Slaves bolted their plantations, usually at night, and made their way to the safety of the Union lines.

Most of the twelve slaves at Lessland joined them and fled together at night—only house servant Douglass and his wife, Sarah, remained with Millie Halsey and her children. Some of those slaves, uncertain about their dash to freedom, returned to Lessland. Planters who woke up to find their slaves gone not only realized that their plantation prosperity was over, but that the enemy was so close that they were now in harm's way. They started to pack up their families and belongings, fearful of the Union Army's return, and headed for safety in central and western Virginia. Ironically, many fled to the Appomattox area, where the war would end.]

June 5
We lay in constant expectation of moving all day. Tents struck. Cannonading was heard in the direction of the river.

🖋 [The Fifteenth moved out the next day as part of a VI Corps reconnaissance mission to cross the Rappahannock at Franklin's Crossing to determine whether Lee's army was still in the Chancellorsville area or had, as Hooker feared, moved toward Maryland.]

June 7 (Franklin's Crossing)
We lay all day on the flat below the hills nearly in front of the ravine coming down and opposite the pontoon bridge, watching the proceedings on the other side of the river where there was occasional sharpshooting and artillery practice. The rebs had sharpshooters in a house towards Fredericksburg but one of our batteries opened up on it, driving them out.

At half past seven the Brigade crossed and relieved part of the 2d division. We were under arms all night.

🖋 [As part of the general reconnaissance, Hooker sent Gen. Alfred Pleasanton's cavalry, along with John Buford's cavalry, to Brandy Station to hunt for J.E.B. Stuart's cavalry. They clashed in what was called the first major cavalry fight of the war, with the North losing over nine hundred men and the South four hundred.]

June 13
Very hot. The regiment was laying at the flat below the high bank most of the day, the enemy occasionally dropping a shell in our neighborhood.

We were in line at 3:30 A.M. and watchful all day. At evening, the six left companies went out on picket.

A bugler coming out on the hills in back of us to sound some call and failing set the whole division yelling "come down off that hill, you bugler." We afterwards had all our calls nearly sounded by a bugler.

A tremendous thunder shower came just after dark, drenching every one but making the withdrawal practicable. Hay was laid on the bridge and the artillery crossed first. Then [came] the regiments, not displayed, last of all the pickets. The lines were formed in the north bank to defend the bridge and pickets were ordered to fall straight back to the river and then along and under the bank to the bridge. Some men of the 10th were there and Sands and Fowler of our regiment sleeping in a tent by themselves when called.

Our regiment assisted the engineers (who seemed, or at least their officers did, all drunk) to drag out the pontoons till daylight. No shots were fired and the boats were all sound. We had men under arms six days and nights.

🖋 [The reconnaissance of the Fifteenth and the cavalry told Hooker that Lee's army was on the move, headed northwest, with Stuart's cavalry in front scouting. Hooker prepared to move his entire army at a forty-five-degree angle to intercept Lee if he invaded the North. It was a hard march.]

June 14 (On the march)

Hot. At daylight, we started directly up the hills (seeing the rebs advance over the deserted pits behind us) and passing through deserted camps and reached Potomac Creek at about one. I saw Huntington Jackson sick with chills at a house and obtained some of "that cherry tree" supposed to have been struck by Washington's hatchet.

At the creek, we witnessed some experiments with the balloon (which by the way we never saw afterwards) and saw the piles of stores abandoned at the 3rd Corps hospital. When night set in and we had been getting ready for a night sleep we were ordered to fall in. We threw the piles of blankets we had collected on the [wagon] and resumed our march. We marched tediously, halting frequently to the railroad and got there about 11. [We marched] more rapidly to Stafford Court House, which we reached about 3:30 in the morning. We men lay down in the road and slept till daylight. I lay in dirt two inches thick, my head in a stack of muskets.

June 15 (March to Dumfries)

HOT. After about half an hour sleep we fell in and resumed our march at daylight. This was the severest march we ever made. The heat was INTENSE. The fine dust being like a closet in the air and was inhaled at every breath. Col. Penrose leading the division unconscious apparently of his speed was overhauled by other brigade commanders in the afternoon who said they had not a company left in line. Scores of men were laying along the road, sunstricken and panting for breath.

A half an hour or so revived the men and by slow marching and with frequent rests the troops marched into Dumfries at dark in good order.

Fowler and I visited the village in the evening for something to eat with very tolerable success.

No words can describe the forlorn, unpainted, dilapidated condition of the place.

✐ [The Army of the Potomac knew Lee had crossed the Potomac and was headed for Pennsylvania, but they did not know his destination. Hooker ordered the entire army to mobilize and move northwest in an organized fashion, looking for Lee and hoping for ground on which to crush him once and for all.]

June 21 (New Fairfax Court House)

Col. Penrose took me aside and privately informed me that he had sent in my name for a 2d lieutenancy and that he wanted all his officers to have a badge he had designed and which Tiffany was to get up. I borrowed $20 from Peter Hardcastle of which I gave him $10.

In the afternoon with Vanderveer and others I walked out a mile or so to see some prisoners from J.E.B. Stuart's cavalry.

Heavy and continuous cannonading all day to the west.

June 26

Reveille at 1:45 A.M. and march at 3. Marched till noon through mud and rain some 16 miles past Herndon Station and Drainsville to the Washington and Leesburg Road where we camped for the night, not far from Drainsville.

The march was a hard enough one and I was footsore and annoyed by the unwelcome visitors in underclothing. The camp was on a field just south of the road.

June 27 (On the march from Drainsville)

Cloudy. Reveille at 2, but did not move until 9 or 10, having to wait for the wagon train to get ahead of us. The train seemed to us about five miles along. After we had started, a handsome black horse came galloping in from the South. Col. Penrose told me to take care of it which I did very willingly until reclaimed. I made two or three miles on him and had rations.

In the middle of the afternoon, we reached the Potomac and after waiting for trains to cross we crossed about five o'clock, our band playing "My Maryland." We were the last infantry to cross. We camped about a mile from the river (no, ten miles).

🖋 [Lincoln had lost his shaky confidence in Hooker after Chancellorsville and replaced him as commander of the Army of the Potomac with Gen. George Meade, whose first major fight would be to stop Lee wherever he found him in Pennsylvania.]

June 28

🖋 [LESSLAND PLANTATION: More planters began to flee the Culpeper area after word reached them that the Army of Northern Virginia had moved out and was heading for Pennsylvania. The local planters were now left completely without protection. Friends urged Millie, weak and haggard looking from running the plantation without all of the slaves, to sell Lessland and leave the area. Some of the women still in the neighborhood offered to let her flee with them. She could bring a wagon loaded with clothes and goods, and her children, and join their own wagons in the general exodus that seemed to grip the county. Millie refused and told them she would stay on the plantation until the war was over. She did not want to leave Lessland to the Yankees and felt that since some friends, such as her mother and "Miss Lizzie" Holmread, were still determined to stay in the area, people would be there to help her if a crisis did arise.]

June 30

Muster Day. Cloudy and rain with showers. We did not leave camp until about noon as we were in the rear and waited for remainder of the Corps and the trains to pass. We reached Westminster (which the rebs are said to have occupied last night) about 5 P.M. and then marched towards Manchester near which place we went into camp about 10 P.M. On arrival, the men were tired and we of Co. D. detailed for fence guard, told the

orderly that he lied (about guard duty). Capt. Walker immediately punished him. The orderly left that night.

The boys stood the march well and I never saw them march better.
There is hardly a straggler. We have travelled through a beautiful country
since we crossed the Potomac.

We are now eight miles from the Pennsylvania line and the rebel cavalry [J.E.B. Stuart] have been and are all around us. . . .

9

GETTYSBURG

July 2–December 31, 1863

[The Confederate Army's success at Chancellorsville, despite high casualties, convinced Robert E. Lee that the time was right for a second invasion of the North. He was certain that the Union Army under its new commander, Gen. George Meade, would try to stop him once he crossed into Maryland and headed for Pennsylvania. One of his aides, A. A. Long, said that Lee hoped the defeat of the Army of the Potomac somewhere in Pennsylvania would give him control of that state, Maryland, and Virginia and cause the evacuation of Washington, D.C., and the flight of the federal government. Others felt the invasion might also cause people in cities such as Harrisburg, Philadelphia, Baltimore, and Wilmington, Delaware, to believe the Confederate Army would attack them. A successful invasion, tied to the unhappiness in the North over the inability of the Union Army to win battles and the just announced and unpopular draft, might even bring about a peace settlement.

Lee's army, with 89,000 men, had a nine-day jump on Meade, who commanded 122,000 men. Lee managed to move away from Fredericksburg and cross the Potomac more than a week before Meade realized Lee was on the move. Union forces then advanced northwest, trying to intercept the rebels. Meade did not know where Lee was headed, and Lee, without his cavalry, which was reconnoitering westward and was out of touch with headquarters, did not know where Meade was or how strong his forces were. The two enormous armies collided by accident at a small town called Gettysburg on the morning of July 1 in a battle that no one planned and that became the pivotal battle of the Civil War.

Union general John Buford's cavalry met rebel infantrymen in Gettysburg early in the morning and, realizing a much larger force was coming up behind them, dug in for a fight to hold off the rebels until the main army could be notified. The fighting, in which one of the North's best generals, John Reynolds, was killed, continued through late morning, when overwhelming numbers of Confederate troops forced the Union line, with the first regiments of infantry joining it, to retreat back through the town and toward Cemetery Hill, a high ground outside of the town. Richard Ewell's corps drove the newly arrived XI Corps back and up to the top of Cemetery Hill, also. Abner Doubleday's men, trying to hold Seminary Ridge, at the western end of town, were driven back to Cemetery Hill in midafternoon.

The Union Army was arriving at the battle slowly, column after column, strung out over miles of Pennsylvania roadways, and still not at full strength. The Fifteenth New Jersey was one of the last units on the move toward Gettysburg. The Union forces holding Cemetery Hill were not strong. Lee, convinced that whoever held the high ground would win the battle, gave Ewell an order to take the hill "if practicable," thinking he would move. Ewell, whose corps already had high casualties, decided it was not "practicable" and did not attack. The delay, and nightfall, enabled the Federals to strengthen the hill and hold it.

Federals kept pouring into Gettysburg and Gen. Winfield Hancock positioned them on top of Cemetery Ridge, a high ground, in a long defensive line connecting Cemetery Hill and, on the other side, two hills called Little Round Top and Big Round Top, in what would appear from the air to be a large fishhook. By the time Meade made it to the town, at midnight, the Federals held the high ground and were dug in for the fight of their lives.

The first day at Gettysburg belonged to the Southerners. They had killed several hundred Northerners and taken nearly four thousand prisoners in driving back every single corps they encountered. Lee, still without information on the Union positions and strengths because Stuart and his cavalry had not returned, had to operate on instinct. The following morning, he devised what appeared to be a sound attack in which Longstreet's men would attack Cemetery Ridge from the right, and at the same time, Ewell's men would attack from the left. Hill's men would cannonade the Federals from the center.

The entire attack was delayed, however, because it took Longstreet until 4:30 P.M. to mount his charge. (He opposed the idea and tried to convince Lee that the rebels should make the Federals attack them.) That gave the Federals time to defend Little Round Top, suddenly left vulnerable when Gen. Dan Sickles moved his men to a weak position in front of it. The Federals got there just in time and managed, with a courageous defensive countercharge by the Twentieth Maine, to hold it against a howling Confederate horde.

The attack on Little Round Top was part of Longstreet's belated attack, which created some of the fiercest fighting of the Civil War in areas around the southern portion of Cemetery Ridge, such as the wheat field, Devil's Den, and the peach orchard. The rebels were beaten back after hours of sharp fighting, unable to take any ground. Ewell's attack, on the northern flank, did not begin until late afternoon either, frustrating Lee, and, despite herculean fighting by his men, was unsuccessful. Two long days of fighting had changed nothing; thousands had been killed on both sides and the Federals still held the high ground.

Still uncertain of the Federals' strength, Lee decided to attack in the middle of their line on the third day of the battle, July 3. He sent fifteen thousand troops under the flamboyant, and fiercely loyal, Gen. George Pickett across a mile-long open field and up gradually sloping Cemetery Ridge. Pickett's men advanced following a thunderous, two-hour-long, 159-cannon artillery attack to soften up the Union line on top of the hill, an artillery barrage, witnesses said, that could be heard as far away as sixty miles.

Despite its double-quick marches and grueling, thirty-seven-mile hike, the Fifteenth New Jersey did not arrive in Gettysburg until late afternoon, July 2, when it was moved to Little Round Top as a reserve backup unit behind the Twentieth Maine and other forces and missed the second day's fighting.

The Fifteenth New Jersey was not on the front line when Pickett's charge began, but was under heavy fire from the artillery barrage that preceded it. Halsey and the others had to lie flat behind the main line as cannonballs and every kind of metal or iron the rebels could find flew over them, cutting hundreds of trees in half. They lay tight against the ground as shells exploded around them, trees fell, and thick clouds of smoke rolled over them.

The artillery barrage, as Halsey reported, was too high. Most of the explosions were well behind the federal line and, despite some casualties, did little damage. The Union artillery barrage was much shorter. The Federals decided to save their ammunition until the actual charge (Meade had correctly figured out what Lee would do). Lee's generals, however, assumed that the artillery barrage had been effective and that federal forces were badly hurt. They also assumed that the Federals had stopped firing because they had run out of ammunition. Pickett was then sent across the field with his mile-wide column of troops, marching slowly and deliberately, flags flying, in one of the most magnificent sights in the history of warfare.

And then the federal guns opened up on Pickett.

The artillery on top of Cemetery Ridge, directly in front of Pickett's men, fired double canister straight into them, and artillery on the Round Tops and Cemetery Hill fired at them from the sides. Hundreds of men fell in the first shelling, bodies blown into the air and into each other, and they kept falling as more and more cannons opened up on them in a grotesque symphony. Still, their rebel yell pierced the afternoon Pennsylvania air. The Confederate soldiers kept advancing up the hill. Union infantrymen began firing at them as soon as they were in range and cut down several thousand in the doomed charge.

A small group of Confederates, led by Gen. Lewis Armistead, waving his sword high over the thick smoke, managed to reach the top of Cemetery Ridge and fought their way over the stone walls there to take on the Federals in hand-to-hand combat, where Armistead was killed. After bitter fighting, the remaining Southerners were pushed back and moved back down the hill. The charge, a disaster, was watched closely by Lee, who, when it was clearly over, rode out to the edges of the field and emotionally told the bloody soldiers straggling back that the blame was all his and that he was sorry.

"Don't be discouraged," he told the men as they wandered back down the hill and passed him. "It was my fault this time."

He moved to the edge of the battlefield and found Pickett. He leaned over his horse, Traveler, and looked straight at Pickett, the hundreds of men retreating past them. "This has been my fight and upon my shoulders rests the blame. Your men have done all that men could do; the fault is entirely mine," Lee said, then dismounted and moved to the side of a bloodied soldier being carried on a stretcher. He took the man's hand and held it tightly and then let go.

The losses at Gettysburg were enormous. The Federals lost 23,049 men killed and wounded and the Southerners 28,063. Hundreds of horses were slain and gun caissons destroyed. There were so many dead soldiers that they were not buried for days. Thousands of wounded crowded small

Gettysburg homes that were turned into hospitals. Gettysburg was a tremendous Union victory, however, a victory that not only stopped Lee's invasion of the North and drove the Confederates back to Virginia, but one that invigorated the Army of the Potomac. The Union Army, so demoralized after frustrating retreats in so many places, had met the wily Lee head-on, taking on his entire army and his best generals, and had badly beaten them. The victory at Gettysburg pumped much needed adrenaline into the Army of the Potomac, which was never the same afterward.]

July 2 (From Manchester, Md., to Gettysburg)

Warm with showers. Daylight found us marching as rapidly as possible towards Gettysburg. No time was allowed for coffee. Halts were barely ten minutes. We passed the wagon train first where we heard that the battle had been going on for a day or two, then the wounded who reported that we had been getting the worst of it. The citizens especially at Littlestown were very kind. Large pails of cool water were kept on the horse blocks in which the men could dip their cups as they passed along. Citizens were seen carrying off the wounded in buggies.

The band struck up going through this village and the marching of the men was perfect throughout the brigade and their SPIRIT was excellent. At a place between Littlestown and Gettysburg we filed to the right into a field and lay for an hour, from 1–2 P.M. No one thought of cooking but every man slept the hour in the blazing sun. We were then moved on a few hundred yards and stacked arms to the left of the road near a little brook. Here we bathed our blistered feet and had coffee. We had made 32 miles in about 15 hours.

Directly about 5 we heard the roar of musketry close on our left to the South and cheers of men and were apparently getting nearer. An officer rode in and inquired for the headquarters, 6th Corps. We all pointed cross the brook where on a little knoll General Sedgwick' Corps flag was flying but every man rolled his blanket and slung it [over shoulder].

The officer scarcely reached headquarters, it seemed, before we were ordered to fall in and the order was half obeyed before it was given. We double quicked toward the firing, passing a few wounded and shells bursting over our heads.

We reached the edge of a woods back of (Little Round Top) as it was getting dark. The "reserves" had turned upon the enemy and driven them from the hill. It is said that both they and the enemy saw our lines advancing.

We stood in line with orders not to unroll blankets for several hours when we were moved to a position believed a stone wall at the top of a wooded side hill between Cemetery Ridge and round top. The 1st N.J. was in front of us at the foot of the hill. The 2d, 3rd and 4th continued our line to the right. We were finally in position a little after daylight.

July 3

At daylight, moved to the aid of the little hill. The morning was very quiet. The wood in front of us prevented our seeing much of the field and we were laying in it when a little after noon several shells came crashing in among us. In a moment we were back in line, which was formed at once and then all lay down. For an hour or two the cannonading was terrific. Longstreet's charge was made to our right. We could not see the rebs, but we could see our own men, and our batteries, horses and men were rapidly killed in the battle and one or two caissons blew up. From much to our left we could hear our men cheer and a heavy gun posted up there seemed to be doing heavy work.

The rebs were everywhere repulsed, our reinforcements were coming up and thousands of deserters and prisoners came in.

The 1st regiment in our front had taken their cartridges out and put them in their socks beside them and picked up extra muskets. They had no design to leave. Their position was not tried.

A piece of shell fell thick among us and we lost in the brigade one killed and 10 or 12 wounded. [Halsey wrote that someone stole his watch during the battle.]

That night I slept with Tunis on top of a very large rock which lay behind our line, without blankets or anything.

July 4 (Gettysburg)

Raining. We were up at daylight expecting a move. As we did not, I joined the 4th and 11th N.J. who lay behind Round Top. The 11th had about 60 or 100 men in charge of the adjutant. Both are terribly cut up. Payson Berry is missing. Ewell, Burroughs, Cory and Baylor are safe, Logan killed.

The regiment exchanged the Enfields they had hitherto carried for Springfields. A company was sent out to haul in all they could carry. The best were selected (and the next morning when we moved the Enfields were left in stack. Company B. had changed theirs at Salem Heights).

All was quiet along the lines. Late in the afternoon, Meade came riding along the lines.

(Above) The officers of the Fifteenth New Jersey Volunteers and friends, photographed on March 4, 1860. *Front row, left to right:* Capt. Cornelius Shimer, Capt. William Cornish, Capt. James Walker, Capt. Lewis Van Blarcom, Capt. Ellis Hamilton. *Back row:* First Lt. Lowe Emerson, Capt. James McDanolds, Lt. James Northrup, First Lt. Ebenezer Davis, Lt. William Cooke, First Lt. William Van Voy, Sutler Sam Young, First Lt. John Crater, First Lt. Edmund Halsey, First Lt. William Penrose (Hunterdon County Historical Association)

(Left) Joseph and Millie Halsey on their wedding day. Joseph joined the Confederate Army within days after Virginia seceded from the United States, and he fought until the bitter end, winding up with his friend Robert E. Lee at Appomattox on the day the war ended. (Mildred Tyner)

Soldiers of the Fifteenth New Jersey Volunteers (Courtesy of John Kuhl Collection)

(Top left) Ira J. Lindsley, killed at Chancellorsville

(Top right) Samuel Stahler, the second youngest soldier in the regiment, who only received his father's permission to join the Union Army after he loaded two large wagons full of hay for him on their farm

(Bottom left) George Thompson, who was discharged after being badly wounded at Spotsylvania in 1864

(Bottom right) Edward Campbell, one of the leaders of Halsey's regiment, who lived out his final days in a tiny town in Colorado, passing away in 1913

(Top left) Ellis Hamilton, at sixteen, the regiment's youngest soldier

(Top right) William Penrose, the commander of the Fifteenth, stayed in the army at the end of the war and retired in 1896.

(Bottom left) Paul Kuhl, who was killed in the charge at Spotsylvania

(Bottom right) William Cornish, who sometimes led the Fifteenth in the Shenandoah Valley Campaign of 1864, was left deaf from wartime injuries

The Halseys of Rockaway lived in one of the largest homes in Morris County, New Jersey. The west wing, the original building (*left*), was the home of Ed Halsey's grandfather, Col. Stephen Jackson, who frequently entertained George Washington there during the American Revolution. To the right and rear were large stables for the family horses and carriages. Ed's large garden, which he cultivated as a teenager along with his father, is to the right, out of the photo. (Rockaway Borough Library)

The manor house of Lessland Plantation, Virginia, Joseph Halsey's home, sat on some five thousand acres of land where a dozen slaves worked fields of wheat and corn. Joe (*left*) and Millie posed for this picture sometime in the early 1880s. The four-thousand-square-foot main house was the centerpiece of the plantation. Joe's law office, not seen, is to the left. A supply building can be seen behind the house. Stables and storehouses were behind it and to the left, and the row of slave cabins was behind the supply building. (Mildred Tyner)

This woodcut shows the Twenty-sixth New Jersey Volunteers ferrying across the Rappahannock River to attack Fredericksburg, Virginia, in December 1862. One of the regiments that crossed with the Twenty-sixth that morning was Ed Halsey's. Fredericksburg was a disaster for the Union Army. (New Jersey Historical Society Collection)

Matthew Brady caught the tragedy of Gettysburg in this July 1863 photo of slain soldiers. The Fifteenth New Jersey did not see direct action at Gettysburg but came under heavy cannon fire on the third and final day when it was held in reserve on top of Cemetery Ridge during Pickett's charge. (New Jersey Historical Society Collection)

The most overlooked units in the war were the Signal Corps, charged with communications. Early in the fighting, this group posed for a photograph in Virginia. (New Jersey Historical Society Collection)

Members of the Second New Jersey Cavalry, part of the Army of the Potomac, rest in front of their tent in the 1864 photo. (New Jersey Historical Society Collection)

Kelly's Ford, on the Rappahannock, was a shallow part of the river upstream from Fredericksburg, which the Union Army used as a crossing on its various forays into Virginia. Ed Halsey crossed it numerous times. (Rutgers University Special Collection)

Union Army soldiers relax after a mail call in the headquarters of the Army of the Potomac. (New Jersey Historical Society Collection)

We had 80 men we picked under Major Boeman and in the night which was so wet we could neither sleep nor make a fire. I started with a detail of 20 men to relieve those who had Enfields without much of an idea where to find them. Happily, I met the whole detail coming in.

No sleep and very wet.

🖊 [Meade did not attack Lee, waiting for him, in the rain on July 4, giving the Confederate Army time to begin a slow retreat. On July 5, the Army of the Potomac began to shadow Lee as he moved toward the Potomac. Meade was reluctant to tangle with Lee again, but wanted to stay close to his forces.]

July 5

Moved at daylight to left to near where we were Thursday evening and halted in the rain for two or three hours. At about 9 our Brigade leading the corps advanced. It moved by the road to right of Rocky Hill, crossed Emmitsburg Road and to Willoughby Run, which we approached very cautiously to find the enemy had evacuated, leaving many of their dead and wounded. Some of them had been there three days. After crossing creek, we advanced in line of battle about four miles and overtook the rear guard of the enemy, near Fairfield, passing thousands of their wounded in tents and barns.

As we were advancing on the left of Hagerstown Pike through a wheat field, to the top of a hill, to the left of us [we saw] a large barn. The owner came to meet us, bowing as he came. In a wood at the top of the hill we heard some shots and when we reached it our skirmishers were engaged. Captains Bush and Walker were not in the line, the line being too short. A halt took place and some eastern men came up on our left sending out a line of skirmishers in a very handsome move. The line advanced at the enemy taking a secesh, Walker, prisoner, frightening an old couple who live in a little house in the woods. We moved through the wood and to an open field beyond, where we halted at sundown. After dark, lines were posted and the regiment fell back to the woods and went into camp. One man in the 3rd was killed. General Torbert had a button shot off.

🖊 [THE WAR: Vicksburg, the port city on the Mississippi River that had blocked all federal army shipping throughout the war, had been under siege by U. S. Grant's army for months. The siege, which tightened a military noose around the Confederate army there, had catastrophic effects.

The twenty-thousand-man army had just ten thousand effective fighting men as half were killed, wounded, or sick. Constant shelling of the city had killed many civilians, destroyed hundreds of homes, and ruined the citizens' will to hold out. Finally, on the Fourth of July, Confederate forces in Vicksburg surrendered. The victory opened up the Mississippi not only for federal gunboats, but for commercial shipping for all of the Midwest. The victory also freed Grant's army for other operations and, importantly, made Grant's reputation as not only a brilliant tactician, but a tenacious bulldog determined to hold out for however long it was necessary to win. The twin wins at Vicksburg and Gettysburg turned the tide of the Civil War in the Union's favor at last.]

July 6 (Gettysburg)
    We camped six miles from Gettysburg. Cloudy.
    We moved up to Fairfield where we halted till about 10 P.M., "in readiness." Then we marched by a narrow muddy road about nine mile to Emmitsburg, which we reached at daylight. We passed through the place and halted for breakfast. We would have fared poorly [for breakfast] had not Davis seized a loaf of bread coming through the town.

    [Halsey later wrote Mary of the post-Gettysburg march.]

Dear Mary,
    It was dark, muddy and raining in torrents but we were all of us tired and sleepy after nearly 25 miles of marching and no sleep the night before and fear of the men having anything to eat as rations had given out. The next morning we crossed the mountains in the rain, fording streams at some places knee deep. In the middle of the afternoon we came to Middleton and for one night rested from our labors. I have been very minute in descriptions for I think these two days were the roughest of my experience in soldiering.
    On the next day, (the 9th), advanced to Boonesboro and on the 10th to Beaver Creek, slowly falling back in the evening. On Sunday we crossed Antietam Creek and moved down to the left of the 5th Corps. Had a sharp skirmish in the afternoon in which we lost two men wounded from our regiment and several from the brigade, and the 15th remained on picket all night, and the next day. That afternoon I went back to Boonesboro to get some papers and on my return on the 14th found the enemy had retreated over the river and our division had gone on to Williamsport. The next day

we marched back to Boonesboro, about 13 miles. Yesterday, we marched through Middletown and down here some twenty or twenty five miles. I've rested here today but expect to cross the river tomorrow, as it is said the rest of the army is crossing.

We hoped that the enemy having been diverted out of the Maryland twice would be given us to rest, but it seems that is not the plan. The idea is to get between Lee and Richmond and if we can only succeed in annihilating that army I am willing to go through a good deal. Our corps is the strongest and freshest in the old army and though the boys are weary and their feet sore, and would be glad to go into camp for while, they are in good spirits and will no doubt give a good account of themselves. The prisoners said that the sight of our Corps on July 2 coming up to Gettysburg created a great excitement among them. Their officers tried to make them believe us militia. They knew we were in the rear and were astonished to find us there when they had every reason to believe we were not in Virginia yet. The militia is a humburg! [worthless] It did nothing at Gettysburg if it was there at all.

🖋 [President Lincoln was furious at Meade for letting Lee's army slip out of Maryland. He hoped Meade would attack Lee between Gettysburg and the Potomac and crush the Army of Northern Virginia. Lee, his army shattered after Pickett's charge and his officer corps demoralized—with many fingers being pointed at Longstreet for his inexorable delay in attacking on July 2—fully expected to be hit with every man Meade had. Lee ordered his army to prepare for a battle as soon as they reached the Potomac, which was at flood stage, preventing a crossing by the Southerners and trapping them with their backs to the river. Meade did nothing, however, and a day later the river had dropped enough to allow the rebels to cross. Meade watched them go. "If I had been up there, I could have whipped them myself," an angry Lincoln told one of his aides.]

July 8

We advanced over the mountain range through a steady rain, up a steep mountain road (itself the bed of a stream) crossing a deep stream five times, wading and fording all the way. This was the Harrisburg or Sedgwick Pass, which had proven impracticable that night for our artillery. At the summit we halted in a cleared field as the rain stopped. In the afternoon, we marched down the valley to Middletown and camped on a hill overlooking the place. Here we received rations (which the men had been without two days) and mail. The men considered the past two days as ROUGH as any in the service, all things considered (15 miles marching).

July 12

I was sent to Middletown to the wagon train to get our regimental returns. Had "Ned" (horse) to ride for the first time. He was very large and I led him through mud and rain a great part of the way. Got my supper just west of South Mountain and slept with Walter Johnson in the wagon train.

July 16

[Halsey, who had now been through three of the major battles of the war—Fredericksburg, Chancellorsville, and Gettysburg, and had nearly been killed twice—was trying to move out of the Fifteenth so that he could be more directly involved in the fighting. He asked his politically connected brother Sam to get him into a cavalry regiment, where he was sure he could see more action.]

July 23

Dear Sister Sue,

Here we are about opposite Hillsborough and only 12 miles from Leesburg. In the evening a large farm filled with grain belonging to a man named Wright was burned as is supposed by a Negro, and lighted up the country for miles. The regiment rested yesterday and we did not move till afternoon, when we slowly advanced some ten miles farther to the place we have stopped probably for the day.

The heat was very oppressive yesterday and the day before and the march was hard on the men. This morning was cloudy and quite comfortably cool. The General has sent word that we will likely remain where we are during the day, the reason being that the horses block up the roads, I suppose. Our corps is in the reserve, I believe. We have not been passed [by others on their way to battle] on the road. Lee is probably in the valley, yet our own troops hold the gaps. Snickers Gap is opposite us and day before yesterday we passed a dozen prisoners who were taken there. One of these was the youngest son of an old lady whose house we had just halted at and she said she had not seen him in two years.

Fauquier County is the best part of Virginia we have seen and seems to have suffered but little from the war. We passed no one, just places. Princeville is only a half dozen little houses.

At Berlin I received a letter from Sam saying a commission had been sent to me, but I have seen nothing of the kind. As we advance more and more into the state it will take longer to get answers and mail. Before I get to Warrenton, which is the direction we are heading, we will get our mail by railroad. I was in hope I could get a commission in [Virginia], so I could get a discharge to make a visit home. Sam has been working for me doing everything he could. I hope his efforts will not be in vain. There is a great probability that some of our mails have been destroyed by the reb cavalry.

Tell the girls I will write them tomorrow if I have a chance.

July 24

We remained at White Plains till dark, when we were ordered towards Warrenton. Marched to New Baltimore over an awful road (for about six miles) and camped about an hour after midnight.

The country abounded in blackberries and guerillas. Col. Penrose went to Washington on leave by trains running for the first time since last fall. I wrote the girls that I had left my underclothing all along the road from Falmouth.

July 26 (Near Warrenton)

[LESSLAND PLANTATION: Ed Halsey's search for his brother Joseph continued when the Union Army reached Warrenton. The community, one of the oldest in Virginia, was a prosperous resort town that attracted hundreds of visitors from other parts of the state and nearby states with its cool summer breezes and lovely views of the Blue Ridge Mountains. It was off one of the main Virginia roads and connected to most of the state, and nearby areas, by railroad trains, which pulled into its low-slung, one-story red-brick depot. It was home to a number of good restaurants and fine hotels, such as the Warren Green Hotel. A neatly designed two-story hotel with long, building-length porches on each level, Warren Green served as host to the Marquis de Lafayette in 1825 and to President James Monroe. The town was anchored by a spacious courthouse square with a two-story red-brick courthouse and nearby law offices (Supreme Court judge John Marshall practiced law there as a young man) and a busy, narrow main street full of two-story brick and stucco buildings and the Presbyterian and Baptist churches. Several prominent Virginians owned summer homes on side streets. They were large, handsome houses, most of them brick or stucco, with oversize, neatly manicured lawns. Warrenton was just twenty-eight miles from Joseph Halsey's plantation and a place where Joseph and his wife frequently visited. Halsey began asking locals there for any news of his brother.]

In the afternoon, I rode with Alanson into the town to get some information about Joseph but could only learn he was very well six months ago. The churches were filled with wounded, cavalrymen, and the streets filled with wagons.

Col. Penrose returned from Washington and Lt. Col. Campbell from the 3rd N.J. which he had commanded since Fairfax. The General was serenaded at dusk.

🖋 [On July 26, the regiment received a general order from the War Department, in Washington, informing the men that the secretary of war had ordered across-the-board reductions in the number of officers in each regiment as an efficiency move. Each infantry regiment was to lose its colonel and an assistant surgeon, and each company was to lose a second lieutenant. Each cavalry regiment was to lose a colonel, one major, and an assistant surgeon. Each cavalry company would also lose a second lieutenant. Halsey fretted that the promotion he was hoping for would be jeopardized. He was right.]

July 27

The day was heavy with office work, yet I finished *The House on the Moon*. We received several days' mail in the afternoon, bringing three letters from Sam, one from Susan, one from Sill.

A commission as 2d Lt. came for me but General Orders 182 prevented my muster. Colonel P. took my discharge up and tried to get it through but it was no use. He seemed very much disappointed as any one and at once recommended me for 1st Lt. made possible by Van Blarcom being promoted to Capt., Co. C.

July 28

The 5th Corps came through from the gap yesterday. It is said that Lee is leaving Ewell in the Shenandoah as a thorn in our side and then went through Chester Gap towards Richmond.

🖋 [Lee continued to move through Virginia, constantly looking back over his shoulder at the Army of the Potomac. Between July and October, both armies were reduced in strength as Lee sent Longstreet to Chickamauga and Meade sent the XI and XII Corps to Chattanooga. Whenever one army was larger than the other, the larger army would try to engage the smaller, and skirmishes occurred from time to time throughout the summer and fall.]

August 1

[In a letter to girlfriend Mary and her sister, Halsey expressed surprise at Mary's criticism of him.]

My Dear Cousins,

We have left Maryland and entered the old campaigning ground. We arrived at Warrenton last Monday and this noon were moved up to the outskirts of the town for duty (in the town, probably). Our division has been divided up—one brigade sent to New Baltimore and one to Warrenton Junction and then moved here. Some think we are to stay here for some time. I am not so sanguine. Indeed I would not be surprised at an order to advance to Culpeper or for a general retreat of the army to Washington.

Meade is said to be a very cautious general, bordering on the timid. He conducted the battle of Gettysburg very well and if I had been in his place I would have resigned and saved my reputation. This army has had singular fortune to make and ruin the name of every general who has had it in charge. It is to be hoped that it will not be the case with Meade.

Halsted, whom you met in hospital, went home with me on furlough in March and never came back. He was reported a deserter here for a long time. He finally reported to Major Jones in Trenton and was sent to Newark Hospital. Old John Johnson I knew well. He never ought to have been in the service on account of his age. He was put in the ambulance corps last winter and when they turned him out he went to the regiment hospital and has been on the sick list ever since. He is a good man but has had a rough time of it. I never believed he would reach Maryland when he started from White Oak.

There is something in the "note" at the bottom of your letter (written by Mary), which I must confess raised no small stir in my brain. "Reports" have reached the "château" respecting "my good behavior." What can this mean? What is the source? Of what nature is it? Let me not burst in ignorance. I am afraid from the way you speak that it is something very dreadful and the "respected friend" feels his good name in danger. Would that the "advice" were a little more definite for I am conscious of so many shortcomings that I do not know where to apply the remedy, fearful that there will not be enough to go around. The reference to certain articles of luxury seems to imply that you do not consider my case desperate—that reformation is possible or perhaps a cut with a "slight tinge of gentle reproach" at my rather egotistical account of our marchings. But enough I am in hopes you will relieve my anxiety and speedily set my mind at rest. I assure you the suspense is great and would not persistent remain in camp an hour after receiving your letter without writing at once for relief. Be pitiful and prompt.

Warrenton is one of the finest places we have seen. It is the county seat of Fauquier County and has a number of fine residences in the suburbs. The people are all secesh and those who have not left the place by their sour looks and closed doors and blinds express their dislike very decidedly to the Unionists. A party of rebel prisoners passing through were cheered by the citizens and the soldiers were half a mind to burn the place for them. They were restricted however, by double guards.

I had a very amusing letter from Sill a day or two since giving a description of affairs at the regiment during the riot excitement. [This refers to fears of riots similar to those in New York that followed the draft in July 1863.] I am sorry I could not have been there to have seen it. Things have come to a strange pass when even loyal New Jersey has to apply to New York to protect their firesides. An officer was telling me today that in his opinion, the 30 days extension granted in N.Y. and N.J. would only be used in re organizing the opposition to the draft, that the quota cannot be supplied by volunteers and then the old troops will have to be recalled to enforce the draft. I hope for better things.

It may interest you somewhat to know that a commission arrived for me a week ago as 2d Lieutenant of Company F, but unfortunately for me it is made worthless by a recent order of the war department forbidding a 2d lieutenant . . . in . . . [small] companies, such as ours. The colonel immediately sent on a recommendation for me as first lieutenant which, if it meets the success of the last, I may hope to be in the course of a month or six weeks, casualties of war excepted. Sam has been trying to get me in the 2d NJ Cavalry but I doubt if I can get away from here.

🖋 [Halsey's references to the draft concerned the July 11 draft ordered by President Lincoln to recruit new troops to make up for the dwindling size of the Union Army. The draft underlined the deep resentment toward the war in many quarters in the North. Despite victory at

Vicksburg and Gettysburg just a week earlier, a large number of people in the North still wanted to quit the war. Antiwar feelings were particularly strong in New Jersey, but the draft engendered the most hostile feelings in New York City.

The draft began there despite the protest of New York governor Horatio Seymour, who challenged its legality. On Saturday, July 11, the first several hundred names of New York draftees were called, and on Sunday the names were listed in the morning newspapers. Most refused to go. Hundreds of draftees and protesters began massing outside government and newspaper offices on Monday. By noon, police estimated the crowds had grown to over fifty thousand. They began to riot during the second selection of draftee names. The rioting continued for three days, led mostly by Irish Americans. The immediate targets of the rioters were blacks, seen as the cause of the war. More than a dozen blacks were murdered by the crowds, some lynched from streetside trees. A black church was burned to the ground. An orphanage for black children on Fifth Avenue was attacked and burned. Police were ineffective against the crowds and federal army units were sent in. They took three days to stop the riots and in doing so killed or wounded nearly one thousand New Yorkers. Others were shot and killed by troops in riots in Boston. Smaller riots took place in Wooster, Ohio; Rutland, Vermont; and Portsmouth, New Hampshire. In New Jersey, where federal authorities feared trouble, the reaction was minimal. Lincoln postponed the draft until the end of the month to give antidraft protesters time to calm down and then reissued the draft order. He added a proviso to the order, however, that permitted any draftee to avoid service by paying a $300 bounty to someone else to serve in his place. The draft was eventually successful.]

August 2 (Camp near Warrenton)

Warm and Clear. Inspection at 8. A church in town having been obtained by Alanson, the Brigade attended service at 10. The band was in attendance, officers in full dress, enlisted men with belts. Alanson preached one of the best sermons I ever heard him deliver.

In the afternoon I got a pass and went with Captain Burt through the town. Had a long talk with a gentleman, a relative of Chancellor Williamson, about Joseph. Wrote to Joseph.

At dress parade, the stragglers in the last guard were brought up, sentenced and addressed by Col. Penrose.

August 4 (Warrenton, Virginia)

Engaged at ordnance papers and involved in rolls. Finished Capt Burt's returns of C Company and also his ordnance. Sent off letter to Joseph. [This was the only letter Ed sent to Joe in the war].

Lieut. Justice being absence from dress parade, sent in the excuse—four cols and a page long—that he had taken too much drink and ice which he was told did not "intoxicate." The excuse was accepted.

The colonel established a school for his officers requiring their attendance an hour each day. Today one of the officers fell asleep and another inadvertently had his back to the colonel for which he was reproved. [This school, mostly for field tactics, was of great advantage to the officers and to the regiment, according to Halsey.] The Colonel was a thoroughly drilled man and gave us many things not in [the books].

Changed mess back to quartermaster and cook with Ben Wolverton for cook. We had vegetables, bread. For a long time our fare has been coffee, pork and hard tack except when a loaf of bread could be picked up at a stray farm house or cheese and sardines from a sutler. "Ben" is a good forager, but said "Let meals take care of itself. Perhaps I can make something and perhaps I can't." The people [around here] are much reduced and the prices for things to eat are high but they will trade anything for groceries.

August 6

It being a day appointed by the President as a day of special thanksgiving, we had a brigade service in the Baptist Church at ten. Officers with belts and men with side arms. In the afternoon the regiment was paid up to June 30. After settling all my duty in regiment had sum of $18 left. Finished the book *The Soldiers*.

August 7

Since we have been in this camp we have been so fortunate as to have our clothes washed in Warrenton, Virginia, regularly [by locals for a price]. Bread is now issued regularly to the men and fried meat of a better quality. Our cook . . . cuts up the meat for us. If there is a good piece we have it and he manages to get vegetables every day.

August 8

About a week ago, a [lieutenant] refused to go out on dress parade or neglected to do so being notified. The Col. sent to him for a written excuse which he refused to send but offered to go in person and see the Col. if he wished. For [not submitting a written excuse] he was court martialed and today his sentence was published—to forfeit $50 per month for six months. Lt. Col. Campbell was president of the court martial at Fairfax and ordered him to take Co. C, which he refused to do point blank. Col. C. at the time appeared not to notice it.

August 10 (Warrenton)

Very warm. Priestly, of Co. E., who deserted and was returned at White Oak Church had been under guard ever since, was drummed out and sentenced to two years hard labor. The man is young and seems a simply, quaint fellow hardly responsible for his acts. He has had . . . opportunities to escape on the march if so minded.

The ceremony was followed by a Brigade drill in the afternoon and then battalion drill.

In the evening, my commission as 1st Lt. Co. D. arrived.

🖋 [Priestly's sentence was later reduced and he returned to the army. He was killed at Spotsylvania on May 12, 1864.]

My Dear Sister Sue,

I sit down surrounded by mosquitoes so thick as to render the work very spasmodic.

At the head of this sheet you have a sketch of the officers pin ordered at Fairfax and just received. It is very neat and has the name engraved on the back. Mine is done with "Lieutenant Edmund D. Halsey" which till now has had no meaning. This evening I received my "papers" and hope soon to sink the "man" in the "officer"—in one sense at least. It seems like an immense barrier or rather gulf between the two. Go where you will in the army and it is recognized everywhere and soon becomes a habit in novices. I value it the more on this account as it will enable me in a short time—providence willing—to make myself independent of home support and perhaps in part repay the money expended on me since entering the service.

[Halsey referred to his officers' papers and the prestige other officers and the men in the regiment accorded his promotion. Halsey felt becoming an officer would make him more of a complete man.]

... My health so far has been excellent and I owe this in a great measure to remittances received from home which enabled me to obtain my luxuries which my pay as private would not afford. As sergeant major things came out about even but then I was already in debt. At present I do not owe a dollar in the regiment and after the next pay day do not intend to.

Let me give you a sample of our living at present. For breakfast we had some good beefsteak and gravy with bread, good coffee and cucumbers with salt. For dinner we had new potatoes boiled, bread and coffee, butter and cucumbers. For supper we had beefsteak, bread and butter and coffee. Not very hard fare, you would say, for a soldier. It is not. Such has been our style for the past three or four days. It costs very little to be sure but not so very much as you would suppose, the substantial food being furnished by Uncle Sam. This is a slight variation from our fare on the march—coffee and hardtack. One day, it is everything a modest man, like myself, for example, could wish and the next nothing but as the saying is "it all goes to make up the three years. . ."

I read in the *Jerseyman* quite a flattering account of the exhibition of the Morris Academy in which I suppose Fred took a distinguished part. I hope he will improve with his opportunities there for as it strikes me, he is a little behind for his age. His correspondence has fallen off very suddenly. What kind of a school have you home for Sally? It is a pity she could not go away from home where she could have some other girls of her own age besides what is found around the Glen. This I suppose is impossible in the present state of things.

Of Joseph no word as yet though I think it is possible I can get a letter to him "sub rosa" [secretly]. [Ed's letter, which he gave to a local man for underground delivery, did reach Lessland Plantation, but was later lost.]

Of course the work on the cemetery this year is indefinitely postponed. If men can scarcely be had to work the farms it is hardly probable there is any gratuitous labor to be had. Perhaps it may be my good fortune to finish it yet. Who knows?

August 14

🖎 [In the morning, Halsey was mustered in as a first lieutenant in Company K. In the afternoon, there was gruesome business.]

Regiment marched at ten about two miles toward new Baltimore where Jewett, 5th Maine, was shot for desertion in the presence of the division. The division formed three sides of a square in two lines. Each brigade a side. Our company was on the left of two lines of the 1st side. The prisoner was finally brought out sitting on his coffin in an open army wagon drawn by four horses and rode slowly around the inside of the square. He was then taken out and shot in the open side of the square. The division then filed by him by the right flank (still in two lines) and away. The body was lying on its face, the balls had come through the back of his head and between his shoulders. I came back with a terrible headache [from it].

🖋 [Executions were rare in either army and almost all were for desertion. Absenteeism was a chronic problem on both sides. During 1864, up to 90,000 Union soldiers deserted. (In the summer of '64, they deserted at a rate of 7,000 a month.) By the spring of 1865, almost 100,000 men had been listed as deserters from the Confederate Army. Deserters, when caught, were court-martialed. An army could not fight if all of its troops fled. However, there were often extenuating circumstances in desertion cases. All executions were also reviewed by high-ranking generals and President Lincoln himself (Lincoln was extremely lenient), and few deserters were actually shot. Of the more than 90,000 deserters in the Union Army, only 287 were executed. Those who were executed were usually shot for desertion during an actual battle, repeated desertions, or if they deserted and joined the Confederate Army and were captured in the enemy uniform.

THE WAR: Confederate bushwhackers led by William Quantrill attacked Lawrence, Kansas, burned half the business district, and massacred 150 men and boys in the continuing guerrilla war in Kansas and Missouri.]

August 23 (Warrenton)
🖋 [Halsey read all the newspapers from home and any he could buy in camp. He was careful to correct any misinformation about the regiment or its members. He fired off an angry, corrective letter to the editor of the *Jerseyman* about misinformation about a comrade.]

Editor,
I wish to correct a misstatement with regard to Captain Edsall, late of this regiment, which appears in your paper. That officer was neither suspended nor dismissed. Having been quite seriously ill for some time before, he obtained leave of absence on the 24th of May for ten days and on the expiration of that leave, forwarded a surgeon's certificate, to the effect that

he was still unfit for field duty. This was considered insufficient on account of informality and on being apprised of the fact, the captain, being too unwell to rejoin the regiment (which those who were acquainted with his disease here anticipated) forwarded his resignation, which was accepted and he honorably discharged on account of physical disability on July 24, 1863.

This explanation I consider no more than is due to the captain and his friends.

🖋 [The editors, who handled Halsey's letters from the front and thought highly of him, printed an apology.]

Dear Sister Sue,

I have been . . . very busy. The duties attending my installation into office and getting accustomed to it were by no means light. Happily, we have been lying still in the mean time. The weather too has been very warm and quite unhealthy—warm days and cold nights. As yet sickness has not become by any means alarming in the regiment.

You have heard no doubt from my letter home of my discharge and appointment as Acting Adjutant of the regiment. Tuesday will be the anniversary of our muster into service. One year spent in the army. I spent four months and ten days as a private, seven months as sergeant major and 12 days as a 1st Lieutenant. My promotion has been rapid though you may think it slow. Recollect that the last was two steps in one and of the twenty five line officers, eight are my juniors in rank.

Today has been for a Sunday a quick day. I attended reveille at 5. I led a guard mounting at 7—unified a detail of 50 men with officers to go to the depot. I attended a regimental inspection and distributed nearly 300 pairs of white gloves all before ten. Being somewhat fatigued after this, I kept perfectly quiet until 4 this afternoon, when I attended a prayer meeting in the church and came back to dress parade at sunset. This getting up a reveille every morning is a phase of the subject I do not much fancy but it has to be done. I have to be present [at it] and at retreat and at tattoo at 9 P.M. The company officers report to me and I take the reports to the Colonel, provided he is awake or in camp. The men now at guard mounting and parade are to have caps on, belts and shoes blackened, brasses polished and white gloves on.

I am sorry to hear from Sill that [sister] Anne is so very unwell in this warm weather. It is hardly to be wondered at that she suffers at such a time when a well person finds it almost insupportable. How is father's health? He has not written me [since Fairfax].

No newspapers have been received in camp for the past two days and we are quite anxious to hear the news from Charleston. Lee is said to have withdrawn his force in front either to make an attack on our flank or to defend Richmond or Charleston. One cannot tell here anything about where either army is or when and where we are to move. It is simply wait for orders.

This letter is hardly worth sending but it is better than none if it shows that I have not forgotten you and that I am as anxious as ever to hear from you all and of everything that is going on—the railroad, the draft, Fred and Sally's school. I do not quite like the idea of your keeping a free children's boarding house in such hot weather and would express myself quite decidedly on the subject if I were you. It will do for one summer, perhaps, but as a general thing it quite loses its interest.

Give my love to all and many thanks for the newspapers.

August 29

✍ [Halsey, distressed over the loss of his watch during the Gettysburg battle, bought a new one from a friend for $6.]

August 30

Clear. I have quite a cold. Inspection in the morning was followed by church, at which Alanson preached from text. Between you and me, a great gulf is fixed.

In the afternoon, I had a picture taken which I forwarded to home in the evening. I read several newspapers. From one, I learned Barret [a friend back home in New Jersey] was admitted to the bar and from another that (brother) Abe was candidate for District Attorney.

✍ [LESSLAND PLANTATION: Ed Halsey did not know that while he was having dinner in camp the previous night, his brother Joseph had arrived back at Lessland, 28 miles away, on furlough for a short visit. Throughout the war, Ed was often within ten miles of Lessland, but the configuration of Union and Confederate lines always prevented any attempt by him to ride to Lessland. He had to cross the Rapidan River, which was usually guarded by Confederate troops, and then maneuver through territory held by the Confederates toward Lessland, which itself was sometimes occupied by the Southern army.]

August 31

Orders to hold ourselves in readiness to march at a moment's notice. Received letter from Sue and [package] of cholera medicine.

September 3 (Warrenton, Virginia)

In the evening I attended the negro minstrel concert given principally by members of the 2d regiment. The performance was quite creditable and highly appreciated by the audience. It was held in a church—the officers occupying the galleries and the enlisted men down stairs or in the body of the church.

September 6

Suffered a good deal from colic, so much so as to get excused from dress parade, Tunis officiating in my place. I was brought around by mustard drafts, vial of laudanum. I slept on the floor of Alanson' tent. The inspection in the morning showed the regiment to be in fine condition. A captain returned from General Hospital without the use of his left arm, effect of his wound received at Salem Heights.

September 7

I am rather weak but otherwise quite well.

We have pickets out every night to guard against guerillas.

September 8

[Letter to Sue, in which Halsey begins by thanking her profusely for sending some unrequested cholera medicine.]

My Dear Sister Sue,

... It could not have come at a better time. For the only time since entering the service, I have lately been troubled in this way [cholera]. This was caused by the cold nights for which we were all or less unprepared. On the march, surplus blankets were thrown away for want of transportation and now all cannot be supplied at once. I am happy to say I am quite recovered and hope will not be troubled again.

This morning we were very much surprised to hear quite rapid cannonading directly in front and apparently but a few miles off. Marching orders were expected every moment but none came and this evening I understand it was a reconnaissance of the enemy's cavalry at Rappahannock Station. They fell in with our pickets and were bluffed off. Our principal apprehensions are from Mosby—"mose" as he is called by the people here. He keeps the country in the rear of us in a state of ferment and occasionally plunders a sutler's train and picks up stragglers away from camp. [Halsey is referring to Gen. John Singleton Mosby, the "Grey Ghost" of the Confederacy, who led a guerrilla cavalry on countless raids against Union soldiers and facilities. Mosby lived in Warrenton.]

The other night a party of these guerrillas rode into General Bartlett's headquarters at New Baltimore and firing several volleys into the General's tent made off before the troops there got aroused. We take precaution to put out pickets every night and perhaps he would find it not so easy to ride into the 1st Brigade as he found the 2d.

I am sorry to say that Quincy Grimes of Company "C," concerning whom you wrote me some time ago, died this morning. He has long been an inmate of the hospital suffering from a most terrible diarrhea. His discharge papers went up and came back approved. He was discharged on the 5th but was then unable to be moved. His friends came in and Mr. Stone of Boonton left here this afternoon with the body. He will probably not reach home before Thursday or Friday. He was advised not to accept his discharge papers and is considered (as is the truth) to have died in the service. He was always a quiet, well-behaved soldier, obedient to orders and much esteemed by all his comrades. It was a fortunate circumstance that he should die as he did while we were lying still and with his friends from home to witness his end.

September 11

[Halsey's birthday] . . . celebrated as circumstances would permit.

September 13

[Letter to the *Jerseyman*]

The regiment now numbers about 275 men for duty—there is some difference between that number and the 960 with which we started a little more than a year ago. Quite a number have been discharged and we met with a very heavy loss on the third of May (Chancellorsville), where our loss was 150 killed, wounded and missing. Many died of disease while encamped at White Oak Church last winter, where our loss was sometimes as high as three a day. Strange to say, the men who appeared best fitted by nature to endure hardships and fatiguing marches have been the first to give out and fall victims to disease, while those that hardly passed examination by the doctors are mostly with us.

The First New Jersey Brigade is now doing provost duty in the town of Warrenton. Our camp is on a high ridge directly east of the town and details are made by companies from each regiment in their turn to do duty in the town. Col. Brown, of the 2d N.J. Volunteers, was appointed provost marshal of the town when we first arrived here and he is obeyed and respected as such.

Before the war, Warrenton was a fine town and it looks quite well yet, but as it has been overrun, at times, by both armies for the last two years, one would not suppose it to look as well as it does. The people are secesh of the rankest kind, and do not hesitate to own [up to] it, but at present their faces are long and their voices sorrowful, for they begin to see that their cause is hopeless. They have heard of the fall of Vicksburg, of Port Hudson, of Lee's Army being driven from Pennsylvania and Maryland, and of General Gilmore's splendid operations against Charleston, and it has a bad effect upon their nervous systems and in vain do they endeavor to conceal it in their looks and actions.

There is a deserter sentenced to be shot near this place on the 18th. He belongs in this Brigade, to Co. H, 4th regiment. His name is Watson, alias Galliger. It is a painful sight to see our fellow men pay the penalty of death for the crime of desertion, but as it is the military law of the land, and as the sentence has been approved by General Meade, I suppose it will be carried into effect on the day appointed, in the presence of the first division, to which the brigade belongs. There has been one executed since we have been here, for the same offense. His name was Thomas Jewett, of the 5th Maine, which belongs to the 2d Brigade of this division, which we were present to witness.

September 17 (Near White Sulphur Springs)
Dear Sam,

I paid $6 for a watch which I had lost a few days after I had bought it. Perhaps I never told you I have lost the one you gave me. It was stolen from me at Gettysburg July 3 as I was asleep, I believe. After the fight, I looked for it and could not find it and I recollect being under a tree asleep just before the fight.

Before the paymaster had done paying Tuesday afternoon, marching orders came and about 6 we "cleared" Warrenton and marched almost to the Springs by 10 and halted for the night. Yesterday we started a little after daylight and moved very tediously, wading streams until we got within a mile or two of where we are now. It was then ten o'clock and dark as Egypt. The brigade might have been considered lost. We halted in the hills till daylight, when we came up and joined the division. We are now within two miles of Culpeper Court House [ten miles from Lessland in central

Virginia] . . . which trains are now running with supplies. A reconnaissance has been made today and the booming of artillery has been quite frequent all day. Upon the result of this reconnaissance depends our moving tomorrow or not. Meade will probably strike at [nearby] Gordonsville which Lee will not yield without a battle.

September 19 (Culpeper County Court House, Va.)

[LESSLAND PLANTATION: Ed Halsey continued to look for his older brother Joseph, who lived just eight miles from Culpeper. He wrote his sisters Anne and Sill about his search.]

Dear Sisters,

This morning, after sending out five companies on picket, I started on a leave for a little while to see the country. I rode first over to the camp of the 2d division, 3rd Corps and saw Jim Burroughs and Hayward Emmell in the 7th N.J. Then I went to the camp of the 11th N.J. and met no one I knew in the rank but Cyrus Talmadge. Captain Halsey has been made major. He introduced me to Lt. Col. Schonover, Dr. Welling and the rest of the staff with whom I dined. There I heard of a Mr. Pendleton who knew a [Joseph] Halsey on the Rapidan. After dinner the Major and I started to see him.

Not finding him in at first, we went on to Culpeper and rode in and through that antiquated town. Description is unnecessary as one or both of you have seen it. Returning, we called at Mr. P's and after waiting for them to get through their dinner I was introduced (one of our generals, French, I think, occupied a large part of his house as his headquarters. I found Mrs. Dr. [George] Morton, a sister of Mr. Pendleton's, and I believe Millie's cousin [Dr. Morton was Millie's uncle]. Mr. and Mrs. P, of course, and some other lady relative.

They treated us very well and invited me to call again. They said Joseph was not in the army but at home. He had been Brigade Commissary in the 6th Virginia Cavalry, but when that system was broken up he lost his position. He had been promised a commission as quartermaster on Loomis' staff should he be made a General. Loomis had been made a General but it seemed not quite clear whether Joseph had received his commission yet. The family was well. Some of Joseph's and Mr. Morton's negroes had taken out, but Douglass remained firm and true—a great help to them. I left with Mrs. Morton's pictures of Father (which they recognized), Emma and Sam.

As we draw our information from the same source—the newspapers—I can give you nothing new in respect to our position. Things seem to indicate an intention on our side to lie still for a few days and I hope Lee will favor our intention.

[Other letters]

My dear cousins Eliza and Mary,

Having just finished a long letter to the girls giving the result of my pursuit of knowledge respecting a lost brother which will no doubt satisfy them of my zeal in the work if not perfectly satisfactory of their curiosity, I am reminded of another not unpleasing duty to perform—to answer your most welcome letters.

They came upon my birthday and a more agreeable present I could not have asked for. I am afraid to say which birthday, for you will think me the yellow leaf. My years become quite a burden and if permitted to survive [the war], my next enlistment will be quite an old bachelor.

Warrenton, as you will notice by heading of this sheet is among the things that were and we speak of that place as of Camp Morris and the last camp at White Oak as things of beauty destined to be joys forever in memory's wilderness, poetically speaking. Six weeks repose undisturbed save by occasional marching orders and four or five hours drill per day was a good deal after being on the go for as long or a little longer time. There we had plenty to eat and drink and a neat pretty camp. Mails were frequent and sutlers in abundance. It closed befittingly.

Monday there was a horse race in the evening. Tuesday we were paid and there a change came over the spirit of our dreams. Suddenly orders came and in less than an hour our camp would have been a desert but for the people of the "colored persuasion" picking up the fragments which were left.

We halted near the celebrated White Sulphur Springs [Virginia] late in the evening [Jeremiah Morton was one of the principal owners of the resort there], the next morning passing the springs, of which I partook quite sparingly owing to my perverted taste which could only detect in the water a savor of eggs of a certain kind. We moved over Hegemans River through Jeffersonton, crossed Hazel Run, through Rixeyville and through two or three other rivers. We arrived at nightfall by some creek, deep and dangerous looking near Stonehorse Mountain. Here we halted. Fires were set on the opposite bank to guide us. The men took off shoes and stockings and through mud, weeds, muck and water the Rubicon was crossed. The brigade being all over moved on marching a half mile farther and again came to standstill. It was now very dark and late and the men were tired and sleepy and hungry and although no orders were given to rest, we were not ordered ahead till daylight when we rejoined the division. It is my impression that we were fairly lost that night.

Today I have been visiting Culpeper and my friends, generally. Since the rain the weather has been quite cool and reminds me very forcibly of winter quarters to which all soldiers seem to look forward as children to a holiday. It is dark and overcast tonight and I think it very probable we will have more rain. At all the camps I saw today the men were fixing up as for a stay and no doubt with Lee's permission they will. One thing is sure if we cross the Rapidan or if Lee crosses there will be a fight. The object seems to be to keep him from reinforcing some other point. Our only fear is he will get in on our flank.

One tragic incident occurred on the march [and] perhaps will interest you. A straggler from a New York regiment attempted to get across one of the fords on a wagon. A Quartermaster saw him and cut at him with a whip to make him get off. This the old man tried to do but, encumbered with his knapsack and traps, being old and tired too, slipped and fell under the wagons and was killed. To be sure, he had no business on the wagon, but it is doubted whether the conduct of the captain was justifiable.

The people everywhere here are strong secesh. Old Mr. Pendleton thought Lee would soon drive us out of this area and his nephew boasted of having two brothers in the rebel army. General John Pope and his army were their peculiar detestation. General George Meade they considered a gentleman. This country was never occupied by the Army of the Potomac before except the 11th corps and perhaps a few more then under command of the hero of Second Bull Run.

But I must close. I am glad to hear that cousin Anne is so much better and hope you will have as good success in curing my sister Anne as the Chief Justice. [Halsey refers to New Jersey Supreme Court head Edward Whelpley, a longtime friend of the Darcy and Halsey families, who was apparently treated by Mary and Eliza when he was ill.] I intended to send you some good book from Warrenton to read but did not have time to make a choice. I sent *St. Olaves* to Anne. It is pretty good, I thought. I learn that two of my Princeton classmates, Gill and Harris (the latter wounded), were taken prisoners of war by our forces at Gettysburg. Huntington Jackson, you wrote, was missing. Has he been heard from?

✍ [THE WAR: An effort by Federals to occupy the upper Tennessee River Valley was thwarted at Chickamauga. Confederate general Braxton Bragg's brigades failed to stop the Army of the Cumberland, led by Union general George Thomas, at several junctures in September, but on September 19–20, aided by Longstreet's division, the rebels, at full strength, engaged Thomas alongside Chickamauga Creek, near Chattanooga. A mix-up of federal orders left the middle of the federal line vulnerable, and Longstreet's men drove through it, splintering the Union Army. Thomas led his men in an orderly retreat to Snodgrass Hill, where he held out all day on September 20 against repeated and furious rebel attacks, earning the nickname the Rock of Chickamauga.

Thomas was ordered to withdraw the next day, but Bragg did not chase him and Thomas left with much of his army intact. The victory was widely hailed in the Southern press, but in reality did not have much effect on the war.]

September 22

Colors, state and national, were presented to the 15th by General Alfred Torbert on the part of the state of New Jersey in a very neat and appropriate speech responded to by Colonel Penrose and by the regiment with three cheers for the general.

General Torbert: "It has been your lot since we have been associated to meet the enemies of our country in deadly strife, upon more than one hard fought battlefield, and although we have not always been successful, your good discipline, combined with your sturdy courage and ardent patriotism, enabled you to sustain the high military reputation of the old Jersey Blues of revolutionary memory. Those starry folds symbolize principles of government, as pure and just as any that have ever been embodied in Constitution and laws. Viewed in this light, the standard I now present cannot fail to fire the hearts and nerve the arms of all of you against the enemies of our government."

Later, a group of officers recommended Penrose for promotion.

[The recommendation, written by Halsey]

To his excellency Joel Parker
Governor of the State of New Jersey

Having learned from a variety of sources that the name of William H. Penrose, U.S.A., Col., 15th regiment, N.J.V. has been spoken of in connection with one of the vacant Brigadierships (Generals) in the gift of the state of N.J., it gives us pleasure to add our testimony to the worthiness of the selection. Intimately associated as we have been with Col. Penrose for several months past, we have had good opportunity of judging of his imminent abilities as an officer and as a soldier and it would be very gratifying to us should he receive the recommendation of your excellency and of the delegation from our state.

On this same day, our old colors were sent to New Jersey. On the state colors are to be inscribed "Fredericksburg, Dec. 13 and May 3, Salem Heights, May 3, Gettysburg, Fairfield and Hagerstown."

September 23

🖋 [The sentimental Halsey cut off a small piece of the state flag being sent to Trenton and mailed it to his cousins, reminding them that the flagbearer, Hicks, was killed carrying it.]

September 24 (Near Culpeper)

About 2 P.M. orders were received to have all trains in readiness to move to the rear at a moment's notice. Considered a preparation for retreat. One officer reported that our reconnaissance yesterday was a failure, that Rosencrans had been defeated and hence we're in great danger. Another said that there was no enemy on our front, whence it was thought that the enemy was trying to flank us. Another said that our cavalry had been driven back by J.E.B. Stuart.

October 3

In the evening, in anticipation of a move, I wrote a long letter to Joseph which I hoped to leave for him. I never sent this letter. Orders for Brigade inspections tomorrow.

October 4

Brigade review.

Re-Enlistment proposed. From the letter to Sam it appears the proposed re-enlistment was for the regiment who went out in 1861 and who were to go home as a regiment to recruit and each veteran was to receive $700 ($400 from the U.S. and $300 from N.J.). An effort was to be made to get the 15th home.

🖎 [It was always difficult to get soldiers to reenlist, so states began raising
bonus money to pay for reenlistees. Sometimes a soldier could pocket $800
to $900, or six years' pay, to reenlist, which made reenlistments enticing.]

October 5 (Mitchell Station, Virginia)

The weather was clear. Marched some 16 miles to two miles below
Mitchell's Station. In this move we passed through Culpeper and
approached Mitchell Station from near the Kirk Place. The Brigade rested
in the fields opposite the Station and we could see rebel officers on Clarks
Mountain to the east. I later learned one of them was General Robert E.
Lee and that my brother Joseph was in the party. After a halt of an hour or
so we moved down the track towards the Rapidan a mile or two and went
into camp in the woods east of our tracks and west of a wooded knoll.

October 6

We are in constant expectation of an attack. Slept with shoes on. At all
times in this camp men were under arms for an hour before daylight. The
brigade we relieved was afraid to build fires for some time. The position
was commanded by the rebel artillery and it was understood we were there
on their sufferance.

October 7

🖎 [LESSLAND PLANTATION: The Halseys and Mortons hoped they would
remain little more than spectators to the civil war that raged around them,
but Lessland and Morton Hall were swept into the war in late September
when the Confederate Army under Gen. Jubal Early decided to use
Lessland as a base of operations to thwart any Union attacks along the
Rapidan River. Joe Halsey did not know that his brother Ed was in the
middle of those Union forces, just miles away from his home. Lessland
was overrun with rebels. General Early moved into the front parlor of
Lessland and lived there for several weeks. His top staff officers occupied
the library. The couriers who took messages back and forth lived in Joe
Halsey's law office building. The officers and family ate all meals together.

The entire Halsey family had to live in the bedrooms upstairs: Joe and
Millie shared one bedroom and sons Morton, eleven, and Og, nine, slept
in the other. Their two teenaged daughters, Fannie, fifteen, and Annie,
thirteen, were at boarding school in Richmond. In that single upstairs
bedroom, with little privacy, Millie had to nurse their baby boy, Bee, eighteen months old.

Even there at the Halsey Plantation, General Early did not feel safe. They could hear skirmishes up and down the Rapidan and in nearby towns. One morning a federal battery fired a random shot across the river at Lessland and the shell landed in the backyard, just ten yards from the granary. Early immediately had his men dig a line of rifle pits over two hundred yards long on the northern perimeter of the plantation for protection of his men. He set up artillery batteries at the rear of the row of slave cabins, about fifty yards behind and in front of the main house, aimed down the road that wound up the hill from the river to the main house.

Hundreds of men camped on the grounds of Lessland. Long lines of bright white rectangular tents lined the fields of the plantation. A wagon park was created at one end, within the shadows of the main house, where dozens of large supply wagons were kept. Several dozen horses were put into Joe Halsey's stables, and hundreds more were tied up to trees and lines near the house. Many were kept at the bottom of a short slope that ran away from the row of outbuildings toward the south. At night, dozens of campfires could be seen from the family rooms and rifles were stacked up in triangles next to most of the fires. Men talked softly in some places and loudly in others, and the faint hint of a harmonica could often be heard from the middle of the nightly clatter. Joe Halsey's plantation had become an armed camp and headquarters for the army.

Next door, the much larger Morton Hall was also transformed into an army camp. Gen. Richard Ewell, his wife, and entire family occupied the Hall itself and his staff joined him there. Hundreds of soldiers camped throughout the six thousand acres of the Morton plantation, and several artillery batteries were set up as defenses. Rifle pits were dug along its perimeters, and hundreds of supply wagons were parked in large squares just a few hundred yards from the main house. Mrs. Morton, so used to feeding her children at dinnertime, now had to serve as hostess to a dozen Confederate officers.

Joe Halsey, who was living at Lessland at the time, gladly turned over his home and Morton Hall to the army. Halsey was home recuperating from a bout with typhoid fever and was waiting for a decision on whether he would be recommissioned in the Confederate Army. He complained bitterly that the army ruined just about all the crops at Lessland and Morton Hall ("the soldiers have destroyed all my hay and the corn nearly so"), but was thrilled to play host to some of the most important generals in the Confederate Army, who frequently dined there. The highlight of the war for Halsey came in early October when his guests for dinner were Generals Richard Ewell and Jubal Early and Robert E. Lee himself, who rode up on his white horse, Traveler, with two aides.

Lee had high regard for Joe Halsey. As soon as Lee took over the Army of Northern Virginia, he began asking around for reputable officers who lived in the northern Virginia area who might be able to suggest attack and retreat routes and suitable campsites for the army. He also needed men who had lived in the area for a long time and could recommend where the river was shallow enough for men to wade across it, springs for fresh water, gaps through mountains, and high ground for reconnoitering. He also needed defensive positions near rivers, on high ground, to repulse any enemy assaults. Several people recommended Halsey because, as a planter and lawyer, he had traveled the area and its roads and rivers extensively for nearly twenty years.

Halsey first met Lee in 1862 at Mount Jackson, in the Blue Ridge Mountains, when he was called to Lee's tent to talk about the geography of the area. He suggested a number of river crossings and campsites to Lee that night and met with the general three or four more times in 1862 and 1863 before Lee came to Halsey's plantation for dinner. Lee was particularly interested in shallow river crossings. He was fighting a defensive war in Virginia and needed to move back from the enemy whenever he wanted. To do that, he needed to know where he could cross such rivers as the Rapidan and Rappahannock with great speed to keep a safe distance between himself and the Federals. He was always able to do that. The Union Army, unfamiliar with the river crossings, was constantly slowed down when the entire army had to wade through water that was too deep. Halsey continued to serve Lee as a geographical adviser throughout the war, and Lee always thanked him for his help.]

October 8
[Letter to Sister Anne]

Dear Anne,

There have been some six or seven in the tent singing and talking and in the rear three genuine contrabands have been having a concert of their own which is somewhat distracting though not unpleasant (Col. P's "Riven" Dr. Sullivan "More" and Lt. Col. Campbell's "Jackson"). The rebel lines cross the river just below us and in front. They have strong works on the opposite side of the river and the guns planted on the hills there cover not only our present position but the whole flat back to the station. You probably know the ground. Yesterday morning we expected an attack for sure. Cars were running all night on their sides, picket firing was frequent and the generals looked for it. The danger is not here now but we have gotten accustomed to it. All sutlers, and all the trains, were ordered back except two wagons to a regiment. Things looked very much as though we would get out of this suddenly some night and not stop till we moved back to Alexandria. I think we are waiting now for an attack first. It is impossible to HOLD the ground. Yesterday it rained all day nearly and our camp was flooded.

I have been reading the novel *Mrs. Itallibetoria Troubles* by Mrs. Henry Wood. Have you seen Alanson yet?

October 11 (Near Brandy Station, Virginia)

Clear. Started from Culpeper an hour after daylight after trains had passed out and moving out in good order. We passed Brandy Station about noon (keeping on the east side of the railroad and the 4th Corps to the west). Arrived at Rappahannock Station in the middle of the afternoon, crossed the river and went into camp on the North bank before dark. The rebels were driving our cavalry who covered our rear all day. We met a sutler at the station with a good stock.

October 12

After dinner the 6th and part of the 2d Corps with cavalry made a reconnaissance or feint, advancing as far as Brandy Station, the cavalry going to near Culpeper driving and punishing the force—not overly strong—found opposing us. Camped till midnight. This movement was a very handsome one, the long lines of battle extending over the plains of Culpeper in both directions and when our regiment happened to go over one of the rolling hills the sight was a splendid one. The movement was a pretended advance to check the enemy moving along the west flank and to give our trains time to get away. It was successful.

October 13

Weather clear. Roused at midnight and marched back to Rappahannock Station where we arrived and recrossed about 3 A.M. Started again at sunrise and marching parallel with the railroad reached Warrenton junction about noon. The bridge at Rappahannock was blown up just after starting. We halted at Warrenton junction for two or three hours, then moved on along the railroad. We passed a large, 40 acre wagon park of the army. We halted for the night at Kettle Run.

[The post-Gettysburg political picture changed as voters went to the polls in state elections in several states in October. Clement Vallandigham, the copperhead leader, was soundly defeated in his bid to become governor of Ohio in a vote that was critical from the White House's view. Andrew Curtin, a strong Lincoln supporter, was reelected governor of Pennsylvania. Republicans in those states and in Indiana and Iowa swept to victory. The elections vindicated Lincoln and kept his critics at bay throughout the fall and winter.]

October 14

Starting at sunrise with some cannonading in our rear.

[The Confederates, under A. P. Hill, assumed that the entire federal army moving through the area surrounding the Bristoe Station railway cut was composed of just one corps. Hill ordered two brigades to attack the Federals, but they were surprised by three other divisions of Federals and an artillery corps. Instead of retreating, the rebels attacked a hastily formed but solid federal line, with artillery in the rear firing over the line, and were badly beaten. The rebel losses were 1,500 killed and wounded and about 400 men captured, plus several cannon. Gen. Carnot Posey was killed and two other CSA generals were badly wounded. Federal losses were 548.]

October 18

My Dear Sister Sue,

I wrote Sam quite a long letter yesterday, giving him a full account of our adventures to date, though I was very uncertain as to whether I would be able to finish it . . . was interrupted by cannonading. It turned out to be no great thing, probably a cavalry fight on Manassas plains and did not affect us.

We left Mitchell Station last night one week ago and crossed the Rappahannock Station the next afternoon, Monday, in order to mislead the enemy or for some other reason. We went back to Brandy Station, falling back again at night. This was a beautiful sight—our long lines preceded by cavalry and flying artillery moving over the slightly undulating plains of Culpeper.

Tuesday night the army moved in parallel columns, with the enemy on our flank, and we reached Bristoe Station.

Wednesday we started at sunrise and moved very cautiously to Centerville and from the heights witnessed the fight of our rear guard (the 2d corps) at Bristoe. The rebs expected to seize our wagon train—and came within 15 yards of our line, lying behind the railroad, before they saw it. Their reception was a tremendous volley and the result was their being driven back to Warrenton Junction.

That night we moved out on the Chantilly Road and with a slight change of position we are still in what goes by that name. The turnpike from Aldie to Fairfax passes through it and here is where our right was turned last year. As near as I can [see], our army lays in the shape of an "S," the front line being the Bull Run stream, the angle at Centerville and our corps at right angles, covering the right flank.

We are under arms every morning before sunrise and every day almost in the few days we have been here we have been in anticipation of an attack. Skirmishing with our pickets occurred only yesterday and we thought it was a sure thing. I cannot say we fear them at all for we have a naturally strong position strengthened by rifle pits and we are three times their numbers. Guerrillas abound in front and in the rear of us, capturing our Brigade quartermaster and commissary between here and Fairfax the day before yesterday and every loose man that straggles. We begin to think that our fears of Lee having a vast army in front of us are groundless—if he has he concealed them well. The report tonight is that we are to make an advance tomorrow and quite a body of cavalry came up this afternoon which seems to prove the idea. Some think Lee has gone into Maryland again and that we are ordered to Edwards Ferry.

The fact is not one of us knows anything about it. Meade deserves a great deal of credit for the maneuver in which the falling back of the army was conducted—no panic, no haste and no abandonment of stores and the enemy severely punished for following too closely. I only hope the rest of the campaign will be as skillfully and cautiously conducted. So far, we have never tried to avoid a fight and never allowed them to fight us at a disadvantage. Meade has to be cautious for he has no reserve and a defeat would be total ruin. What would have been the fate of Baltimore, Philadelphia last summer if the Army of the Potomac had not been in fighting them at Gettysburg. [Who] will answer where Pennsylvania, New York and New Jersey couldn't get a thousand men to stop Lee's victorious march? The defeat of Vallandigham and Woodward and proposed draft of 300,000 new troops are to me much encouraging.

Since leaving Culpeper, we have hardly had a sight at our wagons and the consequences are we are hard up for clean clothes, tobacco, reading matter or edibles. Fortunately, my stock in all of these was good at the start and if we don't move the wagons will be up tomorrow. It's a strong contrast to a Sunday in Rockaway.

October 19

We marched through Groveton to Gainesville, Virginia, and camped a little after dark. There was cavalry fighting all day. They drove the enemy nearly to Warrenton but reinforcements of infantry coming up from below and they were driven back nearly to our camps.

[LESSLAND PLANTATION: While Ed Halsey was on the march to Gainesville, his brother Joe was back at Lessland, thirty miles away, on furlough, and remained there until the end of October. Millie wrote that while they sat in their backyard, they could hear the sounds of battle from cavalry skirmishes at Brandy Station, just a few miles away. Joe tried to return to Lessland as often as possible so that he could work on the plantation, which had lost most of its slaves. He also worked feverishly during furloughs on whatever small jobs he could obtain as a lawyer, using his front-yard office for clients when it wasn't commandeered by the Confederate Army. A study of Halsey's papers indicates a small but steady legal business. Most of his assignments were quite small, but they did supply him with an income to help make up for the ruin of his corn business.

He also used his office at Lessland to conduct commissary business. He sent out and received hundreds of notes concerning the availability and price of food and supplies. He kept careful records of all moneys owed by the army to any food suppliers in the Virginia area.]

October 21

[The Fifteenth continued to move through the north-central area of Virginia. Halsey described the journey in a letter.]

Dear Cousins,

Yesterday we started and felt our way very cautiously to New Baltimore which the rebs left an hour before we arrived a little after noon. On our route there were traces of the cavalry fighting of the day before—dead horses, wounded men—and now and then a dead one whom the rebels had left almost naked as they did over the river. We will be pushed ahead to make room for the 5th corps which lies at New Baltimore. Week ago Saturday morning we were ordered to make a general attack at all the crossings on the Rapidan and only by the merest chance (Russel's brigade being delayed) we were prevented from making the attempt above before the countermanding order came.

November 3 (Warrenton)
    [In late October, Halsey's girlfriend Mary lost her grandfather.]

Dear Cousin,
    Your letter with the particulars of your recent heavy loss reached me last Friday and I take the first opportunity of expressing my sympathy with you in your bereavement. Knowing how much you were attached to him and how rarely death has visited your family, I am very sensitive [as to] how bitter must be this dispensation of [misery] to you. Still, I feel that you have that consolation which is above all other and that the grief which for a time seems inconsolable must yield to its power for your own love to mingle with joy at his happiness. It must be a great comfort to you to think how well spent and useful the life of your grandfather was and the many testimonials to his worth and their esteem by the associations with which he was connected should go to reconcile you for [your loss].

    The papers have no doubt kept you informed of our movements from the time we left Culpeper till we reached here. Though after expecting a battle in a dozen different places for some reason, neither in the retreat or advance has this portion of the army been engaged. There has been some slight skirmishing, and at Brandy Station we lay in support of cavalry who were fighting near enough for us to see the shells burst rather unpleasantly near the enemy in [little] more force than to create a little excitement. The fight at Bristoe we saw from the heights of Centerville and for a few days expected something similar at Chantilly but the rebs were not over anxious to attack us after we got in position.
    The re-enlistment of our regiment I think is very doubtful, although the colonel is quite sanguine about it. We have too much time yet to serve to make it a good move for government. Really, I do not care much one way or the other. It would be very pleasant, of course, to spend a few months in

Jersey this winter, but it is hardly worth fourteen more months service. [The army was trying to get entire regiments to reenlist as a unit at home as a show of strength, and a perk was extended winter leave at home.] As for me, I think if I live out my three years in the army it will be enough for my satisfaction, at least the choice of serving or not is good to have in reserve. I do not wish to speak of my sacrifices (which are slight compared with those of some others) but still, they are entitled to some weight. Had I stayed home it is quite probable I would be by this time settled in the profession I had chosen (law).

Now I have in prospect two more years service and at the end of that time a mind unaccustomed to study with what I had learned and now forgotten about entirely. In a word, to commence life over again as from the commencement stage with this difference, that habits and disposition formed which would make a professional life very doubtful under these circumstances. I do not care to prolong my stay in the service and it is not easy for an officer to resign—in fact almost impossible unless with a damaged character or health. [His fear was that five or six years in the army would force him to start law studies all over again.]

November 5

✒ [Meade, still in charge despite Lincoln's anger with him, decided to pick away at the Army of Northern Virginia, which was arrayed opposite him around the Rapidan, in an effort to dislodge it and make Lee fight him on friendly ground. Small attacks in various places were ordered, but none were effective, and finally, after a number of skirmishes through early December, the Army of the Potomac headed for winter quarters.]

November 7

Marched to near the Rappahannock station where we fell in with enemy's pickets. Disposition made for the attack which commenced about the middle of the afternoon. The 2d and 3rd Brigade supported by us and with remainder of our Corps and 3rd near gallant by assaulted and took the hills and ironworks north of the river with 1,650 prisoners, four cannon and ten flags.

Our brigade was not one of the two in advance because the 4th regiment was with a wagon train and did not get up to the front. The annexed map or diagram I sent home the day after the battle shows the general position of things.

We lost no men though we were exposed to the artillery fire of the enemy.

This attack appears to have been entirely unexpected by the enemy. Our men sprang over their men in the rifle pits keeping out of the fire and not expecting the assault. Our brigade advanced handsomely. General Torbert and staff riding in front. The 1st, 15th and others on the front line. Major Boeman was riding in the rear on the left. Col. Penrose was in the center and myself on the right. A shell struck under the major's horse but did no damage. He was smoking his pipe as he rode.

Just after dark a battery on the edge of the woods east of the railroad about opposite us opened up, the flashes of its guns making a very brilliant appearance.

✒ [The fight on the banks of the Rappahannock was small, but it pushed Lee's main army back to the Rapidan and revived the morale of the Union Army.]

November 8

Raw, clear. Crossed the river on the rebs bridge and in P.M. the 3rd corps having come up from Kelley's Ford and joined our left, we all advanced about three miles and camped on the old camp site of the rebs. Firing in front and to the right of us all day.

November 9

Cloudy with snow squalls in the P.M. About 4 P.M. we packed up and hearing report that the enemy were moving heavy masses on the right towards Sulphur Springs. The corps was moved out on that road to front that way.

The Blue Ridge Mountains appeared very beautiful at sunset, covered with snow while the sun appeared red and fiery under a heavy lowering cloud. I slept in the open air with difficulty . . . seeking warmth.

November 10

[Letter to Emma Halsey, Sam junior's wife]

Dear Sister,

We are now as I understand on part of a farm owned by John M. Batts whose house is now General Sedgwick's headquarters. Last Saturday at day-break we broke our last camp and started a march of about ten miles to Rappahannock Station. The rebels here occupied a strong position in forts we had built on both sides of the river.

The attack was made in the afternoon by the 2d and 3rd brigade of our division supported by others. It was a brilliant affair and resulted in the capture of nearly all of two brigades (North Carolina, Alabama and Louisiana troops) with four pieces of cannon and eight flags. The prisoners said Lee was there but an hour before dark and went away satisfied the place was perfectly safe.

They pronounced the affair very gallant. Neither Meade nor Sedgwick would believe it when first reported. Our loss was quite heavy especially in officers. It is said the 6th Maine lost 17 officers. Altogether some 50 were killed and 300 wounded. Our brigade lost none though shells were very unpleasantly near us at all times.

On Sunday morning we expected to renew the fight and attack them over the river but it seems they had taken wit in their anger and fled. In the afternoon forming a junction with the 3rd corps which had crossed below us on the left at Kelley's Ford with a slight skirmish, we advanced to Brandy Station, with little if any opposition. There was cavalry fighting all day. Yesterday afternoon it was reported the enemy were flanking us by way of White Sulphur Springs so our corps was moved out in that direction to guard against such an attack. No attack was made and today we moved camp to a warmer position with the understanding we are to remain here for two days at least and if the rebels do not attack us we will attack them. There was a little squall of snow yesterday and the Blue Ridge Mountains a few miles to the west are white with it. The wind from that direction comes down cold and raw and last night as I spread my blankets in the "big tent" [I realized] that campaigning in winter is for us a fool of a job.

*[LESSLAND PLANTATION: In letters sent from his office, heated by a small stove, in the front yard of Lessland, Joe Halsey complained to a friend that the Confederate government ignored pleas for compensation by homeowners whose property was occupied by the army]

November 14
[Letter to his cousins after Halsey finished reading the novel *Maurice Tierney*]

Dear Cousins,
I write this with a lead pencil because it is more convenient and comfortable to sit by a fire in my tent than in the office which happens to be destitute of that essential. We have been in the present camp since Tuesday but

no one seems to know the exact locality, it being as near Brandy Station as Freeman's Ford as some say. The quartermaster and I have an "A" tent stockaded some four feet high with a chimney and open fire place made up of stones, much sod and a pork barrel. Orders came in before daylight this A.M. This Corps will be held in readiness to move on very short notice.

November 25

🖎 [In a long letter Halsey sent his brother Sam in early December 1863, he fully described what happened next to the regiment as it tried to maneuver for an attack on Lee's army, dug in at Mine Run, near Germanna Ford on the Rapidan River, near Culpeper.]

We had reveille at 4 A.M. and were all packed up and out on the road by daylight. As we were in the rear of the army our march was very tedious all day, the roads not being the best either. Passing through Brandy Station and the deserted camps of the other corps, we moved to the north of Stevensburg and by dark became entangled in the woods to the east of that place. We crossed the river at Jacob's Mills, I believe, about five miles above Germanna Ford, following the 3rd Corps, and halted for the balance of the night on the south bank. It was then after midnight.

The next morning we were ready to start ahead before daylight, but did not leave the neighborhood till the middle of the afternoon. There was firing in every direction and we were started two or three times. At last throwing out flankers to the right of us, we moved out. In a little while, picket firing in front became heavier and soon warmed into a considerable fight. We loaded and commenced double quicking. Soon streams of stragglers, pack animals, musicians passed us to the rear and then the wounded. Our lines of battle was formed and we expected for sure to go in.

The 3rd Corps who were fighting were breaking in all directions. Russel's brigade went in yelling for them to get out of the way and give the 6th Corps a chance. Howe's division had two regiments deployed to drive up a brigade who had broken without firing a gun. It was now dark and soon became quiet, a few prisoners came in, and on the whole the advantage rested with us—the rebels retiring at dark.

None of our Corps were engaged really, except as I have said; it was July 2 [in reserve at Gettysburg] all over again. At midnight, we were again in motion, having had some three hours sleep, and at daylight, after a tedious march of three or four miles through the woods, came out near Robinson's Tavern, where the 2d Corps had been skirmishing along the pike towards Orange Court House. After going perhaps a mile or two it became evident there was very serious opposition in front and soon we were moved off to the right of the road and after meandering back and forward through the bush and woods, came out on a ridge in sight of the Rebs, posted in heavy force on another hill. I never saw them so conspicuously posted before.

On a large, clear field, especially, their grey lines of battle were very showy, with artillery and rifle pits dotting the face of the hill. Their skirmishers, which were then but a few hundred yards ahead of us, kept blazing away at everything they saw. It soon commenced to rain hard, and did not clear up till late in the afternoon. One of our men was shot through the arm on the skirmish line, but Capt. Walker, who had command of ours, under Lt. Col. Campbell, thinks that we caused more damage than we received. We remained that night and all of Sunday in the same position, expecting every hour the engagement to commence. Movements taking place in the troops around us, and picket firing brisk, with an occasional cannon.

Their position was deemed impregnable right in front, the worst feature being a stream reported by our skirmishers to be nearly waist deep and eleven feet wide, which had to be crossed under their whole fire.

At midnight, we were aroused to make coffee, and at 2 A.M. of Monday we moved out and down to the right. Marching with great secrecy, we got into position about one and a half miles to the right in the woods, formed in three lines in columns of attack. The two brigades of Howe's division on our right, and the 5th Corps on their left. The 2d Corps, with Terry's division of our corps, had gone to the left to attack their right, the 3rd Corps taking our place in the center. Warren was to commence at 8 and we at 9. The enemy were posted in a wood on a hill, at the foot of which was the stream, and between us and it a wide and almost level clear field. It was understood to be a desperate attack, but although it was conceded our loss must be very heavy, we could take it if anyone could.

Our position was gained at about 4 A.M., and with orders to build no fires, with no loud talking, laughing or even stamping, we lay till dawn and then till dusk, though water was freezing in the canteens of the men. As the day opened we began to listen for Warren's guns up the left, but in vain. At 8 A.M. there was some cannonading all along the line and one of our batteries fired a few shells, but five shots from the Rebs made such havoc in its exposed situation that it was ordered stopped. Soon we heard the attack was postponed—Warren having found the position in front of him impregnable, and sent word to Meade he would not attack without orders. After dark, we moved back to our old place when, after being 18 hours without a fire, we busied ourselves getting coffee and thawing out. The night was bitter cold, ice freezing nearly an inch thick, and it is reported some men actually froze to death on the picket line.

In the dawn, just as we started Capt. Cook read to each regiment an order publishing some victory out west. He read we had captured 2000 guns and 20 prisoners or 20 guns and 2000 prisoners, he could not see which.

Tuesday was quiet, comparatively, and it was said the 3rd, 1st and 5th Corps were marching off. As soon as it became dark we started and for a time it was very tedious—the column halting every few steps, and the men not having exercise enough to keep warm. The air was very cold, though a south wind was blowing. It was at least 10 o'clock when we reached Robinson's Tavern, only two miles in the rear. A tannery, some small houses and buildings were fired as the column passed, lighting up our march, and there were crowds of stragglers around small fires by the road. It was thought by some we were going to Fredericksburg, we being on the pike leading straight there from Orange Court House by Chancellorsville. Once fairly started, we made better headway and two or three miles from the old tavern and near the Chancellorsville battleground, we took off to the left through the woods and marching quite rapidly, crossed the Rapidan at Germanna Ford before daylight Wednesday. I think we must have gone five miles further, at least, than the 5th and 3rd Corps, who had been in advance of us before we halted to get coffee, about eight. In an hour or two, we again fell in, but after advancing a mile or two, halted in the woods, and then the report was that instead of going back to our old camps, as we supposed, we were ordered to re-cross. We seized the opportunity to roll ourselves in our blankets and sleep anywhere we could find a soft place.

Hardtack had now become quite an object and there were a good many supperless among the men. Yesterday, starting at daylight, we made the march to this place, arriving here a little after noon. Our wagons came up at dark, and last night we enjoyed a quiet sleep and today the luxury of clean clothes. Rations were issued to the men—letters and papers have informed us as to what is going on at home and elsewhere and now [we look] forward to sutlers to supply us with what might be called necessary luxuries. Last night there was an order that "the enemy were reported crossing at Raccoon and Mortons' Fords, and we should be in readiness to move at a very short notice." It proved to be a false alarm. This P.M. there was distant cannonading, which would seem to indicate that they were anxious to find out where we are. Tomorrow we propose to change our camp a few yards, to better ground.

There were some things which were unfortunate for us. Confederate cavalry General J.S. Mosby tried to burn our train, but failing in that, burned some 14 or 15 army headquarters wagons just on the rear of them. The 4th Virginia cavalry also struck the supply and ammunition wagons of the 5th Corps over the river and destroyed the most of them, running off the mules. General Bartlett lost all his baggage and he said he had nothing left but what he had on. The cold made the sufferings of the wounded much worse, and I am glad there were no more of them. A train of nineteen army wagons (you know the style—heavy, without springs) came by filled with our wounded from General John Buford's cavalry, lying in the bottom without straw even, some of them having just had amputations performed. As the road was long, rough and frozen, their situation was terrible. One of our men, sick with diarrhea, died in the ambulance on the 2d.

🖋 [THE WAR: U. S. Grant arrived outside of Chattanooga with reinforcements in late November to break the siege there. On November 23, the Union Army captured Orchard Knob, a mile in front of Missionary Ridge, where the main Confederate force was located. On November 24, Hooker and three federal divisions climbed slowly up nearby Lookout Mountain, through a fogbank, and seized it. The following day assaults by Gen. William T. Sherman and Hooker on Missionary Ridge failed, but an afternoon attack by Gen. George Thomas and the Army of the Cumberland succeeded, and the ridge was taken. CSA general Braxton Bragg retreated with his army after a strategic loss.

Meanwhile, in another part of Tennessee, Longstreet's division moved on Knoxville in an attempt to take Fort Sanders, where Ambrose Burnside's Federals had set up strong defenses. The dawn attack was made on a cold Sunday morning and the rebels had to run across freezing ground covered with a recent sleet, making footing difficult. The Confederates hit the fort with considerable force and managed to get one of their flags onto the top of one wall, but were slowly beaten back and defeated. Longstreet, knowing Grant's army was moving toward

Knoxville with reinforcements, withdrew and Knoxville was never threatened again.]

December 5

[Halsey wrote a condensed version of the battle to cousins Eliza and Mary and then launched into speculation.]

Dear Cousins,

You seem to think from what I said of farming that I was getting discouraged or had the blues. It may have been so but that was not what made me say it. It was from the settled conviction that my habits and mode of thinking were changed and as extremes meet it was quite probable, if I should be spared so long, that I would go to California or settle down to some quiet farmers' life when the war is over. I spoke of farming because it would be in accord with another plan I have always considered my duty to carry out to take care of what is left of our family, my father especially, should they ask it. I do not pretend to any extraordinary merit in this particular and may very probably be mistaken in my knowledge of myself . . . if I think as I do now. August 25, 1865, I would hesitate to do anything which would in any way draw me from that purpose. That consideration out of the way, it is quite as probable I should go to California as anywhere else. I believe I am too lazy and think too much of my own "ease and quickness" ever to be ambitious. However, what is the use of talking about anything which is so far off and from plans which there is so little likelihood of being realized?

The girls write me from home that Anne's rheumatism is improving and all the rest well. They have just had a visit from Sarah Willard which they enjoyed ever so much. I am very glad of it on Sills' account especially she has so little recreation. Since I have been out, she has not been away a week at a time and with all the care of our household . . . with Anne helpless and only one girl, sister Sue deserves a great deal of credit. . . . She has done her duty. You who know her so well will pardon what others would consider the unpardonable sin of bragging of one's relatives. I am proud of her and not ashamed to say it.

December 21

🖋 [Halsey spent the Christmas holidays visiting his girlfriend Mary, friends, and relatives in Rockaway and Morris County and, since there was a deep cover of snow on the ground, went sleighing most afternoons. He returned to the Army of the Potomac on December 28.]

December 29

✒ [LESSLAND PLANTATION: Joseph Halsey returned to the army after a furlough home at Lessland. He wrote a long letter to a neighbor who had moved his family and slaves away from Culpeper to Appomattox for safety. Joe explained why he turned down an offer to sell Lessland but told him how he worried about his plantation and his family. It was one of dozens of letters Joe Halsey wrote to friends in and out of the army during the war, and they all at the same time expressed worry and pride about Millie and his children.]

Dear Sir,

I am glad to hear that you have purchased a place that will answer at least as a retreat for your servants and a place of refuge in an emergency. I mailed a letter for you at Rapidan yesterday on my way to camp in which I stated my embarrassments about Lessland. If I could get a good tenant for Lessland, I should like it. Perhaps it might suit Colonel Porter's family to occupy it for a time, but I am so situated that I can only be absent for a night occasionally on my own responsibility and can have but few opportunities to manage matters at home.

I dislike to sell Lessland for Confederate money unless I could get a very heavy price and be able to save at least a part by another investment in productive real estate. Confederate money seems to be closely guarded and threatened with utter confiscation by our own government in its heedless upkeep, tinkering with its obligations as by any Yankee edict. Land cannot be constitutionally confiscated . . . under either government and law must sometime resume its sway over society under any issue of this war.

It will, however, be extremely difficult if not impossible to raise supplies at Lessland from its exposed condition, if the Yankees persist in another campaign. . . . Yet, I will see what can be done to do the best with the property. If I could get a tenant there and with the damages and what means I could raise, buy a small temporary home and move the family and stock where they could make their living I would prefer it. But whether without the sale of Lessland I could do this is the difficulty.

I think the farm will be quite safe [until April] and I think the severest part of the winter is over. It is too cumbersome to move anyway and I think it would be well to let the family remain until that time.

We shall remain here (camp) some three weeks, I presume, and then move back to recruit [for the army] unless the Yankees become troublesome. Where we shall go, I do not know. I would like to have home matters comfortably arranged before we leave if I could, and I had some ideas about the middle of January of trying to get a 30 day furlough if possible. I have never had a furlough indulgence for over 24 hours since I have been in the army, now nearly three years, and if our regiment goes back merely to recruit and in winter quarters I might possibly get General Lee under the circumstances to grant a little time to arrange for my family in their present exposed position.

The damages done to Lessland [by the Confederate Army encampments there] are too heavy to be overlooked and yet without close preparation not a thing will be done nor a cent paid to me, though I doubt if the government profits on the operation. By that time, too, possibly the financial policy of the government may at least be shadowed forth and some idea found of what the country is to expect from the wisdom or folly of our legislators.

[Halsey went on for a page describing his plans to purchase flour from a Northern town and have it hauled to the center of the state for the army, enabling the cooks to use it to make bread, ending a bread shortage. His letters were full of rather unique schemes to supply the army by moving goods from one area of Virginia to another. He also asked his friend if he had any cotton textiles that Joe could buy for his wife.]

Give my love to the children. I wrote to Fannie and mailed it yesterday, will write to Annie soon. Morton and Ogden wrote to Annie by yesterday's mail. I hope you all have a pleasant Christmas, though it is gloomy enough in the seriousness of the country here.

December 31

✒ [Halsey and other Union officers held an all-night party December 31 through January 1 to celebrate New Year's Eve, ending 1863. The war droned on.]

10

ORDER IN THE COURT

January 22–April 30, 1864

[The new year found Lieutenant Halsey wearing yet another hat for the Union Army—judge advocate. Because he was a law student at Princeton before the war and had planned to eventually take the New Jersey bar exam, Halsey, like many other prewar lawyers and law students, was asked to be a judge advocate for his brigade's general court-martial boards. His job was to present the case and evidence against the accused—and to offer legal advice to him—to a board of from five to thirteen officers, which would then decide the guilt or innocence of the accused or reduce or modify the charges. The board would then pass sentence, which could range from merely docking a soldier's pay by a few dollars a month for three or four months, to execution.

Generals convened court-martial boards at odd times and in odd places. They were usually established when there was a backlog of cases—as many as twenty. They tried to hear as many as they could in single sessions to avoid taking time off from the war for the tribunal but, given the pace of the judge advocate and the cases, usually only heard two to four per session. Many cases were heard in the winter, when the army was in camp, and few during campaigns in spring and summer. The boards were assembled to give a fair hearing to soldiers charged with crimes and to levy light sentences for minor army infractions and heavy ones for major insubordination. Court-martials were indispensable to maintain discipline in the army, particularly in 1863 and 1864 when there were so many desertions. The army felt that the strongest way to prevent the desertion of many was to harshly punish the few who were caught. Court-martials were also an effective way to preserve discipline and order within brigades and companies and to stop soldiers from verbally or physically assaulting their superiors or from refusing to obey orders. The war's court-martial boards heard thousands of cases.

The judge advocate's job was to present all the facts of the case, explain army punishment on all charges to the board (members of the different boards, who rarely served more than six months, were usually not lawyers and did not know much about army rules and regulations), and to give adequate advice to the defendant. His job was also to notify board members of upcoming trials (members were usually from different companies and regiments), keep records of each case, preserve the paperwork, and to forward the trial findings and sentences to headquarters.

The judge advocate's responsibility as a lawyer or law student, however, was to assure that each defendant received a fair trial and that the prosecution of the case was just, nonprejudicial, and balanced. They had the same responsibility to the legal system in the army that they had in civilian life, and usually even more because in the army they did not present cases to judges steeped in the law, but to army officers who knew little about the law. Most judge advocates fulfilled their responsibilities fairly, but in minimal fashion. They usually notified board members in advance, but only worked on cases on the day of trial, kept records, and did little more.

Halsey went well beyond established codes of responsibilities for judge advocates in his work, plunging into it with the same earnestness he displayed as an adjutant. He kept dutiful records of the appointments of each judge to his trial board and made certain each was notified of upcoming trials several days before the cases and then on the morning before the trial. On the day before the trial, he rode out to the camp of the defendant and conducted a long interview with him in order to present his defense. He then conducted an interview with the commanding officer who had brought charges in order to present the prosecution. He collected the names of witnesses from the commanding officer and the defendant and interviewed those witnesses. He made certain all witnesses knew when and where the trial was going to take place and demanded their presence. He kept detailed records of the fifty-seven trials he worked on as a lawyer. (Unfortunately, in most cases the details of the crimes themselves are not described, merely the military charge, such as desertion or misconduct, but information in his diary and letters fills in some gaps.)

"Special" court-martial boards handled minor cases and could not impose sentences of more than a loss of a month's pay or a month in prison. Halsey served as a lawyer for a "general" court-martial board, which heard major crimes and could impose long prison sentences and order executions. The board's work was difficult. All cases, military or civilian, have extenuating circumstances. Civil War cases had extenuating circumstances exaggerated by the nature of the war. Some desertion cases were simple and some were extremely complicated, involving men who rushed home to be with wives giving birth or men who simply did not understand the terms of their enlistment.

The rapid growth of the army from just a few thousand men to nearly a million created enormous problems with the issuing and interpretation of orders. For example, dozens of men who honestly believed they had ten-day furloughs to go home were brought up on desertion charges. Men who routinely argued with bosses in the civilian workplace were arrested and court-martialed for doing exactly the same thing with superior officers in the army. Men who fled in the heat of battle to save their lives were sometimes charged with cowardice. The judge advocates' job was to present these circumstances along with the cases and argue for fairness, and not simply by-the-book justice. They had substantial influence in the presentation and outcomes of cases.

The boards' punishments were inconsistent. Punishment for the same crime could range from a $3-per-month reduction in pay for several months to three years in prison. Some deserters were put in prison for three years, and others who had deserted two or three times, but had lengthy and complicated stories, received light sentences. New recruits were held to lesser standards than old veterans. Drunks were not only protected by God, as the adage goes, but by court-martial boards. Officers were rarely charged with anything.

Judge advocates had to suffer politics. Defendants who had political connections in the army were looked at with more lenient eyes than those who had none. On April 30, 1864, Halsey was judge advocate in the case of Pvt. George Adams, of the First New Jersey, charged with desertion. Adams brought along five different highly regarded captains as character witnesses. He could have been shot or sent to prison for several years, but the sentence for the well-connected Adams was merely an extra month of service and the loss of four months' pay. The boards' decisions were usually confirmed by the reigning general, but they were sometimes overturned for political reasons. One general told the board he did not want an officer sentenced because the officer was a trusted aide and friend of his and was needed immediately for service. The general tossed out all charges against the officer and had him reassigned to his staff the next day.

There was comedy, such as the case of Pvt. Peter Clancy. The young private from New Jersey was a low-level aide assigned to help maintain General Torbert's personal headquarters tents. Torbert had a sweet tooth and kept a large stash of candy secretly hidden in a chest under a bed in his tent, which was cluttered with tables, chairs, boxes, and piles of paperwork. Clancy found the candy stash and, cautiously taking just a few pieces every few days so the losses would not be noticed, fed his own sweet tooth.

One day Torbert returned from an inspection early, caught Clancy in the act, and became incensed. He brought charges against Clancy and had him court-martialed for the sugary thievery, harrumphing that the theft of candy was symbolic of what was wrong with discipline throughout the entire army. Halsey presented the case with a raised eyebrow and a tongue firmly planted in cheek. The court-martial board found Clancy guilty, as they had to because of the evidence and an eyewitness, the general. However, they merely gave Clancy a slap on the wrist with a light sentence since the case was so frivolous.

When he heard that the candy thief had been dealt with lightly, Torbert became enraged. He fired everybody on the court-martial board, except Halsey, appointed a brand-new board, and ordered Peter Clancy tried all over again. Halsey told Torbert that a soldier could not be tried twice for the same crime, and Torbert told him that this was the army and, oh, yes, he could. Caught between an irate and rather foolish general and his own conscience, Halsey carefully stalled the second Clancy case for months while at the same time promising Torbert that Clancy would be brought to trial as soon as the backlog of cases was concluded.

Every time the Clancy file rose to the top of the pile of court-martial cases, Halsey put it down on the bottom again. Finally, Torbert was promoted and transferred out of the area. Halsey promptly tossed out the second case against Peter Clancy, the notorious candy thief, who was never again ordered to stand trial.

Halsey and the boards he served realized that war fever brought the army many soldiers who were probably either too young or too old to fully understand military discipline. Several extremely young soldiers who deserted were given light sentences. One, just sixteen, became homesick, went back to New Jersey, and did not return for five months. Instead of putting him in front of a firing squad, which it could have done, Halsey's board, on his recommendation, sentenced the soldier to forfeit a year's pay and make up the time he was gone. Leniency was extended to extremely old soldiers, too. On May 2, 1864, Halsey tried a desertion case against Pvt. Still Hendricks and noted in his prosecution that Hendricks was an elderly man whose patriotism led him to enlist. At Halsey's urging, Hendricks was not only spared jail time, but sent home where he belonged.

Court-martial sentences took many forms, and sentences were often devised to humiliate the defendant as well as punish him. A common sentence for a soldier who stole something was to forfeit pay and to spend an hour or more each day for several months standing at attention with a twenty-to-thirty-pound knapsack hanging around his neck. Also hanging from his neck was a large sign noting his crime. A man who stole something would have a sign that read THIEF. A man who beat up a fellow soldier would stand for an hour or two each day with a sign that said RUFFIAN.

Halsey's boards were fair. Cases brought to trial in the army during the Civil War almost always ended in guilty verdicts, but in over 10 percent of Halsey's cases, following a selective presentation of the case by him, not-guilty verdicts were handed down.

There were harsh sentences for harsh crimes, but, again, Halsey's boards were not as rigid as others. Desertion was a major problem in both armies. The Union was riddled with desertion, and in 1864 alone, over ninety thousand soldiers had deserted. Getting out of the army was just as easy as getting into it. Deserters simply wrote their families that they wanted to come home and had civilian clothes mailed to them, which they donned and literally walked out of camp. Some convinced doctors and nurses in camp hospitals that they were much sicker than believed and won medical discharges or simply left the hospital and went home unnoticed.

Many soldiers in uniform left the army after particularly harsh fights and found many civilians, particularly in Southern states, eager to help them get home. Some just ran in battle and kept running.

Union desertions were so frequent that guards had to be posted on all the Potomac River bridges to catch deserters trying to make it over the river on their way home. The high command saw it as the most heinous of all crimes, but although 287 Union deserters were sentenced to death during the war, Halsey's boards, at his urging, never ordered an execution. They were tough in desertion and other cases, though, and did hand down more than a dozen sentences that imprisoned soldiers from one to seven years.

Ed Halsey was frequently unhappy about the outcomes of cases and took extraordinary steps to rectify them. In one case, he argued that, technically, the soldier had not violated a particular section of the military code as charged and interpreted the code for the court-martial. The board turned him down. After the session, Halsey went up to the president of the board and tried to get him to change his mind, explaining once again that the man was probably not guilty. The president refused. Frustrated, and convinced an injustice was being done, Halsey then rode several miles on horseback to division headquarters and spent nearly an hour trying to convince an army general that the man was not guilty. He failed, but it was an example of how strongly he felt about fair trials.

Halsey was the judge advocate, but he was also a soldier who felt for the weaknesses and disorderly binges of other soldiers. In one morning in 1864, two defendants in his trials were sentenced to three years in prison each and a third was sent to jail for seven years. Halsey wrote his sister that the severe sentences made it one of the worst days of his life.

Although Halsey wrote friends during 1863 that he might turn to farming or move to California when the war was over, his appointment as a judge advocate in December of 1863, and his one year of service in that post, probably reaffirmed his desire to stick with the law as a profession when the war ended.

His first case was during Christmas week, 1863, but he plunged into the full docket of cases on January 4, 1864, with the case of James Dolan.]

January 22

Feeling blue. Finished the novel *At Odds,* then *The O'Donohue,* and my cases all written up for court tomorrow.

🖋 [THE WAR: President Lincoln signed papers to direct the owners of plantations in counties and states occupied by the Union Army to hire back their former slaves at a daily wage and ordered military officials in those areas to supervise the new policy, aimed at stabilizing the Southern economy in the postwar era by sustaining the production of cotton, tobacco, and sugarcane for the owners and providing new jobs for freed slaves.]

January 24

I received from Mary a pair of very neat hospital slippers made of carpet soles and cloth worked with red gump [a dye]. So very busy reading the novel *My Hard Cash* that everything else was a nuisance.

February 3

In the evening, I attended a meeting of the Adelphi Society, a literary society gotten up by the enlisted men under the supervision of Alanson and holding its meetings every Wednesday evening in the chapel.

February 9

🖎 [THE WAR: Col. Thomas Rose led a group of 109 prisoners of war in a daring escape from the Confederate Army's notorious Libby Prison, in Richmond. The men dug an elaborate tunnel underneath the walls of the jail, a converted warehouse, emerging on one of the city's back streets. Although two drowned and forty-eight were recaptured, fifty-nine men reached federal lines and safety.]

February 10

[Court-martial]

Prisoner: Pvt. George White
Charge 1: Violation of articles of war.
Charge 2: Conduct prejudicial to good order and military discipline.
Finding: 1st charge. Guilty of leaving his regimental guard without being regularly relieved. 2d Charge: Guilty.
Sentence: To forfeit to the U.S. $10 per month of his monthly pay for five months and carry a knapsack weighing 30 lbs. every alternate hour for 20 days from reveille to retreat in front of his regimental guard house.

🖎 [Halsey, dissatisfied with the army's interpretation of the law, talked to the board about it. Unhappy with their interpretation, he took the case all the way up to General Torbert and discussed it with him at length.]

February 12

[Letter to his brother Sam]

Dear Sam,

For some reason our sick list has increased with alarming rapidity lately, without any assignable cause. There were 35 on the list this A.M., double what it was last week, chronic diarrhea being principal trouble. Of the whole number, one fourth are recruits, many of whom never ought to have been here. Of 54 recruits ... 15 have been rejected by our surgeons as unfit for duty.

🖋 [LESSLAND PLANTATION: Millie Halsey not only had to raise two small boys, breast-feed a baby, plant corn and potatoes, look out for Yankees and run the plantation in her husband's absence, but also had to pay his bills and collect money owed him. It was complicated and time-consuming work. Today she received three checks from her husband, which he told her to turn over, sign on his behalf, and distribute to three different people, including a Mr. Miller, whom they had to buy cornmeal from after the Confederate Army took all of their corn. Miller, Joe Halsey told Millie, "is an extortionist" and ordered her not to buy anything else from him. She was also told to drive to the plantation of W. H. Martin and collect $135 that he owed her husband and to visit a local business-man to collect another $100 that was owed. She also had to take money her husband mailed her and drive ten miles to Culpeper, with the Union Army scattered throughout the area, to deposit it in the bank.]

February 13

I was appointed Adjutant by Regimental order 13.

🖋 [THE WAR: Gen. William T. Sherman's army left Vicksburg and headed for Meridian, Mississippi, a railroad junction, where he planned to tear up railroad tracks to ruin the Confederate supply routes. Sherman's army of twenty-five thousand men met little resistance and destroyed with a vengeance just about all of the town of Meridian, burning or tearing down the railroad depot, an arsenal, some storehouses, office buildings, a hotel, and some stores. "Meridian . . . no longer exists," he wrote.

Sherman was not rebuked for the destruction of civilian property, despite protests from the local Southern politicians. His success at destroy-ing Meridian was a precursor for his legendary and destructive March to the Sea later.]

February 16

In the evening we were enjoying ourselves but our amusements were constantly arrested by our chimney catching fire.

February 18

[Court-Martial]

Prisoner: Pvt. Nathan Culver, 15th N.J.

Charge 1: Conduct prejudicial to good order and military discipline

Charge 2: Neglect of duty
Plea: Guilty
Finding: Guilty
Sentence: To carry a knapsack weighing at least 30 lbs. every alternate
hour from reveille to retreat for 30 days in front of the regiment guard
house and to have a placard placed on the knapsack with the word "thief"
painted on it in large legible letters and to sleep with the guard during the
30 days.

February 27

We broke camp about ten o'clock, leaving behind us about fifty sick
convalescent and supernumeraries. Marched to Culpeper—about five
miles—and passing through the town turned southwest and north of Fox
Mountain and went into camp a short distance of James City.

We met a soldier's wife [who] said her husband's wages were $11 a
month and flour was $150 per barrel and bread $5 per pound. The town
itself is a beautiful place with two or three nice churches, a court house.
Most buildings are on a street with a rolling country all around.

🖋 [The green recruits were extremely apprehensive about any movement
in the terrain and almost shot both the colonel and an orderly.]

March 1

A cavalry force under Stedman were at our lines this morning. They
knew nothing of Custer but about ten we heard the latter guns close by and
Stedman's cavalry were out to help him. In the middle of the afternoon all
the cavalry came in presenting a sorry appearance. Horses were hollow and
jaded and like the men withered. By the side of the column walked hosts of
negroes, hurrying along, all ages and both sexes, some with horses. The cavalry had passed us by dark and drawing in our pickets we followed them
back to the river. I was ahead looking for solid ground to march on. It
seemed muddy, but the men did not grumble much.

🖋 [LESSLAND PLANTATION: Joe and Millie Halsey discussed the abandonment of Lessland many times between the spring of 1863, when the Union
Army poured into the Chancellorsville area, and the spring of 1864. Joe,
away with the army most of the time, waffled. Millie was always insistent
on staying. In the spring of 1864, she wrote her husband: "I am disposed to
stand my ground, especially since there seems to be no opening for me in

any other direction. And, of course, there is no argument necessary to prove that home is the best place to be, when let alone."]

March 3
    [Letter to Sue]

My Dear Sister,
    I received Sill's letter which was accompanied by one from Carrie Jackson, who wished to thank me for attentions to Alfred and his wants. [I have not written often lately] because my time has pretty well been occupied by duty, not on account of my attentions being distracted by other correspondents that I seem to have forgotten you.
    On Washington's birthday, the 1st regiment gave a grand dinner at which many distinguished guests were present: John Hill of Boonton, Mr. Cobb (and Miss Wandell) with others ladies and gentlemen too numerous to mention. On their account I suppose our corps was received on the 23rd. This review was like all others except as respect to guests and for me personally. I served on general staff of the brigade which gave me better opportunities for seeing things.
    Wednesday and Thursday followed without anything of interest except a raffle for a horse of Capt. Whitehead, who had broken his arm and was going home. This came off Thursday night and was attended by nearly half the officers of the Brigade, more out of compliment to Captain W. than for any other reason. Friday night came orders to march and the next day about ten o'clock leaving about fifty sick in camp, we started.
    The day was very pleasant and the roads hard dry and (not dusty). It is six miles to Culpeper and we passed this there about one, marching quite rapidly we into camp near James City some three or four miles outside our lines. This march of fifteen or sixteen miles came rather hard on our men, who had been so long in camp and there was more straggling than usual. Early the next morning, our brigade leading, we were off again. James City, which we first came to, consists of a shop and house together and a store and dwelling house together one side of the street and a dwelling house on the other, with a few out buildings laying around, on the whole looking very old, forlorn and miserable—Meriden would suffer in comparison. Being outside everything, we were obligated to march a little cautiously having flankers on either side and pickets or rather skirmishers ahead.
    Passing Thorofare Mountain, we soon came to Robertson's River, which was gallantly forded and then came a rush for the town about three miles

on. We entered it I guess about noon, meeting no enemy of force. Two regiments went out to west of the town and two to east, towards Orange, ours went straight through and halting at the outskirts threw pickets out. The colonel was fired [upon] once. We established headquarters and proceeded to make ourselves acquainted. Only our brigade was over the river the next day another being thrown over to support us if necessary.

Opposite our quarters lived an old man with (among others) one interesting daughter and we soon proceeded to make advances. Our efforts were successful so that by noon of Monday, our whole staff were on terms of intimacy. The lady had an old piano of the most antique style I ever saw and with no pretensions to time, howbeit Dr. Sullivan played quadrilles on it and Miss Maria sang and played the "Bonnie Blue Flag," "When This Cruel War Is Over" and to our great delectation, Miss Maria and her whole family were extremely secesh but on parting with them they all expressed themselves disappointed.

Our tent was pitched in the yard of a woman who's husband is away in the army. The town itself is a beautiful place with two or three nice churches, a courthouse, mostly on one street, and with a rolling countryside all around.

Monday morning about 2 A.M. General Custer with about 1,500 cavalry and two guns passed through our lines on the road and about one in the P.M. we could hear his artillery. From a high hill on the picket line one can see for twenty or thirty miles and almost directly to the south there was heavy smoke rising all the afternoon. At dusk I was sent out about a fourth of a mile to bring in the pickets, which I accomplished with my usual ability, as you might suspect. Drops of rain were then commencing to fall and all night it came down steadily. Tuesday morning found a part of the cavalry force under Stedman at our ports. They knew nothing of Custer, but about 10 we heard him closer by than we did the day before and the returned cavalry were sent out to help him. About the middle of the afternoon, they all came in presenting a sorry appearance in the rain which was continuous all day. Horses hollow and covered with mud, men wet and muddy too, [coloreds] hurrying along by their side, towards the north, of all ages and sexes, some with horses and some without. We were there under orders and as soon as it came dark, the pickets were brought in and formed as our rear guard, our regiment being in the rear of everything. Notwithstanding the mud and rain, it rather snow for it had turned to that. The men did not grumble much and the river was safely recrossed and we camped for the balance of the night on this side.

March 11

My Dear Sister Sue,

We are in expectations now of the usual preparation for the spring campaign and everyone is wondering how soon it will commence and what will be its character. General Grant is said to have arrived yesterday for the purpose of consulting Meade as is supposed and reviewing and superintending the much talked of reorganization of the army. It is said our corps and the 1st are to be merged but we know nothing about it as yet. The ladies have all been ordered out of the army as soon as practicable. This is a preliminary. Yesterday and today have been very rainy, this afternoon furnishing a violent thunder storm, the mutterings of which a good way off are still occasionally heard. This will necessarily delay any movement were any intended and indeed it is hardly considered possible to move the whole army much before the middle of next month.

Ann writes me that Fanny has been sold and that the Dr. has the colt to break. If I had been home I would perhaps have objected to the sale. As to the colt, I make great calculations on the beach and reckon on her being just right by the time I get out of this if I should be so fortunate. In being promoted to adjutant it becomes my duty to provide myself with a horse and expect to pay about $150, at least for that commodity. As for saddle and bridle, I trust to being able to pick them up. A McClellan saddle is worth about $30, but by giving a bonus of one sixth that amount to some teamster one can provide himself one.

As for clothes, I am pretty well provided, perhaps too expensively for a campaign. I bought a rubber coat yesterday and have sent for a pair of blue corduroy pants which will quite set me up and might to last me till fall. One little thing I must ask some of you to send me is a tobacco pouch. You need not be shocked. It is an essential with me. If you haven't time to make it, tell Sill. It should be 6 or 7 inches long and four or five wide. I have been waiting for some of young lady friends to make me a present of one but they seem to have forgotten it and content themselves with mittens of which I have now three pair on hand. Summer being at hand, their importance diminishes while that of the other raises proportionately.

I hope the Dr. will succeed in renting some of his mine lands. It will relieve you of so much trouble and may be no end good to you. Many thanks for the *Observor*s which I receive regularly.

March 18

[Once again, Halsey met someone who knew his brother and asked for information, of which there was little.]

There was a general jollification in the regiments and in the evening there was a minstrel concert in the quartermaster's tent. A recruit named Ayres, the principal performer, [and] Hedges of the 2d N.J.

Had a call from Mr. Tierney of Virginia who lived about two miles from camp who knew Joseph. He was grateful for three canteens of whiskey but wanted to buy a barrel!

March 19

Getting over the party and reading *Eleanor Victory*.

Colonel Penrose left for five days leave. The quartermaster [who does not like Penrose] celebrated the absence of the colonel with a little fandango.

March 21

I sent Sam the watch he had given me and which I had lost at Gettysburg and which was returned to me by Elkins. I also sent him my red cross badge [regiment insignia].

March 24

I visited Mr. Churning, Joseph's friend, in the afternoon. He has a son in Joseph's regiment and saw Joseph the day after the battle of Rappahannock.

🖋 [LESSLAND PLANTATION: Millie welcomed her friend Elizabeth "Miss Lizzie" Holmread back home again. The social gadfly and adventurer, who had long ago decided the war was not going to curtail her shopping, had visited stores in Washington, D.C., and, to get there, had sneaked through two separate sets of Union lines. She returned by boat and sneaked past both sets of Union lines again plus federal gunboats blockading the Potomac River.]

March 26

[Court-martial]

Prisoner: Pvt. Peter Clancy, 4th Regiment
Charge: Conduct prejudicial to good order and military discipline
Plea: Guilty
Finding: Guilty
Sentence: To forfeit his detail and be returned to duty in his regiment.

🖋 [Clancy was accused of stealing candy from General Torbert's personal candy stash in his tent. The general, outraged that the candy thief received nothing more than a slap on the wrist, disbanded the entire court-martial board two days later, leaving Judge Advocate Halsey in place and surrounding him with an entirely new board. Halsey considered it a tremendous compliment that General Torbert did not dismiss him, too.]

March 27

   Col. Penrose arrived from New Jersey bringing my commission as adjutant.

March 29

🖎 [Court-martial. It was a light week for the newly convened, post-candy-theft court-martial board. Pvt. John Hazard, of the First New Jersey, was found guilty of desertion and forfeited pay and had to serve time to make up for the time he was AWOL. Sgt. Michael Hogan of the Third New Jersey was busted down to private after pleading guilty to desertion. Pvt. Christian Schniber of the Second New Jersey was acquitted of misconduct charges.]

April 3

My Dear Cousin (Eliza),

   You will be pleased no doubt to learn that I have received my commission and have been mustered as Adjutant. There was one thing about this I did not like so well. All new musters now are made for three years and they are very particular about being mustered back before the time a man has the commission in his hands. Ergo, I had to conform to the rules and my time of service is now four years and a half instead of three. I go out March 28, 1867, unless sooner or shot. A long time, isn't it? I believe I have a season ticket now for sure. What do you think of it? Won't I be OLD enough to commence the study of law by that time? I had to do it in order to have a man mustered in my place and to get my pay as Adjutant.

   I have just been in to have a talk with Alanson. He says Nettie is to take a part in the great Sanitation Fair in New York and be one of the salesmen. You will probably attend with Mary and Sill writes me that she intends to be there. I would like to be there myself but circumstances render it impossible. Sometimes I think I would give nearly all I am worth (not much to be sure to anyone but myself) to see you all for an hour or so. When Miss Wardell was here she stayed with Mrs. Penrose one night and in the morning as she came out to get into an ambulance I stood close by and was in hopes she would recognize me but as she did not seem (which is not very strange inasmuch as we only met once) I thought I had better not thrust myself on her notice. I spoke to Mr. Cobb on the review but don't think he recognized me, either. We have been in daily anticipation of a grand review by General Grant for the past week or so but as yet the weather has been too strong and rainy for it. We are not very anxious for we know that after a review comes a movement and are in no hurry to give up our present pleasant quarters. This is destined to be the theater of operations in the next campaign and the fighting we all expect to be bloody and desperate. I hope we will be successful and that this army will be allowed to enter Richmond in triumph. It is their right, I think.

But I must close. There are half a dozen letters I must answer but I will do no more this night. Write to me soon and give my love to all.

Attended church in the morning. In the afternoon, called at The Globe, on a Mrs. Wagner, who was cousin to Mary Glassel (Joseph's first wife) and had a pleasant call. [Halsey knew many of Joseph's relatives and friends from previous visits and letters, so it was easy for him to seek out people for information.]

April 5
🖋 [Court-martial. The ever-vigilant Halsey championed the case of Cpl. Amos Parsons, Fourth New Jersey, and convinced the board to acquit him of desertion charges.]

April 6
🖋 [LESSLAND PLANTATION: Millie Halsey was startled to see her father, Col. Jeremiah Morton, ride up to the front porch of Lessland with six of the most important generals in the Confederate Army, all eager for dinner. She rearranged all the chairs in the dining room so as to seat Colonel Morton and Generals Jubal Early, Richard Ewell, Joe Johnston, William "Grumble" Jones, Junius Daniel, and John Pegram. She apologized profusely that she had to make dinner from the scraps that were left in her kitchen and only had a short supply of corn to offer them. She cooked most of the dinner herself, most of the women slaves having fled when the Union Army invaded the area.

Whatever key postdinner military conference the generals had planned was destroyed by the arrival of Millie's friend, the buoyant Elizabeth "Miss Lizzie" Holmread, a bright-eyed social gadfly and notorious

Orange County busybody who was determined not to let anything as silly as a civil war interrupt her pursuit of eligible young men in Virginia or her travels. She intercepted General Early coming out of the dining room as she arrived and talked him into giving her an extremely detailed briefing on the placement of all Yankee military camps so that she could plan the safest route to visit someone in Winchester whom she suspected was going to throw a party.]

April 9

[Court-martial. Pvt. Jesse Kenny was found guilty of being AWOL and was ordered to forfeit pay for the time he was gone and make good the time (eleven months).

LESSLAND PLANTATION: Joseph Halsey wrote Millie that he would try to sneak away from camp to see her again as soon as possible. He was stationed at Ashland and might be able to ride to Lessland soon. Halsey, who loved his wife very much, missed her desperately when he was away. Whenever his regiment was stationed within ten or twelve miles of home, he would ride to the plantation to spend the night with Millie and then get up at dawn and ride back to camp.

Joe's letter, like most of his letters, mixed news of the army with concern for Millie and the plantation. They also showed him to be a devoted father who did everything he could to keep his attractive teenaged daughters away from the war's shadow and the soldiers of both armies. A bit of a gossip and aristocratic snob, Joe always had some tidbits or criticisms to add about the way people looked, dressed, or carried themselves and worried constantly about his appearance and his horse.]

My Dear Wife,
   . . . I have a dry little office [at Ashland] with good stove and my horse is stabled close by so that I am personally more comfortably fixed than on the wet ground in camp. I draw supplies from Richmond. I went down on Thursday last and being detained, spent the night at Mrs. Pierce's [his teenaged daughters were staying in Richmond at the Pierces', family friends, for protection during Grant's campaign in northern Virginia] and returned to Ashland to breakfast the next morning. The children are well. I slept on a lounge in the parlor. There was no fire there during the afternoon and night. John Willis' daughter Jane was occupying your mother's room. As I left, Fannie said to write you to send her some buttons. I shall

probably go to Richmond twice a week as long as we stay here, going down in the morning and returning by the 3:30 P.M. train in the afternoon. I cannot thus see the children often as they will be at school and their boarding house is too much like charity for me to patronize much.

I have not been able to get any clothes yet.

It has rained here all day, now pouring down, wind from the East, and the slashing rain floods the camp. This is the poorest country this side . . . the worst spot in the poison field, and yet Ashland struts some fine cottage buildings filled with handsomely dressed people. A great many from Fredericksburg are here. Dr. Edward Barber, son of J. B. Barber, of Fredericksburg, called to see me yesterday. He looks ten years older than I do.

. . . I would not have you remain at Lessland if you feel personally unsafe, or afraid to remain, still I would hold on till the last moment and if what little we have there be lost, it is time enough to grieve over it when the loss occurs. But to scatter things, giving the house a half abandoned look, will, I think, invite rather than repel destruction. If you go to Appomattox you could live there without buying supplies until next fall, certainly, but where they are to come from I do not know.

I shall be very busy for some days having my accounts for February and March to make up and now a double set to keep. Write me as often as you can.

I am glad Miss Lizzie got through safe [on one of her trips to Washington in which she sneaked through Union lines]. If she does not get through the blockade she may be of service to you amongst the Yankees, if General Lee has joined the "retreaters" so as to leave you in the lines. My own belief is Grant's army is greatly exaggerated and his "name" seems to be acting with some as Hooker. Nor is Grant the best strategist in the world. Why does he break up two corps of his army and put them in to fill up other [corps] if he has been heavily re-inforced? This is all staff [not soldiers]. He cannot feed a large army by that one railroad line and these rains will delay his teams of horses.

I will send you some new issue (cotton) as soon as it can be had.

Give my love to all and tell the boys to help take care of everything. Hope your father will succeed in getting any damages question settled. Fannie and Nannie say they need their shoes. Send them up and see [that] they are made [at a Richmond shop]. Do not plant potatos until the old moon.

[As always, Joe worried about Millie's comfort in the bad weather and, as always, added a dig at President Jefferson Davis.]

PS: I hope you can get more fire [from the four fireplaces in the house] for this chilly weather. If you wish real Richmond elegance, put out the fire, sit by the door, shiver and look anxiously hopeful that you may not keep fast more often than Jeff Davis requests.

April 13
🖋 [LESSLAND PLANTATION: Millie Halsey heard another rumor that Yankee troops would attack plantations on the Rapidan River and packed her bags, again. She waited and then unpacked. She had followed this routine for several weeks, but each time remained at Lessland. She could not bring herself to leave, no matter how close the Yankees seemed and no matter how many rumors she heard about the whereabouts of the Army of the Potomac. She wrote Joseph.]

Dear Husband,
[People] predict this great battle of the coming campaign is to come off around us. I feel like dispensing with advice which is to move my things southward. Mother says she expects we will all be in Appomattox by the summer. Yesterday, she advised me to move my best things back to the neighborhood [the town of Culpeper]. I have packed and unpacked so often from the fear of danger that I feel utterly demoralized.

🖋 [A distraught Joe Halsey wrote back immediately and told his wife to leave Lessland if she wanted, but to stay if at all possible. In their letters, all of which ended in loving regard for each other, Joseph and Millie often discussed the abandonment of Lessland. Neither wanted to give it up to the Yankees. Lessland, and Morton Hall, had been Millie's home all of her life. Lessland was the symbol of her love for Joe and her family. She was determined to stay there as long as she could. The husband and wife finally agreed, after long talks at home and in letters, that Millie would keep her things packed, horse and wagon ready, and children prepared. If the Union Army actually attacked Lessland, or seemed prepared to occupy it, she would flee on a designated safe route, taking her mother with her.]

April 14
🖋 [Court-martial. The court passed a flimsy desertion charge against William Campion, First New Jersey, up through the ranks with the recommendation that charges be dropped.]

April 18

Our Corps was reviewed by General Grant. It looks larger than ever. The old troops are consolidated with the 1st and 2d divisions and a new, 3rd, division is added of troops mostly new in the field. It numbers at least 25,000 men.

Grant looks just like his pictures—very plain and unperturbing.

Fresh troops are arriving daily.

[LESSLAND PLANTATION: Miss Lizzie Holmread continued to amuse Millie Halsey and her mother, as she did throughout the war. By mid-April, Confederate camps were being set up throughout the area, and Miss Lizzie, who seemed to have a new boyfriend every month, had fallen deeply in love with one of the men who manned an artillery battery for the Confederate army, or, as Miss Lizzie described it, "fired cannons." It turned out, though, that he was also an accomplished singer and accompanied Millie and her mother and Miss Lizzie to Morton Hall, where, after a jovial dinner, he sang a medley of songs as Millie Halsey played the piano with great enthusiasm. ("I made that piano talk!" she bragged to her husband in one of her few upbeat letters of the war.]

April 27

[LESSLAND PLANTATION: The Confederate Army, constantly foraging for food and supplies through Culpeper and Orange Counties all spring, decided to set up permanent headquarters on the grounds of Lessland, to the consternation of Millie Halsey. Lessland Plantation was an ideal campsite for the Confederate Army because it was within view of the Rapidan River and just ten miles from Culpeper, the county seat and a town at the convergence of several main roads.

Hundreds of troops from the Texas Brigade, under Gen. J. P. Robertson, set up their tents on the northeast corner of Lessland, within one hundred yards of the manor house. They commandeered the entire plantation for military use. A barn was turned into a jail and bars installed in its windows and special locks on its doors to hold any Union soldiers who were captured (it is uncertain if any prisoners were detained there). General Robertson used the other outbuildings for storage. Military wagons and carriages lined the roads in and out of Lessland, and a wagon park greeted Millie's eyes when she woke up every morning. Neither she nor the boys got much sleep as bugles constantly sounded throughout the camp for weeks. The couriers constantly arriving on horseback and the streams of supply wagons pouring in and out of Lessland kicked up dirt and dust that at times seemed to cover everybody like an extra set of clothes. Hundreds of rifles were stacked up all over the property. The night was littered with hundreds of troop campfires.

The general told Millie his men needed Lessland's corn to eat and agreed to pay her $262 for hundreds of bushels of corn. The army used up all of the corn the family planned to sell for profit plus all the corn the Halseys wanted to keep to feed themselves. (Robertson paid in what turned out to be useless Confederate money.) Pieces of artillery were set up in her front and back yards. Dozens of pickets were ordered out to the far corners of Lessland to watch for Federals. Millie felt patriotic about letting the rebel army camp on her grounds, but she also felt annoyed that her family's life was turned upside down. Robertson told Millie he had no idea how long the Texas Brigade would be stationed there, but the federal invasion of Virginia led Millie to believe they might be there all summer. Instead of being just another plantation in Virginia, merely a bystander to the war, Lessland had suddenly become part of Robert E. Lee's army.]

April 29

[Court-martial. Pvt. Hugh Lippencott, Tenth New Jersey, was acquitted on desertion charges.

Severe apprehension began to settle among the soldiers of the Army of the Potomac in the dying days of April. The review in front of Grant was an ominous omen of a major campaign deep into the heart of Virginia. Men speculated that 1864 would be the last year of the war, the year that the Union Army would take Richmond. The Confederates knew this, the men agreed, and would dig in for one final, brutal campaign. Rumors spread of a dreadful battle ahead somewhere on the way to Richmond. Special religious services were held, and Halsey, searching inside himself even deeper than usual for his faith, decided to formally pledge allegiance to Christianity. He was joined by others as many men in the Fifteenth and in the Army of the Potomac feared their doom in the rumored campaign in Virginia. Halsey not only reaffirmed his faith in God, but filled his letters with depression and homesickness. He scampered about camp to find pictures of himself to send home. He wanted everything to be just right in case he died.

LESSLAND PLANTATION: Millie Halsey rarely complained about her difficult circumstances at Lessland as she continued to run the plantation with little slave help, raise three children, balance the family's books, care for her mother at Morton Hall, and live with armies camped in her front yard. In the spring, though, she complained bitterly to her husband that the neighbors never gave her credit for anything because the Mortons had money. "I have a rough road to travel sometimes—in many pilgrimages—having the reputation of my family of having nothing but a flowery bed of roses to journey on!"]

April 30

🖋 [Edmund Halsey wrote to Mary. She'd asked when he thought the army might move into spring operations, and he started by telling her, in an ominous phrase, that "the time is short." He took great pains to make light of his own fears.]

Dear Mary,

. . . As to pictures, I had but two and thought that sending them home as a central place the illumination of their beauty might "radiate" so to speak. This made trouble for Sue wanted one. So did Sam. With difficulty, I raised one from the quartermaster, who had one to spare. This I sent Sue, leaving Sam in the lurch. The article has now departed and it is impossible to get any more. I had one for you but courtesy compelled me to present Mrs. Penrose with one. As to the reenlistment, it is a necessary consequence on promotion and I am very sorry to say they consider that sufficient compensation without furlough or bounty. I would like to have gone with you to the Fair. Sills' letter after her visit was very interesting and Alanson hears from Neddie, who has one of the tables there, how grand a time they are having. Some officers from our regiment on leave of absence dropped in there and were introduced to Neddie. Their attention was called by a little wooden cross which I had given Alanson and he had send to Neddie. This had been found on blue velvet ground and inscribed "This cross was cut by an officer of the 15th N.J. Volunteers from the tree which George Washington cut his hatchet." This called forth exclamation "Why I'm from the 15th" and someone said "This is Miss Haines, your chaplain's sister," whence the introduction. Everyone says the Jersey Department was the best in the show and the tables more beautifully served (this is a nice place for a compliment, but I repair knowing how little you like them).

Our Corps were received Monday by General Grant, a plain, unassuming looking man—just like his pictures. The corps looked splendid, supplied with white gloves, well dressed, and marched well and larger than ever since the division of the 3rd has been placed in it. Everybody anticipates lively times this spring, more so than ever before.

I am sorry you think me so "homesick" from my letters. I assure you I am not at all that way, except (very naturally) I see nothing in this life which makes me prefer it to home. I am simply more serious where I settle down to write and there you both know what a "plain, blunt man" I am and how matter of fact. While I am writing tonight there is a quartet in the same room playing dominos and a whole band in the tent adjoining making night melodies with song and guitar accompaniment, no unusual thing in this ranch. So you see we are not without our amusements. Why a night or two since we played twenty three games of whist at a sitting!

The 10th N.J.'s Col. Ryerson arrived last night from Pennsylvania where they have been "enforcing the draft." They have never been in the field and are much commented on by the old vets. It will be sometime before they hear the last of "coal" in its many shapes and are styled the heroes of Pottsville. The regiment [10th] was very large indeed but since they have been ordered to the front they have lost heavily by desertion. Still, there is more of them than two of our regiments.

But I must close, hoping to hear from you soon again and to see you face to face some day this side of March 28, 1867. Give my love to all the family and believe me.

11

THE WILDERNESS
CAMPAIGN

May 1–May 7, 1864

[Ulysses S. Grant was named commander of the Union Army to win. He knew that to win he had to defeat the Army of Northern Virginia and eventually take Richmond. In early May he decided to cross the Rappahannock and move southeast to Richmond. He did not know where the Army of Northern Virginia was, but he was certain they would meet somewhere between the river and Richmond. He decided to move through the Wilderness around Chancellorsville and then through the Virginia countryside toward Richmond. The Wilderness, thick, treacherous terrain that had thwarted Hooker and his men in the Chancellorsville campaign, stretched for twelve miles. Grant told his generals that somewhere on the other side of it they would probably meet Lee. They did not anticipate meeting Lee, or anyone, in the thick forests.

The army marched through the Wilderness with great trepidation. The veterans, who had fought against the Army of Northern Virginia so many times, remembered that Lee liked to attack them where least expected. They remembered, too, that when it was dry, the Wilderness was a firetrap in a battle, and they remembered the desperate fires that had burned so many men to death at Chancellorsville. As they marched through the Wilderness with Grant, they remembered, too, that it had not rained in a long time and that the Wilderness was dry . . . very dry.]

May 1, 1864. Sunday.

I made a public profession of faith and took the sacrament. The chapel was full. Nearly the whole regiment being present. About 20 were admitted to the church at the same time.

Col. Penrose and Emerson both had a talk with me in the afternoon and seemed in serious mood. Sgt. Wyckoff and his friends returned from a "jubilee" they had brought from home [shared liquor].

May 2

🖎 [General Torbert, promoted to a cavalry command, accepted flags from New Jersey and bade farewell to the New Jersey Brigade. Halsey wrote down his emotional remarks practically verbatim and sent them to the *Jerseyman* for publication. Torbert's speech was a chilling reminder of the awful rumors of an upcoming Armageddon that drifted through the Army of the Potomac like a fatal whisper.]

"In every home circle they [families] are offering their devotions for your safety and comfort. Throughout the length and breadth of our land are seen the evidence of their goodness and care. Go to the hospital, there they are. Go to the Sanitary Fair—and there they are. Go to the Sewing Society, and nimble fingers are busy for your welfare and care. . . .

"Your valor and bravery is beyond question. Of that I need no proof. But don't forget the sacred trust you take upon yourselves in accepting this bright and beautiful flag. Remember that only the brave deserve the fair and he who proves recreant to this flag would receive no favor at the hands of the noble women of your native state.

"You are about to enter upon a campaign of no ordinary magnitude. The great question of civil and religious liberty is to be settled. Remember the motto of the brave and lamented Kearny, 'Nulla vestigia reiroranm,' and keep well in view, always, that your Brigade was never known to falter. March on to honor and victory, letting your watchword be God, your country, and the ladies. Whatever my place in life may be, I shall always revert with pride and pleasure to my connection with the 1st New Jersey Brigade. Accept this flag. It may be the last gift you'll ever receive from me. The destiny of men, and nation, is in the hands of One 'who doeth all things well' and whatever may happen, let us not fail to be encouraged to do our entire duty to each a flag as this. If our national emblem goes down, we go down with it and of our once glorious country nothing will be left but its mouldering ruins to tell the sad tale of its former glory. But this can never be, our eagles and the red cross must ever lead us on to victory.

"The thistle of Scotland may die, the shamrock of Ireland be broken and trodden down, the black eagle of Prussia close his eye and droop his pinion, the Lion of old England paw the earth no more, the Lillies of France be crushed and buried neath the mire of an absolute despotism, but the star of American liberty, ever bright, ever beautiful, shall shine on."

🖋 [Court-martial. The board was harsh, sentencing Tom Colligan to five years in prison for desertion and William Lloyd to seven years for participating in a small mutiny.]

Gen. Charles Griffin's first division, the federal column farthest along the Orange Turnpike, met the enemy shortly after dawn on May 5. They encountered heavy fire coming out of a thicket from Gen. A. P. Hill's division. Grant, when first told, did not worry about it. He assumed it was a small Confederate force and of no consequence and ordered Griffin to attack. Griffin's men moved off the road and into the thick forest that surrounded them like a beautiful but thorny blanket. The men who had been there a year ago, at Chancellorsville, worried. They remembered how tangled the forests were and how easy it was for an entire Confederate army, such as Jackson's in 1863, to move out of that woods like an avenging angel. The new men found they could barely move. No one could see more than a few yards in front of them. The line moved forward tentatively, inches by inches. The Confederates, hiding in the trees, and many lying on the ground, well protected, kept up a heavy volume of fire, and the Federals, unable to see anyone, simply fired toward any loud concentration of musket fire their ears picked up. An hour later, unable to gain any ground, Griffin reported to Grant that the enemy force was much larger than he'd assumed.

The enemy was, in fact, the entire Army of Northern Virginia. Lee had moved in on Grant, determined to surprise him in difficult terrain and defeat him. He had his entire army on a long line in the forests and was ready to move in. Grant, fearing the worst, tried to move his forces up. Hancock's Corps was still several miles away, and Burnside's men were strung even farther out. Both were ordered up as quickly as possible.

The entire federal army soon found itself dug in at different spots throughout the Wilderness, unable to make any movement because the enemy was invisible, hiding among the bushes, prickers, groves of trees, and tangled vines of the forests. Men fired at noises. Eerie moments were frequent. Troops could not see as far as the regiment next to them in line, and many regiments, trying to move, found themselves totally unsupported and caught in crossfires by the enemy. One regiment tried to mount a charge and found itself right next to a Confederate brigade and had to surrender. The Federals, who outnumbered the rebels under Hill by 38,000 to 14,000, made no headway. It was an invisible battle against an invisible enemy on killing fields.

By noon, so many volleys had been fired by both sides that smoke hung like low fog over the forest, making vision even more difficult. Thousands of minié balls crashed into stands of trees and brush and started fires, the same kinds of menacing fires that had rippled through the area during the battle of Chancellorsville a year before, fires that raced along the ground, fed by dry leaves and beds of millions of dry pine needles, and men who were there before became petrified.

Some small fires moved slowly through bushes that lined the roads and fields and burned up some patches of grass, and then large fires, started in the middle of the heavy jungle set groves of trees on fire and moved inexorably toward the troops. The fires began to make movement impossible. Wounded men became trapped in front of fires and were burned to death as they struggled to haul themselves to safety. Dozens of soldiers, pinned down by rebel fire and unable to move, watched in horror as their comrades, lying wounded in an open area of the forest, were killed when the fires caused their own cartridge belts to explode into their stomachs. Others, unable to move, watched as comrades suffering no more than leg wounds, but immobile, burned to death just yards in front of them, screaming.

That day and night on the killing fields, over two hundred soldiers on both sides burned to death in the forest fires that swept through the Wilderness for miles. Later, many said it was the worst night of the war. The wounded men being consumed by the fires howled for help, but no one could get to them through enemy bullets and the forest fires. Men begged for food or water, which never came. Many called out the name of their beloved back home and then became silent. Moans from dying men on both sides could be heard for miles in the still night. The smell of the night was different on this night than on any other during the war, too, as the odor of smoke and fire mixed with the odor of the dead bodies.

The Fifteenth New Jersey moved into the battle that morning with other regiments from the New Jersey Brigade, directly next to the Tenth

New Jersey, and stumbled and bumbled through the woods like everyone else. Finally, it was ordered to work as a covering force. The regiment was stationed on a small hill between two fierce segments of the battle and came under sporadic fire all day, but did not attack again. Halsey moved between the Fifteenth and Tenth on instructions to keep the lines even in the morning attack.]

May 5

Broke camp a little after daylight and moved and soon had evidence of the enemy in close proximity. Our pickets being in as it became evident that a fight was at hand.

Colonel Penrose directed me to count the muskets in line. I did so, with the help of the Sergeant Major who counted the left wing and made 429 men in line.

We even moved about in the woods in a confusing manner until afternoon when we were found the 10th N.J. on the right and 12th on the left of front line. Old regiments in two lines. The advance was ordered about the middle of the afternoon.

Our orders were to "guide left." Advancing, we found ourselves crowded and that the orders on our left were to "guide right." Col P. sent me to Col. Brown to tell him this during a temporary halt but Brown, who was sitting on a log with his staff about him, only said he would be up presently. Cooke and Paul were annoyed but said nothing.

Again we advanced and found ourselves alone with the 10th. I rode back and forth between Penrose and Ryerson to keep the two in line. At another halt each of these colonels [signed] the other to be in command of both.

The firing now grew heavier and bullets whistled about us but another line seemed ahead of us. Directly, we came into an open field on a hill. Here General Sedgwick and Captain Cooke each gave us orders. The latter trying evidently to get the Brigade together again, but Sedgwick ordered our regiment forward into a gap and we went in, seeing no one of the 10th or the rest of the Brigade.

Where we went was to the right of a Brigade where two companies of the 95th Pennsylvania had been holding the ground. The leaves were on fire and scattered over the ground were the dead and wounded of the rebs and our 5th Corps men (the 5th corps was on our left when we first started).

The position we then took we held unchanged until the night of the 6th. The rebel line crossed the turnpike. In front of our left was a clear field on the other side of which were the rebels. Our right was in brush which prevented anything from being seen. The 7th was in our sight.

The enemy fired shell and cannister into the woods but we were lying down and lost in the day but a few men. Capt. Vanderveer was wounded [with] five or six men.

At nightfall when things had apparently quieted down, an awfully exciting scene was enacted. Beginning off on the left came a roar of musketry growing nearer and nearer, both armies evidently firing, caused as we supposed by an advance of the enemy. Every officer of our command shouted 'don't fire' and stuck up the muskets of such of the men as offered us to do it. This stopped the firing along the line. Shortly after the same thing came from the right, coming up to within regiment or so of us. There was no advance but each army in close quarters believed the antagonist moving to attack.

This over, we settled for the night. Capt. Hamilton took a few men a half dozen yards to the front and found a picket line. The enemy were so near that their muskets Col. P. thought were our men and twice sent me to Hamilton to tell him to make his men stop firing and I brought back (I had only ten paces to go) that it was the enemy [and not Hamilton]. In this way we passed the few hours of darkness. I slept a few minutes, waking between two half rotted bodies, one reb and the other a 5th Corps [man]. The dead lying thick about us and some wounded out in a field to our left between the lines crying out for water and to be carried off. This night was perfectly hideous.

🪶 [On May 6, Grant ordered his men to attack at dawn. Every division except Burnside's was just about in place, but the attack foundered. The rebels, concentrated in well-fortified woods and in command of several roads, offered too much resistance. Federals and rebels, trying to move huge forces of men through thick forests, both tumbled out onto roadways throughout the jungle and met in cluttered groups of battle. Roads were hopelessly bottled up and forces stalled. Fires continued to start and burn through the area. Grant's battle plan, a good one, misfired from time to time as men were not ready to attack. An early-morning attack by Hancock amounted to little because Burnside's men, supposed to be in place at 9 A.M., didn't arrive until after 2 P.M. There were victories for the Union in parts of the Wilderness, though. In the afternoon, Hancock's men beat back rebels in several areas and at Tapp's farm almost won the battle, and the war, when they found themselves not only within striking distance of a vulnerable rebel force, but of Robert E. Lee himself.

Hancock's men fought against the division, with Lee in plain view riding back and forth to rally his men, for more than thirty minutes and seemed on the verge of victory. Lee then ordered artillery up to pummel the Federals and drive them back and the opportunity was lost. Both armies struggled throughout the day with heavy losses. Finally, at 4 P.M., Lee ordered a general attack against the northern wing of the federal army. The attack drove Sedgwick's men, and the Fifteenth New Jersey, into a temporary retreat late in the afternoon, which was halted late in the night. The outcome of the battle, despite heavy losses (Union casualties were seventeen thousand, or 17 percent, and Confederate casualties were seven thousand), was a victory for the Confederates as the Federals were forced back, unable to dislodge a much smaller force.

Once again, Halsey's diary shows how much more responsibility Colonel Penrose was giving him in battle.]

May 6

As new pickets came in Hamilton was hit in the arm (and both thighs), from which wounds he afterwards died. The musketry and shelling were almost incessant on either side of us all day. The open field in our front prevented the rebs from attacking us. Their officers could not get them into the open. In the afternoon, things grew more quiet and tools were brought up with which we then threw up a rifle pit. Col. Penrose also had his and my horses brought up.

At nightfall, we again heard the roar of musketry in our right. This time an advance in earnest by the rebs. We could hear the yells and firing passing around to our right and directly balls were coming in from the front and behind. Col. Upton took his second line and moved off towards the right and Col. Penrose was left in command of the front line. General Wright came along and I sang out to him: "We're all right here, General."

Darkness by this time had come in. Colonel P and myself rode off to the right a little way but found the woods filled with our men, some with prisoners and all in confusion.

Late at night, the regiment was around and moved quietly to the left out in to the road and down the road for a mile or so. Men stopped and trailed away and held their canteens with one hand to protect their rattling. The enemy were within easy call.

Moving down the road a mile or so, we turned to the left, crossed a clear field and then to right, going into position parallel to the turnpike and facing north. It was about daylight when the position was taken.

Rivers, Col. P's darky, saved the mule and an axe in the route of the rear, but my new haversack, rubber overcoat and Col P's new uniform all fell into rebel hands. We made a change under Colonel Upton and did not hear of losses or doings of other regiments til the next day.

🖎 [Halsey's dry prose does not adequately describe the scene in early evening, when the right flank, and the Fifteenth, seemed to be routed by a rebel attack under Gen. John Gordon. Men who ran made it through the swarming lines of soldiers to Grant and told him the line was broken and all was lost. They were panicky. After scolding them for their lack of belief in the army, Grant sent reinforcements but they found that Sedgwick had rallied his men by taking veteran regiments and regiments who had not seen much action that day, including the Fifteenth, to stop Gordon's attack. Sedgwick had done such a brilliant job that Vermont regiments who arrived as reinforcements raised their hats to him and cheered as they arrived. The move, and the stand of the Jersey regiments, saved the army.

LESSLAND PLANTATION: As usual, Millie Halsey and her neighbors were misled by Confederate wire services, which sent news flashes over telegraph wires that the South had soundly defeated the North in the Wilderness, taking more than twelve thousand prisoners.]

May 7

Hot. At daylight we began to dig a rifle pit along the road and sent pickets to the front. I went out to the line and found they connected with nothing on the left, passed along that way and soon came to a line of pickets facing ours! I found the officer of the day and reported [it].

I made my way back to the regiment from the left. An attack was made and handsomely repulsed to the left of us early but the rebs felt our picket line all day. We lost five men on the skirmish line during the day. In the afternoon . . . there was firing all about us and once in the afternoon we were in the rifle pit expecting an immediate attack but were only engaged by our skirmishers.

After dark, we moved along the road to the right to near the "mine" and near the turnpike where we halted for an hour or two. We moved from here with the rest of the N.J. Brigade with whom we had again fallen in. About midnight, we moved on to the pike towards Chancellorsville. About 2000 prisoners at the time marched along the side of us. On the road to the south of us could be heard the rumble of wheels.

[The men realized as they marched along the Brock Road that they were not moving north, in retreat, as they had in each previous invasion of Virginia, but south—toward Richmond. They would not be going back to Falmouth or anywhere else again. In the middle of the night, as the men moved slowly south on roads clogged by weary men, wagons, and ambulances carrying the wounded, the flow of blue-uniformed men was interrupted by a short, squat general, coat unbuttoned, head down, cigar stuck into the corner of his mouth, riding his horse at a deliberate trot through the ranks and headed south. "Grant! Grant! Grant!" shouted the first men who saw him, and soon there was a roar of approval from one hundred thousand men, strung out over several miles of darkened roadway, as U. S. Grant took them . . . south.]

12

THE WAR COMES TO LESSLAND PLANTATION

May 8–June 8, 1864

[LESSLAND PLANTATION: Millie Halsey's worst nightmare came true shortly before 9 A.M., May 7, when she looked out the window of the rear parlor of her home to see five Union soldiers peering into the windows of the icehouse behind the main home. The five then went to the granary, the corn house and the wagon house, looking through the windows of each and muttering something to each other. They marched to the stables and unhitched five horses there and shooed them away, laughing as the horses took off across the meadows toward Morton Hall.

Millie backed away and went to the other side of the house to see if there were any more Yankees and spotted two slowly approaching the front gate on horseback ("They looked like the dregs of the earth," she wrote in a note). She slowly walked out the front door, down the porch steps, and to the gate to meet them.

"What do you want?" she asked them politely.

The two men dismounted and moved forward, opening the gate, and approached her. Afraid, she backed off one step.

"We want some meat," one of the men said, closing the gate behind him.

Millie walked away from them and motioned them to follow. Carefully walking a wide path around the great house, where the children were, she led them to the meat house.

"It would be unchivalrous for men to walk into a lady's meat house," she said.

The men demanded that she open the door to the building and she did, her anger rising.

"You specialize in robbing women who can't forage for themselves?" she said. "To rob the weak is no mark of bravery."

The two soldiers ignored her and filled up a bag with meat and started to leave in silence, mounting their horses. Suddenly, Millie's nine-year-old son, Ogden, hiding in a woodpile when she thought he was safe in the house, emerged and shouted at the soldiers, "You shouldn't take something that is not yours!"

One of the soldiers looked angrily at the boy and then turned to Millie and told her they would like something to eat and would search the house to find something. She backed toward the door of the kitchen house at the rear of the big house and stopped in the doorway, hands on each side of it, trying to stop them with the movements of her body.

"We'd like something to eat," said one of the soldiers, and then both men raised their carbine rifles and, laying them on their horses' necks, aimed them at her.

"There's nothing here to eat," she said as sternly as she could, her body shaking a bit from fright, her voice rising to show false bravado, her young son Ogden standing just ten yards away.

"We'd like something to eat," the soldier repeated in a louder voice, pointing his rifle higher, directly at Millie.

Looking at her son, she turned to the soldier and compromised, fearful they would both be harmed if she refused to let the soldiers eat anything. "There's nothing ready right now, but if you'd like, I'll see if the servant can prepare something," she said.

The two men dismounted and, rifles in hand, walked into the kitchen, Ogden right behind them. Millie grabbed Ogden from behind and whispered to him to keep quiet and not say anything to anger the men. Dode, the servant, prepared bowls of soup for the two men, who sat down at the table.

Dode was looking out the window and spotted one of the Confederate pickets stationed at the perimeter of Lessland walking down the hill. She shouted that a picket was coming and the two Union soldiers stood up and looked out and saw him. They took a few quick gulps of the soup and ran to their horses and galloped away. Both Millie and Dode breathed a sigh of relief.

Millie Halsey wrote down her brush with death in a notebook and tore out the narrative and mailed it to Joe, with a letter, two days later.]

Dear Husband,

I have not had time to write you, but cut out a leaf of my note book to give you an idea of our movements. I want to see you dreadfully.

We [Millie, the children, and the few slaves left] planted corn all day yesterday. We were glad to hear that [the army] had made a successful raid. I don't know where your regiment is now.

I have not seen a newspaper for an age. There is no mail. The postmaster left and his replacement left. All mail is now through Orange County.

I am very anxious to see you.

SPOTSYLVANIA

✒ [Grant, pushed back in the Wilderness, was taking the army south toward Spotsylvania Courthouse and then to Richmond. Lee, sensing Grant's every move, tried to stretch his army in a semicircle around Grant and attack him on May 8 in what became the first day of the battle of Spotsylvania, which turned into the bloodiest bath of the bloody war for the men of the Fifteenth New Jersey.]

May 8

Hot. About 7 o'clock we passed through Chancellorsville. The rifle pits of the old battle field were all in shape. I noticed a skull lying in the road. We passed our ambulance in one of which was [the dying] Hamilton.

Turning abruptly to the right, we went near Todd's Tavern and came up with the 5th corps, who were engaged with the enemy a little after noon. At first, we moved to the right but not General Warren, who asked me in a very excited tone, "Whose Brigade is that?"

I told him "Colonel Brown's N.J. Brigade." He asked "Who will show me this Col Brown? Where is Colonel Brown?"

I brought Paul to him and said, "here is one of his staff."

We were then countermanded and moved up to a piece of wood, sloping eastward behind where General Sedgwick was afterwards killed. Here we lay down in the wood for a little while. The enemy shelling us significantly.

The 3rd regiment was deployed as skirmishers. The 15th was ordered to advance across the field and develop the enemy in the opposite wood. Col. P. sent me out to the skirmishers to order them to direct their advance at a certain point. Changing his mind, I went to tell them to guide in another point. By this time, the line was well across the field and the 15th in line of battle behind them.

As the line approached the road it was evident the 15th was too short and Col. Penrose sent me back to get another regiment. I rode up to Colonel Brown and gave my message and he asked what regiment he should send and Paul or Farley said the 1st (which seemed the only one nearby). I told Col. Hay to get up his regiment and Col. Brown [taking] my word and I telling him I would show him where to go. Col. Hay ordered the men up and forward. I rode along with Col. H. and had half crossed the field when we met the 15th coming back. Both regiments lay down until dark.

After the charge I rode back to the rear and found Dr. Sharp and saw a hospital with Alanson in attendance in a slight hollow the other side of the road. Our badly wounded, who crawled off the field, were taken there.

Generals Warren, Sedgwick and Meade were together in the woods in our rear and Col. Penrose reported to them. Col. Campbell's horse was wounded and his men tried [getting him out from under it] but he lay in the grass until darkness enabled him to get in. Other wounded did the same. A sergeant was killed after the charge when he sat up. Captain Van Blarcom was wounded and left with the enemy.

Alfred Jackson was killed.

The 10th New Jersey afterwards attacked to our left and a whole division I believe tried the same spot.

After dark, I got up the regiment and reformed it, then moved it back to the woods where we camped for the night.

Col. Penrose insisted on our spreading our blankets in a little hut outside of where General Sedgwick was killed on a knoll but at dawn the rebs put so many balls in our shelter that even he was ready to scamper back, dragging out blankets after us.

We lost about 100 men in this fight. The 15th had dashed like a "sling," as Col. Campbell expressed it, through the rebel lines, driving them from their pits but were soon enveloped by superior numbers and there was nothing for it but to get back.

✒ [One of the losses that hurt the most was Ellis Hamilton. The boy who joined the regiment at age sixteen was shot through both legs on May 6 and nearly bled to death. He was taken to a hospital at Fredericksburg and then removed to a better one in Washington, D.C., but he died on May 16.]

May 9

All the morning we lay in the woods from which we had started the charge of the day before. Another Brigade lay in the same place but we were not moved out. The ground sloped to the east and being covered with rebel sharpshooters and pickets had [us as] fair game. Rubadeau (our color sergeant) was shot dead and the same ball wounded another man in the leg.

About noon, General Sedgwick passed by us and inquiring why we were massed as we were, ordered our Brigade out. Colonel Penrose started . . . put me . . . at the head of the column to lead it, he remaining to start each regiment successively as the ones before filed out. I had reached the outer edge of the woods, perhaps a hundreds yards, when Colonel [reached me] and in a low voice said General S was hit and put his finger to his face, shaking his head to indicate there was no hope for him. He had ridden to the edge of the wood and was standing in the road on his horse, little back of where Colonel P and I slept (perhaps 20 feet) when he was almost immediately shot.

The regiment headquarters lay for a short time in a grove back of and a little north west of the former position. Here, Col P was directed to take command of the Brigade, irrespective of rank.

Colonel Campbell with the 15th and 1st was ordered to feel around the enemy's right and get to the Brock Road if possible. We moved out to the north through a swamp, coming out on a hill, cleared and having an old deserted log house on it. The regiment was here deployed and skirmished eastward down the hill and through the swamp driving the rebs, swinging a little to the right. Sgt. Budd of Co. F was badly wounded. I rode back by Colonel P's order about an hour or two afterwards to report to General Russel that our men commanded the Brock Road with their muskets (Gen. Russel's headquarters was where we first halted after moving out of the woods in the morning). We lay here all night. We built a fire in the old log house but had to put it out as the rebs fired at it. We were in the skirmish line all night, headquarters now being the old log house.

No supper and no breakfast.

[On May 9, 10, and 11 the Federals made several unsuccessful attacks on the Confederates, who had dug in before them in an elongated U-pattern of breastworks, with Ewell's corps holed up at the very tip, or "angle," of it.]

There has been heavy musketry for the last half hour on our right and orders have just come to be in readiness to move to support the V Corps which is now engaged. At dawn, we advanced and swinging round to the right at almost right angles with our former lines, met difficulties which halted us. . . . In the P.M. [we] made charges in connection with regiments of the Excelsior Brigade which were failures as the "white diamonds" ran both times (I forgot to say that on Tuesday afternoon, while we were with General Mott, the balance of our Brigade, Russel's and Upton's made an assault in which they took 900 prisoners but were finally compelled to fall back with heavy losses). At last the 1st was deployed as pickets and their ammunition being exhausted, ours next after dark and finally both came in to our old position and went to rest at 3 A.M. Wednesday morning, losing out of our regiment between 3 P.M. of the 9th and the night of the 10th twenty two men killed and wounded. In bringing in our regiment acting as guide, I got my face all cut up, the scars of which are still visible, riding through a pine woods in the dark and lost my hat. I considered myself lucky in escaping.

[On the Eleventh, responding to critics in Washington who complained of heavy losses, Grant sent off his most famous wire to Halleck, telling him that he proposed "to fight it out on this line if it takes all summer." The stern telegram thrilled Lincoln, who knew now that he had the right man at the head of his army. Whenever Grant was criticized for anything, Lincoln would waive off the charge and tell the accuser, "Grant fights!"

On the Twelfth, Grant decided on a massive assault on the Confederate lines, targeting the "angle" of the breastworks where he thought the Confederates could be cut in two and then routed. He sent Hancock's division in at dawn and parts of the VI Corps at 9 A.M. A total of twenty thousand Federals attacked in one of the largest, and bloodiest, assaults of the war, an assault that became a funeral for the Fifteenth New Jersey.]

May 12

Thursday morning, the 12th, was a sad day for our regiment. Early in the morning, a part of the 2d Corps assaulted and captured a part of the enemy's line of works (where we had attempted a charge Tuesday and capturing a large number of prisoners). We were told that the corps had captured 10,000 prisoners and 28 guns. Our cheers were interrupted by rebel shells which showed they were still in position. Our division was ordered in to relieve them. There was desperate fighting here, the enemy making every effort to recapture the works and did.

We moved out again past the rifle pit of yesterday, then to the "Angle" (in the works). It was raining furiously. The road was lined with wounded. The musketry in front was continuous.

Suddenly we moved to the right of the angle by the flank and then facing and in a single line charged, with our regiment on the extreme right. The next 20 minutes were horribly fatal to the 15th. As soon as we came out of the woods, the fire of a quarter of a mile of rifle pits opened up. The right wing was almost entirely swept away in an instant. The left succeeded in getting to the works and captured a flag and about 100 prisoners, but all came back in a few minutes who could. In this charge and during the day all of which we were under fire, we lost four officers killed (Walker, Shimer, Justice and Vanvoy), missing (Lt. Fowler) and two wounded (Capt. McDanolds and Lt. Penrose) and over 150 men, the best we had. Justice had just waved his hat in front of the rebel rifle pits when he was killed. Only one man was left standing in the color guard.

A white oak tree was cut in half [and fell] from bullets in front of us.

At nightfall we were moved about, those who remained. At midnight we were halted and lay down in the rain and in silence till morning.

In the morning, the losses were footed up (of the 429 men we started with, 130 remained).

In the afternoon, we moved down to where the fight was and buried a few of our dead. General Fould's body was found but we had no time to bury it as we were ordered into the rifle pits and kept in a state of watchfulness all night, the skirmishers being driven in three times. It was raining constantly.

The rifle pits were filled with rebel dead, piled up and our men lay thick on their sides next to them. [At another juncture, Halsey wound up in a former Confederate rifle pit and noted that—"a leg or arm could be seen moving in the dead mass."] The next morning we were moved down to near where we are now and relieved. . . .

Tuesday night we were on picket all night and in a sudden dash of the rebels, the 1st regiment running without firing a shot, we lost one man killed, one wounded and one missing. At 3 A.M. yesterday morning we withdrew our line and marched three miles, I should judge, to our fighting ground on the right to support what proved to be an unsuccessful charge of the 2d Corps and then marched back again, arriving at about 2 P.M. yesterday, sleepy and tired. Today we have been digging rifle pits. Tonight we are expecting orders to move to support the 5th corps, which is having some hard fighting to our right, judging from the sound. We are told though today we were to rest here for a day or two.

Of the 2,800 men in our Brigade, but 1,100 are left. Our whole division is cut up the same way—but our Brigade is very much demoralized, having lost so many officers, especially.

✒ [The Fifteenth went into the history books on May 12. Its losses that day gave it the sad distinction of having the second-highest percentage of soldiers killed in the Civil War in a single day. One of the hardest losses for Halsey was the well-liked Lt. George Justice, the actor, shot and killed in the charge at the Angle. He left a widow and seven children. Right after he was shot, his friend William Housel ignored a withering fire from the Southern line and rushed right into it, bayoneting to death the man he saw shoot Justice. Housel later said it was his proudest moment.

Also killed that day was Capt. Cornelius Shimer, whom Colonel Penrose tried to prevent from becoming an officer the year before. Shimer was buried on the battlefield. Also killed was Capt. James Walker, who some said had the fullest beard in the army. Residents of Lafayette, New Jersey, his hometown, raised $350 for a permanent monument to him in the tiny village.

Halsey, usually restrained in his diary and letters, was emotional after the Wilderness and Spotsylvania. He wrote a fatalistic letter to his father.]

My Dear Father,

... The fighting has been unusually desperate and continuous, beats the Seven Days Peninsular fighting. The odds have been first on one side and then on the other. It is believed that we have the decided advantage now on the whole. The army is, however, exhausted and I am afraid a slight reverse would be terrible in its consequences.

... Everyone seems to look upon himself as doomed and considers it only a question of time. Our order was read tonight on this very thing, exhorting the men by the memory of their losses not to be discouraged or listless but to cover their efforts by victory, seeming to show that the struggle is yet to come which will end in victory in Richmond or defeat in the fortifications of Fredericksburg. God grant we may be successful. ...

I trust that the good providence which has watched over me hitherto and covered my head amid so many dangers will continue to keep and protect me that if it should be my lot to fall that I shall not be unprepared and that the changes as far as I am concerned will be for the better.

✒ [LESSLAND PLANTATION: Unknown to Ed, his older brother Joe was behind the rebel lines at Spotsylvania, watching his army repulse the heroic but fatal charge of the Fifteenth New Jersey and other regiments at the Angle. His view was different from Ed's, naturally, as expressed in

his account of the battle in a letter to Millie, but the heartbreak he felt
was the same.]

My Dear Wife,

General Lee keeps his men in their breastworks with several loaded guns
each and suffers Grant's drunken legions to come up close before sweeping
them down like hedge rows. . . . The Yankee's line of officers is terrible.
Sedgwick, Wadsworth, Talbot, Ogglesby, Conch, Warren and Stevens are
reported killed, Seymour captured. . . . General Lee will then [at Richmond]
get supplies and ammunition in time to keep his line and destroy Grant if
he persists in storming his works. We have but little to fear from Grant's
Army now.

[But Joseph realized how bad the killing at Spotsylvania was for his
army, too.]

. . . Our regiment has but two captains left. Two are killed, two are
wounded and three are captured and several good men are lost. Stuart is
dead. The 5th regiment had three captured, and their colonel killed and
only has five commissioned officers left. Col. Collins of the 15th was also
killed, so you can see Lomax' Brigade did their full duty, even against
such odds.

I have been with the trains since last Thursday, working my horse, trying
to stand a hard campaign in a barren country. . . . It is impossible to buy corn
or flour anywhere. The army is reduced to the lowest allowance and people
in the country are almost destitute. I never saw such a state of things before.

. . . So far, Providence smiles upon us and I trust will give us a glorious
victory and with it peace and liberty. . . . I still think the Yankees will be
terribly conveyed this summer and our peace be confirmed by a merciful
and just God.

✒ [The charge at the Angle, which dislodged some of the rebels but not
all, was the last major assault in the Spotsylvania campaign, which, with
heavy losses, wound up a draw. Grant would plunge on . . . south.

LESSLAND PLANTATION: The day after the two Yankee soldiers threatened to shoot Millie, Confederate officers in the area made certain that
troops either slept over at Lessland or were on guard duty there twenty-
four hours a day (usually, five guards were around the house each day).
Officers arrived most mornings or evenings for meals to keep Millie and
her children company.

Slaves Ned and Washington, who fled during the Yankee raid, returned. Millie and her two sons joined them and Douglass and Dode in planting potatoes, which took hours in the hot sun. In a diary, Millie wrote of how hard she and her children had to work with most of the slaves gone and the hot sun beating down on them.

On May 15, after the battle of Spotsylvania, hundreds of Confederate troops scattered through Orange and Culpeper Counties looking for food wherever they could find it. Over 150 arrived at Lessland when they saw storehouses from the road. The pickets on duty had to protect Lessland and its food from their own army.

The Fifteenth New Jersey marched around Virginia for the next few days, sometimes with other infantry and sometimes with cavalry, uncertain where they were headed, or where the war's twists and turns would bring them. Death was all around them. When they marched through Chesterfield, they walked down a road littered with dozens of dead cavalry horses left by the rebels. There was the din of fighting in the distance every single day. On June 1, they reached a small tavern named Cold Harbor, which, although no one knew it, was going to be the site of one of the most devastating battles in American military history.

LESSLAND PLANTATION: Millie's ordeal with the Union soldiers did not surprise her neighbors. Everyone in Culpeper and Orange Counties seemed to have a story about marauding Yankees stealing food and ordering local women and children to fetch supplies for them. Millie did not mind the loss of her food—she could always grow more food. She was worried about the safety of her two sons and her attractive teenaged daughters, due home from boarding school in Richmond any day.

Her fears for her children, particularly the girls, were heightened in the middle of the month when she received a letter from her husband warning her to be just as careful to watch out for Confederate soldiers as those in the Union. "You may be annoyed by straggling cavalry. Say NO to all applications and you may save yourself much trouble. Roper's Brigade has a very LOW reputation, especially his western regiments and many of his men are mere brutes of low passions and propensities. They are badly spoken of wherever they have been," he said.

The Yankee raid, and his warning, started her thinking of a daring plan.

COLD HARBOR

The Union Army had spent the entire month of May trying to wedge its way past Confederate forces to make it to the slippery shadows of Richmond. It had to cross several rivers to do it, and it seemed that on the other side of every single river, whether the Rapidan, the Rappahannock or the North Anna, the Confederate Army was waiting. Stalemate followed stalemate in the Wilderness, Spotsylvania, and in numerous small skirmishes—stalemate at a dreadfully heavy price—but the army was making progress. By the beginning of June, Grant and his Federals had managed to crawl to within five miles of Richmond and only had one more river to cross, the Chickahominy, before they could enter the Confederate capital.

Cold Harbor tavern hugged an intersection of roadways just a few miles from the river and was held by rebel cavalry. Grant sent cavalry under General Torbert (Halsey's old boss) into the junction to clear out the rebels on June 1. The rebel cavalry retreated back to Lee's main army, and Lee then advanced on Cold Harbor, determined not to let the Federals use it as a base to cross the Chickahominy later and move on Richmond. Several rebel attacks failed to dislodge the Federals at Cold Harbor, and enough federal corps poured in during the morning of June 1 to continually repulse the Confederates. One of the most important charges that drove the Confederates back involved the VI Corps and Halsey's Fifteenth, which suffered heavy losses as it not only had to fight the enemy, but wound up being shelled by its own artillery.]

June 1

We started at daylight and reached Cold Harbor when the cavalry were fighting about noon. The air was filled with dust which made everything—men, horses all one color. We halted at the hotel for an hour or two. The cavalry dismounted and [was] fighting in front of us but a skirt of wood concealed the enemy and our pickets.

About noon our lines were formed. The 3rd brigade and 2d Brigade to the right of the road, the 4th brigade to the left of the road and to our left the 2d division (but I do not think they joined in the charge). Our regiment was in the 3rd line and as the rest of the division advanced we lay still. As the line passed the skirt of woods the musketry began. We could SEE nothing, but a shell or solid shot struck Oliver of Co C, as we were lying on the ground, on his head, throwing his body up in the air. Shot and shell flew over us but he was the only one hurt. Two or three men carried him back to the rifle pit by the hotel and I went and brought them back to the line. Directly, an officer appeared at the edge of the wood and beckoned us forward.

We rose and advanced through the wood, where we got a view of the whole field. The lines which had charged ahead of us had disappeared obliquing to the right. The 1st N.J. was coming back by the road. A rebel battery to the left of our front at once opened fire. Col. Campbell ordered a half wheel to the left and we moved rapidly forward to a small knoll about 150 feet from the battery, where we halted and opened fire over it, silencing it more or less effectively.

A little to our left and first believed to be behind the top of another knoll was the 3rd N.J. (Captain Wahl being conspicuously waving his saber, the top of his hat suddenly turned with a bullet) who were firing into the enemy. They afterwards fell back to us. To our left was nothing and we apprehended that the enemy would soon flank us as a wood a short distance off in that direction would enable them to do so easily.

To [prevent it] a battery of ours to the right started opening fire, its shells dropping in among us. Word was sent back without success. Ogden Whitesell ran back by the Colonel's order to have it stop but the stupid or frightened captain insisted upon his fratricidal work until threatened with being fired on by us.

We kept at this firing till night. The muskets became too hot to hold. Under this fire, the 10th came up with little loss and formed behind us.

Between the firing, which kept up till late, the men dug a sort of a pit with their tin plates and later spades were brought up and we dug a good rifle pit a few feet in front of the old pit in some places and at other places [new ones]. . . .

In our charge, we lost 30 or 40 men, among them Sergeant Major Voorhees, Wyckoff, one of the best men of the regiment, a man of a frank, open countenance, always in good humor, enduring every hardship without [complaining] and never shirking from either danger or work. His death was an irreparable one to the regiment. I believe he was a perfectly consistent Christian man and I had been most intimate with him since we were at White Oak church. He was a beautiful writer and caught as well the proper way of doing the work of the adjutant's office, relieving me to a great extent of the drudgery of the office.

These losses rendered our numbers to below 200 again, nearly equalling our gain from the two regiments.

✒ [The federal plan was to hit Lee with all they had early on the morning of June 2, but the attack was delayed until late in the afternoon because Hancock's corps was late in arriving. The Union Army spent most of June 2 replanning the assault, but the Confederates spent the day furiously digging rifle pits and building trenches and breastworks. The men in charge of the defensive design used the unusual design of the ground—wildly separated stands of thick trees, creek beds, ravines, rapidly rising and dropping hills, grassy depressions—to build a unique defensive fortress that enabled the rebels not only to fire at any attackers straight on, but to use the odd pits and trenches to fire from a number of different angles.]

June 2

Lying behind works under orders to charge at dark, but postponed by rain, lost several men by sharpshooters.

We lay in our pit, anxiously looking at the wood in our left from which the enemy could at anytime make our position. . . . We lost one man here. He had been digging a grave in the hollow behind the pit for one of our men and came up to the line and asked Colonel C. to send a man to help him lay the body in. Col. C. asked him if the grave was deep enough. At the same time the acting orderly of Company C asked him if he wanted a man. Instantly a musket ball struck him in the face and he fell dying at our feet. He was laid in the grave he had dug. We widened it for two.

The battery in our rear (which fired on its own men earlier) troubled us again and one of its shells was sent back to the captain as evidence that they were falling among us. We could see the shell in the morning, when the sun rose behind the battery, from the time they left the gun, and it gave us a feeling of relief to see them pass over our heads.

The dust and smoke was such that the sun could be looked at any hour of the day nearly all the time we were here.

✒ [The attack finally got under way on the morning of June 3. The three main attacking forces were the XVII Corps, the II Corps, and right in the middle, the VI Corps and the Fifteenth New Jersey. The enemy opened fire as soon as the blue line of battle began to make its advance. As federal soldiers moved closer and closer to the main Confederate breastworks, they were cut down by musket fire and artillery snugly set up in the zigzagging trenches and ravines where thousands of well-protected men in gray uniforms waited. Every regiment that charged was caught in the enfilading fire from two and sometimes three sides and cut up. The Fifteenth New Jersey was one of the few regiments that made it to a reasonably safe place, where they stayed all day and then survived the night.]

June 3

Hot. Early in the morning we had orders to charge, General Russel standing in among us and ordering the advance. Col. Campbell said "we will when the line gets up to us," referring to the line of battle seen approaching from our left rear—it was Gibbons division of the 2d Corps. As we first saw them, the rebels saw them and opened fire on them. They had to cross the same wide field we had passed on the 1st, every part of it swept by the enemy. In this line was a new heavy artillery regiment which advanced in a handsome line but was cut down like grass. A few reached the rebel rifle pit and were probably taken prisoners. It was the most sickening sight of the war, and the sight of these bodies strewn over the ground for a quarter of a mile and in our sight for days will never fade from my recollection.

In this line was an old regiment from Massachusetts. They seemed to catch the position at once and neither going back nor forward with distinction, like the new regiment, they came up to us.

General Russel seeing the fate of this line did not urge us forward to the same fate and to lose the hold we had. The 10th advanced to the knoll ahead and entrenched.

The battery behind us wounded four of our men and would have killed me had I not been sent along the line to the left a moment before. The shell tore up the little shelter tent we had struck up to keep off the sun and under which I had been lying.

After dark we moved over into the first line, relieving the 10th.

A charge was made to our left at night as we could tell by the musketry. The fusillade continued along the line.

We felt safer at night in one respect. After the charge of the morning our men held the woods to our left and a rifle pit was dug open in the intervening space during the day. First a man crawling on his face [crawled to us and we] threw up a little dirt to cover him. Behind him [came] others. . . . We dug a rifle pit. Rebel bullets fell in the loose dirt, throwing it up [in the air] but they did not stop the work.

Another incident. The ground behind us was as dangerous to cross as that in front. To get water our men would run the gauntlet of the enemy's fire. The man would take a dozen canteens and run as fast as he could to a little building half way back where he would have a rest. His comrades watched the race, the bullets striking the dirt sometimes close to the feet of the runner and often another would ask permission to go until Col. C. told them to stop, that he believed they had enough [water].

Our cook took the meals for Col. C. and myself after things got quiet at night (about ten) and before daylight in the morning (about 3) and between times we went hungry. Once he returned with our breakfast before we lay down to sleep. So far as sleep was concerning, Col. C. and I took turns to keep half of the line officers awake and half the men awake at all times. It required the greatest effort of the officers to keep the men awake.

🖋 [The June 3 attack against well-fortified breastworks and trenches was a disaster. A direct charge against a dug-in enemy with breastworks set up to give the enemy a variety of angles and sight lines had no chance of success. No army on earth could have taken those breastworks. The Union Army lost seven thousand men in the assaults, most of them in an eight-minute period that Halsey described as "sickening," and did not seize any ground. Grant, who always defended his strategies, despite the casualties, later said he should never have made the attack.

Including the Cold Harbor casualties, the Union Army lost forty-one thousand men in a single month, over 40 percent of its soldiers (the Confederates lost thirty-two thousand and 46 percent of their total). The carnage in Virginia in the spring of 1864 brought a whole new spate of complaints in Northern newspapers for a peace settlement, and Grant came under severe criticism in the press and in Congress for the continual heavy losses. Lincoln, stunned by the casualty figures, never wavered in his support of Grant and told him to keep plunging on toward Richmond. Again, whenever critics wailed about Grant, Lincoln would look them straight in the eye and tell them, "Grant fights!"]

June 4

Hot with showers.

I ran the gauntlet of the rebel bullets which whistled around me as I ran, having a feeling that if I was maimed or fell I could not get away in safety and proceeded to list the men, taking a list [with me]. Leaving them in line in a rifle pit near the battery, I had a wash . . . my face. . . . At dark, I [went] to the line, getting there between the fusillade of the enemy. The men mingled with those of the 15th and I lay down and slept entirely

unconscious of fusillades and of a heavy shower which left me in a puddle
of water when I woke in the morning.

June 5

Rainy. We lay behind the pits all day, exchanging shots with the
enemy's sharpshooters. Their rifle pits were not 20 yards off.

One man, David Husted, of the 3rd, running after water, halted
behind an apple tree. The enemy (fire) fairly barked this tree and would
eventually have hit him had not our men risen up and opened a general
fire on the enemy which gave them something else to think of and Husted
watched his chance and saw it. He understood what his comrades were
doing for him.

We have 216 muskets, having lost 52 men since the morning of June 1.

[On June 6, the Fifteenth lay close to the ground all day as the general
bombardment from both sides continued. On the seventh a truce was
declared so that the bodies of the dead could be collected, but Halsey speculated that pickets from both sides had arranged the previous night to
stop firing through the night and morning anyway, prior to the official
ceasefire.

Halsey wrote home.]

... It was a singular sight to see the men of both armies standing up
looking at each other curiously while between the lines both parties mingled
exchanging papers (to collect bodies). Our men went out and exchanged
with them shaking hands most cordially and returning unmolested. This
good feeling was kept up until this morning about 8, when it seems the rebs
were dissatisfied with our digging pits in the rear or anticipated something
from us (which they had reason to) and determined to put things on the
old footing. So one man sang out "you had better get down, you Yanks!"
and immediately both parties got under cover.

[On June 6, Halsey sent a summary of the battle to his brother Sam.]

Dear Sam,

Our losses since the first of June: 12 killed, 26 wounded and 14 wounded
so slightly as since they have returned to duty—total, 52. Our regiment,
having received some 120 from the 2d and 3d (who have gone home leaving their vets with us) is now 233 for duty. [We have] the Delaware

cavalry . . . not drilled at all, made up of boys and undisciplined, they are not much account. Our division, I fear has lost some 1000 or 1500 some men since the first of June in this place. Why we are waiting here I cannot understand. The enemy is too strong in front to be charged now and we are certainly not resting any if constant digging and watching in trenches can be considered duty.

Rumors have been floating for some days that our Brigade is to be relieved but I don't see where the relief is to come from for the rest of the army seems to be equally engaged. Another left swing movement, I suppose, is intended. Heavy works are being thrown up in our rear, which seems to indicate a stay.

I do not wish to destroy a hope though ever so slight, yet I am afraid Alfred is not living. Some six of our men missing at the same time (two from the same company) who were taken and recaptured by Sheridan report that they saw nothing of him among the prisoners.

I closed my last letter rather abruptly, the reason was the rebs opened a battery upon us and followed it with musketry obliging us to keep low. So I handed the paper as it was to the postmaster asking him to take it to the rear to Alanson and requested him to direct it to you.

I have asked you for quite a number of things, but for fear I may have made mistakes I will ask you again to send if convenient the following little articles: a tooth brush, comb, typographical map with roads, a compass and good lead pencils. My diary I feared has too little room for each day. Should you send me another I will send you mine. You might ask father to send me some money occasionally.

✒ [Once again, Ed Halsey did not know that his brother Joe was watching the battle from the commissary wagons of the Sixth Virginia Cavalry, which was fighting at Cold Harbor under General Lee. Right after the battle, Lee sent Joe Halsey to Richmond to look for food. Lee was certain Grant would again try to take on the Army of Northern Virginia at another spot along the Chickahominy in order to move on Richmond and that soldiers and residents there would need supplies if the attack bogged down into a siege, as Grant's 1863 attack on Vicksburg did.]

June 8
✒ [LESSLAND PLANTATION: General Robertson's brigade pulled out of Lessland in early June. (Robertson, an unpopular man, was soon relieved of command and sent to the backwaters of Texas for minor duty.) Millie

was extremely upset. She had no slaves left to help her except Ned, Washington, and Douglass. Most of her neighbors had fled the Culpeper area for the safety of the western part of the state. Despite all of the problems the occupying Confederate Army had caused her, it at least offered protection against the Federals, who were moving about the area and could frequently be seen.

To protect her children, Millie moved the entire family out of the posh living rooms on the first and second floor of the manor house and set up an apartment in the basement of the building. She, the servants, and a friend put iron bars on the windows of the basement and added several strong, bolted locks to the door connecting the basement to the first floor of the house. They dragged some beds and pieces of furniture down the narrow staircase into the basement—what could fit. Some light came through the barred windows and a thin wood floor offered protection from the dirt. The basement was cool because almost all of it was below ground, but it resembled a dungeon. Millie and the children stayed upstairs or outside most of the day, as long as no Union soldiers were in sight, and hid in the basement as soon as the sun went down. They stored food in the basement in case they came under siege. Millie also kept weapons there for defense. She never wanted to be in a situation again where soldiers could stare her down with rifles when she was defenseless. If she had to, she would shoot soldiers.

Outside, the plantation fell into ruin. Little was done on the farm, grass and weeds began to grow high and dry, and summer winds kicked dirt and dust all over the manor house and into the basement apartment where the Halseys were holed up. The Confederate soldiers had taken all of the Halsey corn, leaving them with nothing but some meat. The soldiers had trampled vegetable gardens, ruining all the vegetables. Earlier, Yankees had raided Morton Hall and occupied the main house for a night, then rode off with most of the food stored in Millie's mother's back houses. Both plantations' lawns and gardens were destroyed by horses' hooves and wagon ruts. Little food was on either plantation. The war that Millie Halsey was so afraid of in the spring of 1861 had trapped her and her children at last.

Millie learned that her husband had left Spotsylvania and moved to the Richmond area on permanent assignment as the Confederate government expected Grant to attack the city within days. "The cavalry was running through on the Central Road yesterday and will run up the Richmond road today," he'd written on May 15. "General Lee will get supplies and ammunition in time to keep his line and destroy Grant."

She frowned at the rest of his letter, though, which explained that as one of the officers in charge of procuring food, he was having a difficult time supplying the army.

During the second week of May, too, after the Yankee raid, Halsey learned, to his great surprise, that his two daughters in Richmond, always healthy, had suddenly become very sick. He had visited with them in early April and they seemed vibrant. He agreed with Millie that they should get to Lessland as quickly as possible so they could recuperate.

Frustrated by his inability to crack the lines of the Army of Northern Virginia, Grant decided on a wildly different tactic and ordered the army to swing east and then south in a wide crescent and assault the city of Petersburg, below Richmond. He believed that if he could quickly take Petersburg, he could move north and take Richmond within days, striking so quickly that Lee would not have time to move his army in front of Richmond to protect it. The Union Army moved out of Cold Harbor, and its ghastly memories, on June 12.]

13

A SUMMER TO REMEMBER

June 19–September 4, 1864

[While Halsey and his comrades were completely engaged in fighting in the Wilderness, one of the greatest emotional tragedies of the war for New Jersey, involving many of his friends from Rockaway in the Twenty-seventh New Jersey Volunteers, occurred on the swollen and swift-running Cumberland River in Tennessee. The Union Army was bogged down in a slow crossing of the Cumberland. The fast-running river prevented a normal crossing by pontoon bridges or rafts, and soldiers had to string a series of ropes, tied together, from one bank of the river to the other. Rafts were then sent moving across the river, adjacent to the rope lines, at a snail's pace. Soldiers formed lines on the edges of the rafts, held on by comrades, and hand over hand, pulled the raft across the raging river toward the heavily wooded banks on the other side as water beneath them tossed the raft from side to side and up and down.

Suddenly, one of the boats broke free from the line and twisted and turned as the current caught it. The boat moved away from and then back toward the rope line. An officer on the boat screamed to his men to lie down to let the boat drift under the rope, intending to have them rise when they passed the rope and attempt to bring the raft to shore somehow. He reasoned that if they all lay down on the boat, no one would be knocked overboard by the rope. The men panicked. Some fell to the floor of the raft, as instructed, and could see the tightly pulled brown rope about to pass over them, but most stood up, flailing at the rope with their arms to stop the boat and prevent it from circling out of control and going down into the hard-swirling rapids of the river.

The men who did catch the rope pulled down hard on it and others scrambled to help them. Too many men gathered on that side of the raft and it capsized, one end sinking deep into the river and the other end towering high up into the air before going down and then turning completely over. All of the men were tossed violently into the river, which sent them swiftly downward into rock formations and deep pools of water. Some crashed against the rocks and some were sucked down toward the river bottom by the currents and undertow. Thirty-three men drowned within minutes. Nineteen of the dead were from Company L, the Rockaway boys.

"I was on the capsized boat, but caught the boat again after she righted. It is not fair to impute the blame to anyone," said Lt. Stephen Pierson, of Rockaway, one of the survivors. "The boat was let loose from the upper rope and, floating down, struck a lower rope. Had the men kept their presence of mind (and laid down) all would have been safe. But they clung to the rope, the swift current swept over us, and in a moment we were all in the water."

The nineteen deaths were the largest single number of men killed from Rockaway in any single engagement of any war and one of the worst single-community tragedies in the country, North or South. All were buried together in the Rockaway Presbyterian Church cemetery with full military honors.

The dead included Joseph Class, Jesse Demouth, Lemuel Degraw, James Fuller, Lewis Green, B. K. Miller, John McCloskey, Ed Nichols, William Ockaback, William Weaver, Thomas Dell, James O'Neil, Rolson Peer, Wilson Pittenger, George Shauger, Eliakim Sanders, Sam Smith, James Shaw, and Gideon Bostedo. Their coffins were lowered gently into the cemetery where Edmund Halsey had been the gardener before the war began, the same Edmund Halsey who was supposed to be the lieutenant of that very same regiment—and could have been on that very same raft—before his father talked him out of it.]

June 19 (Petersburg)

[The Fifteenth was one of the many regiments on its way to Petersburg to help in Grant's assault there. Grant decided to attack Petersburg, which lay south of Richmond and which was defended by only 5,400 men under Gen. P. T. Beauregard, and then, after capturing it, move north on Richmond. The semicircular sweep of the Union army east and then south to Petersburg completely surprised Robert E. Lee. He was certain

that Grant would simply nudge slowly south from Cold Harbor toward
Richmond, continually attacking Lee's rock-solid lines, continually losing.
He never expected Grant to sweep around Richmond to try to take
Petersburg and then move on Richmond.

The first assault at Petersburg was on June 15, by the XVIII Corps and
Kautz's cavalry. They had some success, particularly with Hinks's colored
division pushing thousands of Confederates back into a series of trenches
built for the defense of the city, but when Hancock's II Corps arrived at
nightfall, the Federals declined a marvelous opportunity for a surprise
nighttime attack under a full moon that illuminated the entire area. Some
reasoned that a full moon would provide enough light for the troops to
see where they were going and that an evening raid, unexpected, would
succeed. Several daytime attacks of the trenches followed through June
18, but by then Lee had had time to move the bulk of his army, over forty
thousand men, to the Petersburg area, securing it from direct assault. His
men flowed like water out of a vase into the dozens of long trenches the
army built there for the protection of the city and settled in to defend it
against what appeared to be a wide-ranging siege. They dug themselves
into the long, narrow trenches, precursors of trench warfare in World
War I, and waited for Grant's next move.

Grant was determined to take Petersburg. He needed a victory after
the terrible losses of men at the Wilderness, Spotsylvania, and Cold
Harbor. Grant was a winner, the victor of Vicksburg (Lincoln called him
his "pit bull"), and he had not been winning lately. The dour general had
come under much pressure during the last few weeks because his casualty
rates were so high. He was convinced that if he took Petersburg, he could
push Lee's army back to Richmond and then defeat it, take the
Confederate capital, and end the war. Determined to win, Grant settled in
for what turned out to be a tedious ten-month siege of the city.

Halsey and his comrades in the Fifteenth were supposed to be part of
one of the June 15–18 assaults, but arrived a day late. They did not attack
but, for the time, became part of the siege army.

Halsey wrote to his brother Sam.]

Wednesday morning we were moved down to the right about a mile
and taking a position in a cornfield in a line, our corps marching from one
branch to another of the James River and proceeded to throw up breastworks, the sun being very hot, and the ground dry. We passed a quiet night
undisturbed by alarm save the distant booming of artillery, which was an

every day affair. The next morning we moved back and took a similar position near the river and . . . in pits waited for the wagons to pass through. About 4 P.M. "the general" again sounded and we moved down to the river at a place called Live Oak, about five miles south. There the whole wagon train was crossing on pontoons and our corps was embarking. We took until midnight to get on board and after an hour or two we were roused up at Bermuda Hundred.

Here we were til daylight, disembarking. We marched up the Appomattox past Point of Rocks and halted after a march of five miles about an open field when the heat was about unsupportable. We passed Butler's headquarters and his men were all about us seemingly in summer quarters. They have works which are the strongest I have seen yet and I believe impregnable if half defended. Our men having gone a different route (I did not come up till last night), we were badly off for food and glad to get at the Sutler's which we stationed hereafter lying in the field an hour or two we moved off to the right in a woods and lay till night when the general again sounded. From 12 to 2 we were out in the field as we had halted in the morning, expecting to make an attack but we finally put back again.

All the afternoon, half the night and yesterday morning there was very heavy cannonading in the direction of Petersburg and news was received of successes there by the 18th corps and especially by the Negroes. Some 19 cannon were captured from the rebs. [They] were reported at Butler headquarters yesterday though constantly expecting orders we did not move and lived from hand to mouth. At 4 in the morning, we were started for this place where we arrived about 9 or 10 and have been laying in an open field since. The rebs threw a shell or two in our direction as we came up the south bank of the river but did no damage. Our batteries on the right and left fired a shot every little once in awhile which so far has been feebly responded to. There are four lines of pits in front of us (the 1st is within 500 yards of the city), which we captured yesterday. The city might have been taken last night, it is reported, if the troops on the left had come up. I think Burnside and Hancock and Warren are all on the left of us. The newspapers can give you a better account of the general position of the army than I can.

I have just received letters from Sue and Eliza Howell, reporting all well but anxious. It is impossible to write very often and people must not wonder if letters asking about their friends are unanswered when we scarcely find time to write for ourselves. Should we ever go into camp there will be enough back writing to do to last me a month. No reports have been made [by me] since we started [the campaign].

If Sam P. [Ed's cousin, the new minister in Rockaway] is in earnest about a chaplaincy, he can perhaps get appointed to the 4th NJ Vols, but as Alanson says, I would not exchange a good settlement I liked at home for any chaplaincy.

*[THE WAR: The marauding Confederate warship the *CSS Alabama,* which had terrorized the seas and sunk sixty-nine Union ships during the war, was sunk off Cherbourg, France, by the federal warship *Kearsage.* It was a hard blow to the Confederate Navy.]

June 20
*[LESSLAND PLANTATION: The war had crept to the edge of Lessland in May and stayed there. As both armies maneuvered through Virginia during the Wilderness and Cold Harbor campaigns, Lessland and the surrounding plantations and towns found themselves within the shadows of the cannons of both the Army of the Potomac and the Army of Northern Virginia. Both armies alternately occupied area towns such as Culpeper, Warrenton, and New Baltimore, all within miles of Lessland, and several battles had been fought so close to the Halsey plantation that Millie and the children could hear the shots and see the smoke. Both armies set up large camps on both sides of the Rappahannock and the Rapidan Rivers. Millie Halsey was fearful that Lessland would be shelled in any battle that suddenly erupted in the countryside around her. She was absolutely terrified that their two teenaged girls, both attractive and blooming into womanhood, back from boarding school in Richmond, would be harmed by marauding Union soldiers. Her husband wrote to warn her about straggling Confederate soldiers, too, particularly those of Roper's brigade. She feared for her daughters, stranded in the middle of hundreds of thousands of men from both armies. She was afraid that despite all the precautions she had taken, such as the bolted locks on the doors to their new home in the basement of the manor house and the bars installed on the basement windows, harm would come to her family.

Her fears reached their peak one morning in early May when, with her two small boys, she walked to the edge of Lessland and could see, on a distant mountain, the Union Army encampment with artillery pointed directly at Lessland. One week later, the two Union soldiers arrived looking for food and pointed their rifles at her. Terrified for the girls, she decided to spirit them out of Lessland and Virginia to safety. Millie was certain that if anybody could get them out of the war zone, it was Elizabeth (Miss Lizzie) Holmread, her close friend and acknowledged gadfly of the Culpeper County social world. Miss Lizzie, as some said, could be Dizzy Miss Lizzie at times, but she had managed to drive to and from Winchester without being stopped by Union or Confederate guards and had just returned from a shopping spree in Washington, D.C., during which she slipped through two lines of Union soldiers and a Potomac River boat blockade as well. If anyone could get the girls to the North, and safety, it was Dizzy Miss Lizzie. Holmread, who loved to trek off on adventures of any kind, got them past Union and Confederate camps in the Virginia countryside to Washington. As did their mother, Miss Lizzie explained to them both exactly how to get out of Washington and north to the Halsey home in Rockaway. Lizzie left them in Washington, and the two girls, Fannie, sixteen, and Annie, fourteen, two strong, independent, well-educated girls, like so many of the Halsey women, were on their own.

Fannie, her letters at the time show, was a practical, levelheaded girl, just like her mother, who had the maturity of a much older woman. The girls had no trouble getting to Washington, despite anxiety as they went past Union camps, and took a night train out of the capital by themselves and spent eight days traveling to Newark and then on to Rockaway, New Jersey, where Millie hoped her father-in-law, Sam Halsey Sr., would care for his grandchildren, as he had told her he would in a spring letter in which he begged the entire family to flee Virginia for their safety and to come to Rockaway.

"I have determined to remain at home whether for weal or woe, as it is the only chance of preserving my roof. . . . The step [the children] are about to take is fraught with considerable difficulty and danger, but I trust wisdom and strength may be given them. I therefore commend them to our heavenly father and yourself," Millie wrote her father-in-law.

She should not have worried. The Halseys disagreed on politics, but not family. The two girls arrived in Rockaway, unannounced, on the Morris and Essex Railroad on June 28 and made it by foot across the village of Rockaway to the Halsey home on the river, where at first they thought no one was home. All was quiet on the outside because Sam was at the grist mill and Cornelia was in the village. There was no sign of life in the stables or barns directly north of the main house. Fannie and Annie walked through the open front door and peered about the parlors, which were empty. Then they climbed the stairs to the second floor, where they found their aunt Anne lying in bed, her wooden crutches leaning against the wall next to her pillow. Anne could not believe the sight in front of her. Tears in her eyes, Anne pulled herself up, swung her legs over the side of the mattress, got out of bed, grabbed her crutches, stumbled away from the bed and across the room to the girls, and hugged them.

Joseph Halsey was livid that the two girls had been spirited away from Lessland and the South and wrote his wife he was "startled, surprised and mortified" that she had sent them North on what he called "a desperate adventure."

"In times of profound peace you would have hardly judged it prudent to start two helpless schoolgirls off on such a trip utterly unprovided with means and unprotected and under such a sleazy escort as Miss Lizzie. Your family pride and position would have shrunk from throwing your children out as beggars upon anybody's charity," he wrote in a heated letter on the Fourth of July, and added that Millie's decision was far worse in wartime. "The whole country is full of sharpers, armed and without money, and you start your children with a carpetbag and a ninepence to cut their own way as best they can 300 miles into the enemy's country where you can never hear their troubles nor true condition and from which there is no return except at the pleasure of the brutal despotism at Washington."

He was also annoyed that the escape of the girls once again underlined Southerners' view of him as a transplanted Yankee. "Your action places me in a very embarrassing condition myself in the Confederate service, a northern man by birth and forever liable in Virginia to suspicion (however unfounded) and here goes the report that two of my daughters have been sent to Yankeedom to live and be educated. We are all too poor to live, too unpatriotic to endure a moment's pinching sacrifice and longing for the fleshpots of our vile enemies?" Joe scolded.

Finally, realizing he could not undo the damage, he prayed for the girls. "I hope a merciful providence will protect and shield those thoughtless children from the thousand perils that seem to me to encompass their path," he said, and told his wife not to do anything so "extravagant" again. (Halsey had a remarkably low opinion of his daughters, who had done well in school, comported themselves with dignity at all times, and in their sprint to the North, showed more courage and sagacity than most men.)

Jeremiah Morton told Millie he was "pained and astounded" at her actions. He, too, was aghast that two Southern belles, the pride of Dixie, were spirited out of Virginia to the heart of the Union at the very time when the South needed every able-bodied man to fight and every able-bodied woman to run the plantations and stores back home to keep the Confederate economy going.

Despite the outcry of criticism from her husband and father, Millie Halsey hoped she did the right thing. As a woman, she sensed real danger for her two daughters in a land overrun with straggling soldiers from both armies, men who were starved for food and affection and a long way from home.

Millie spent many sleepless nights through the rest of the summer because she had no way of knowing what had happened to her loving girls. All mail was cut between the North and South, even to nearby Virginia, throughout much of the summer of 1864, and a fretful Millie ("I am a lunatic for doing this") feared the worst for her daughters.]

June 24 (Near Petersburg)
🖋 [Most of the regiments in the Union Army spent their time digging long trenches during the siege of the city.

Halsey wrote his sister Sue.]

Since last Saturday afternoon, we have had a quiet time, laying still. There is occasional firing to the right of us from Petersburg and this morning a little far to the left but we have been allowed a temporary season of rest. Our Sutler is up with stores of tobacco and other necessaries and were we [assured] that the stay would be of any duration we might make ourselves quite comfortable. Our baggage wagon is up too, so that whatever is left in our valises we can get.

I say we have rest. Five of our companies have been on picket since Sunday morning and the men and officers in camp have had their entrenchments to make—ground to police and muster rolls and other papers to make out. I have been to work two days hard on a return for May and haven't [finished] it correct yet. I would have written home sooner but for that now I am waiting for a return from a company. This morning we were drawn up in line to be received by General Wright [we] [looked bad]. There were 96 muskets in stock, some 120 being on picket and 30 on guard. Their appearance was gay as might be expected. I thought I was the hardest looking officer in the company but concluded on inspection there were some a little worse. With a private cap, duty ragged coat, private pants too short to wear over boots which had not seen blacking for weeks and rusty sword and scabbard imagine how prepossessing was my appearance. If I had known it in time, I might have got a better fix from the wagon but the summons came too suddenly and besides I have no time to dust up for an hour or two for a five minute inspection.

I received a letter from Fred yesterday which was very entertaining indeed. I must try and write him if we stay here another day. When you write him, tell him how much I was gratified with his letter. I must write to Father next to get an advance of money. We have now four months due us and all are very short of funds. I have been expecting an installment from Sam every day. Taking the campaign together, we have done remarkably well in the eating line, much better than we had reason to expect.

The reason of this halt is probably the increased sickness among the men or perhaps awaiting reinforcements. Another flank movement now would take us away from Richmond and to go directly forward must be by siege or attended by great loss of life. The 2d Jersey Brigade now lay close to us. Their division was flanked the other night and lost very heavily. The 7th N.J. lost its colors and Major Halsey [his cousin] of the 11th is missing.

I will leave this open until the mail comes in which we expect in an hour or two. As for Alfred, I wrote to Fannie in this—all I know or could say about him is that nothing new has transpired since. If alive, he will be heard from—if killed it will ever be an impossibility to find his remains. People at home never can realize how difficult it is in war for the living to provide for the dead.

At Spotsylvania, we might have buried more of our killed of the 12th if not all had it been rightly conducted, but so much pain was taken with the five who were buried that twice as many more left for the 2d Corps to bury. Hence, Fields, for one, never can be brought home as Leggo proposed. His body had been found but as they were about bringing it in we were ordered off. Some 450 rebels and many more of our men lay together in a space no larger than our garden. Judge the difficulty of bringing them so as to reorganize each one.

Give my love to all your family. I would give two months pay to see you all, but that is in the hands of one with whom has the issues of life.

PS: If you see Sam before I get a chance to write him, say I am anxiously awaiting the receipt of the soft hat and the light flannel black coat would [be] very acceptable in this hot weather. If sent at all, now is the time.

🖋 [Later that night, Halsey wrote his cousin Eliza when he felt a twinge of emotion about the regiment and asked her to talk to the veterans in Newark about the war to see what it was like, even though she did not share his opinions of soldiers.]

Dear Eliza,

... You can learn more from the wounded than I could write, and do not think too lightly of them because they are uninteresting and light specimens of humanity. They are a fair sample of our soldiers and their patriotism and their misfortunes would cover up a multitude of deficiencies. Perhaps if you were to see some of your friends here you might not consider them quite so prepossessing, and war would be stripped of much of its glitter. There are a good many sick I am sorry to say who spend the whole time of this enlistment nearly in or about hospitals, who never see a fight, but the wounded have stronger claims on our sympathy. They at least have exposed their lives.

As we approach Richmond, the difficulties seem to increase. At Cold Harbor we were the nearest to it but found obstacles which were insurmountable. I think Grant's plans will be to swing around until the city is isolated from its supplies and thus compel its evacuation. How he will succeed we cannot tell. One thing is certain—I think the campaign is likely to be a long one and I will be well if the summer finishes it. God grant that it may be decisive and that this war which never seemed so terrible before may end. It makes me sick to look at our regiment or brigade, but our [heavy] loss is but little over the average for the entire army.

[Halsey closed this, one of his most touching letters, with even more emotion.]

... I feel very grateful to you both for your earnest wishes and prayers on my behalf and can but feel that the petitions which have been put up to [God] on my behalf have been heard and answered. May God bless you and grant that I may be enabled to thank you at a far distant day in person for your kindnesses.

June 29

Hot and excessively dirty. We were reviewed, say rather drawn up to be looked at, by General Wright. There were 96 muskets in stack, 120 being on picket and 30 on guard. Their appearance was as might be expected.

At noon "the general" was sounded for "pack up" and we moved at about three P.M. the corps going down to Ream's Station to meet the cavalry and to tear up the railroad. We went by the Jerusalem Road part of the way and arrived at our destination at 11 P.M. and camped in the trench. The march was so dusty that objects could hardly be distinguished and was about 8 miles. Arrived at our destination [in the morning] and began at once tearing up and destroying track.

✒ [The track they destroyed was that of the Weldon Railroad, a direct line in and out of Petersburg. The ruined track forced the Confederates to supply Petersburg by wagon.

LESSLAND PLANTATION: Millie Halsey, alone with her two boys and some of the returned servants now, kept track of her husband through his letters, visits from her father, or word of mouth from neighbors. Joe had moved south to Petersburg, following Grant's army, to secure provisions for the Army of Northern Virginia there when it appeared that the army and city might come under siege.]

July 2
[The Fifteenth soon left the trench area.]

At daylight came the long expected orders to move and after waiting for other troops to get out of the way, we were soon on our way and marched back to near our old camp by noon.

But not to the old camp, but to an open, unsodded corn field whose surface had been pulverized by many feet. It was just large enough to keep its dust in the air. We proceeded to fix up our headquarters when other headquarters had been falling heir to furniture taken from some house. We made a bough house, fixed up with bricks at the ends (a mahogany bedstand at one end) and table in the center, made of pine boughs and stakes through which the cool breezes blow. Bands are playing at various headquarters and the Johnnys are not in too close proximity. Some ten contrabands (freed slaves) came in to us—which the men call the "proceeds of our raids"—we labor under one difficulty—want of water.

By digging five or six feet we get enough to drink but the horses have to go a good ways to drink out of dirty pools.

The whole country seems a swamp with no running streams in it. The ones we crossed were black, nasty streams.

An order has been received allowing officers to draw two rations with the men "owing to their inability to pay" which is adding insult to injury. We have four months pay owed us.

July 11
[The regiment was moved to Washington, D.C.]

We moved out at 8 and by 11 were embarked on the "Governor Chase" for Washington. We had a good time—a good dinner, an opportunity to dress up and NO DIRT. The brigade and regimental headquarters were on board and with flags flying, bands playing we sailed down the river saluting and being saluted by gunboats. We touched at Fortress Monroe at nightfall and in the evening were in Chesapeake Bay.

We are on our way to Maryland as usual, rather later than last year, earlier than in '62.

July 12
🖎 [The citizens who lived west of Washington, D.C., were amazed to see the Confederate Army marching through their villages on July 11 and on the morning of July 12. Lee had sent Gen. Jubal Early, a hard-bitten veteran, to attack Washington, D.C. By then, the Union capital was the most heavily fortified city in the world, with seventy-four huge cannon batteries surrounding it. The capital had few troops, though, since U. S. Grant had ordered all available troops to join the Army of the Potomac for his Virginia campaign. Early hoped that an attack—with Fort Stevens (Halsey referred to it by its original name, Fort Massachusetts) his first target—would be met with little resistance. He believed victory there would leave him an open road into the capital itself. Early, severely criticized for not attacking Culp's Hill on the first day at Gettysburg when he misinterpreted an order from Lee, once again waited too long to mount an attack. He began his assault in the afternoon, giving Union riders all morning to rush to areas of Washington with orders to round up whatever soldiers they could find, including old men in the home guard, to support the soldiers at Fort Stevens.

The Federals had so much time to rush to Fort Stevens that President Abraham Lincoln joined them, delighted to finally be an eye-witness to the war. Lincoln alternately knelt and stood up on the parapets of Fort Stevens as bullets whizzed by him. Finally, an infantryman a few yards away from him, future Supreme Court justice Oliver Wendell Holmes, yelled at the president, "Get down, you damned fool!"

Early's raid was a failure and the capital was safe.]

Hot. We landed in Washington about noon and lay for a little while near the landing. Here I settled with a file of men a difficulty arising from a bill. A vendor has been keeping a slate bill for $2 in payment for a couple of glasses of his mixture. Made two excursions into the city, the last one with Dr. Hall, to get our pay. On returning the second time, I found the Brigade had gone out. I caught up with them before they reached Fort Massachusetts. As we galloped up a rebel shell burst over our heads. We could hear the sound of fighting ahead but it was now so late that we went but little farther. We camped in a yard. The citizens seemed unduly glad to see us.

July 13

In the morning, the Major, Alanson and Dr. Hall visited Washington and I expected to do the same when they came back but about 11 we were ordered forward following the rebels who had marched off in the night.

The paymaster came up and paid the whole regiment.

Passing by Ft. Stevens (formerly Fort Massachusetts), Ft. DeRussy and our old camp, we advanced from Tennallytown on the river, our division leading. We made I suppose 12 miles to near Morford's, meeting the opposition and camped.

✒ [The VI Corps was sent after Early, who was headed back for the safety of the rolling Shenandoah Valley, in Virginia.]

July 17

✒ [The Fifteenth left the Washington area and marched toward Leesburg. A shell killed Robert Chambers, of Company D, the last of the four Chambers brothers killed or wounded in the Union Army. Halsey wrote in his diary that the shell that killed Chambers exploded so close to himself that he felt heat burns from the shell on his neck for days.

The regiment was ordered back to Washington on the twentieth, and along the way, Colonel Penrose tried to set a trap to snare the elusive Gray Ghost, Gen. John Singleton Mosby, but failed.]

July 24

Visited Washington with the major (Boeman). We attended church (Dr. Sutherland preached) and put up at the Metropolitan Hotel for the night. The major could not sleep for a while, so amused was he at the posh surroundings.

July 25

 [Washington. Halsey and Boeman were just two of hundreds of soldiers from the VI Corps enjoying a needed break from the war amid the bars of the capital.]

Rainy. We were in the city shopping and enjoying ourselves generally during the day.

The 6th Corps was "in force" in the city, having apparently the freedom of the city.

At night, [remembering] we moved at daylight, I started back alone at midnight. The road was lined with drunken soldiers making the best of their way back.

 [On July 26, the army left town and headed for Virginia once again to chase Early. Halsey processed promotions for fourteen men in the company.

The weather was so hot on the march that on July 30 sixteen different men received a doctor's permission to fall out and rest from heatstroke.

THE WAR: Back in Petersburg, Gen. Ambrose Burnside finally carried off his brainstorm and blew up his tunnel beneath the rebels' defensive perimeter of the city. The crater left by the explosion was 250 feet long, 30 feet deep, and 35 feet wide. Burnside waited an entire hour before sending troops into the crater, though, giving the rebels time to regroup around its edges to meet the attack. Lee himself moved to within five hundred yards of the crater and got almost fifteen thousand troops around it by the time the Federals began their attack. The blast left a sloping grade on the Union side for the Federals to charge into the crater, but no slope anywhere else for them to get out.

The Union general directly in charge of the attack, Gen. James Ledlie, a former engineer who helped build the mine, sent thousands of men forward, but they were all trapped and casualties were high, particularly among black soldiers, who fought bravely there. Right after he sent the men into the crater, Ledlie himself hid in a bombproof shelter four hundred yards in the rear and finished most of a bottle of rum while the fighting raged. The explosion and charge were a complete failure. The Federals suffered 3,798 casualties in an attacking force of 20,000 to just 1,500 casualties for the Confederates.

"It is the saddest affair I have witnessed in the war," said General Grant. Within days, General Ledlie was relieved of duty and General

Burnside was given an extended leave of absence and never recalled. (Ironically, after the war the bungling Ledlie became the chief engineer for the Union Pacific Railroad.)]

August 4 (Near Frederick, Maryland)

✒ [Jubal Early was determined to avenge the destruction of private property in Virginia, including the Virginia Military Academy (VMI), by the Union Army in the spring of 1864, despite Robert E. Lee's orders not to war against civilians. Early sent Gen. John McCausland to the small town of Chambersburg, Pennsylvania, in July to demand $500,000 to make up for the destruction of VMI. If the town refused, he would burn it down. Town leaders could not raise the money and four hours later the rebel army torched it. The fires destroyed 70 percent of the town, including 400 buildings and 274 homes, and left over a thousand men, women, and children homeless. The destruction of the town was quickly used as a precedent for Union generals to destroy property.

Halsey wrote home.]

Dear Sam,

Everything arrived yesterday. Immediately, I had the desk up and have been working hard night and day. Everything to be done correctly. I have to do [things] myself now that the Sergeant Major is dead. He knew as much about the business as I did and could write enough sight better. I find the regiment has lost by death in the months of May and June 111 men. This does not include the missing nor those the report of whose deaths are not officially received, no officers. We have about 200 absent, wounded and four dead officers. One is supposed to be dead, one in Richmond with a leg off, one home with a leg off, one in Washington wounded and one discharged for wounds.

✒ [On August 6, cavalry commander Gen. Philip Sheridan, just thirty-three, was named by General Grant commander of the Middle Military Division (Army of the Shenandoah), which oversaw the VI Corps and Halsey. Sheridan, who spent the early days of the war as a quartermaster, was given a field command in May of 1862 and skyrocketed to the top of the Union Army with a succession of victories. Sheridan, a thin man who stood only five feet five inches, was nicknamed Little Phil by his men. His panache and flamboyant style, and bravery in leading men in battle, made him incredibly popular among the troops.]

August 15 (Near Strasburg)

An oldish man, probably the landlord, sitting on a porch, saluted us as we passed the hotel. Col. C asked him how his business was lately.

"Customers were plenty, but business was bad," he answered.

Instead of going back where we started from, Col. P. posted us on the hill in front of the one we had occupied looking directly into the town. Here we kept up a fire with the rebel pickets on the right. Some sharpshooters in a house were particularly annoying.

Directly, Col. Halstead of the Corps staff came out and ordered us in again, to form our former line, somewhat to our relief as we could see the enemy crawling around on our right.

Col. P went back somewhere to explain his movement and we settled down in quiet.

As we were laying along the line with no expectation of being disturbed, saddle off my horse, a rebel line of battle appeared coming steadily across our whole front. I saddled my horse and rode back to Col P's headquarters to give the alarm, finding no one had an orderly there. I returned to the line to find it engaged. On the left of the pike, the 8th Corps fell back and the rebs brought up three pieces of artillery and began shelling us. Their line came up to our picket line which fell back to the woods and assembled, laying down, awaiting a further advance. I went to the right and brought Col. Lay and the 10th up to the right of our line. Some of our pickets still retained positions in natural pits in front and kept up a fire on the enemy.

For some reason, the enemy advanced no farther but directly returned and we pushed our pickets out to the former lines. It was about dusk and Col. P. came rushing up. We lost seven men wounded and two missing. We understood that the enemy lost eight killed, 40 wounded.

🖋 [During the fight, Halsey issued three thousand cartridges to his men.]

August 16

🖋 [A house was pillaged and each man was examined by order from headquarters to find missing property. None was found.]

August 17

We were in the rear of the infantry and passed through Newtown (Virginia) about daylight and reached the stream near Winchester about 8

(18 miles). By request of General Torbert, commanding the cavalry, our brigade was left with him while the rest of the corps and the 8th went on over the Occoquan [Creek].

At first only part of the regiment was deployed and they with the cavalry kept back the enemy's cavalry from now until about four, where the enemy deployed and infantry skirmish line. The rest of the 15th was then deployed. The 10th on the left of it. The 4th on the left of it. Our men held their own against the skirmishers without difficulty, but at dark the enemy having learned that they were fighting only their skirmish line arrayed in two lines of battle, overlapping us at that. It was swiftly a rout, with the color guard and some of Company A who were to the left of the pike. I went straight back to the town, the enemy's line showing way to the east by the flashes of their muskets in the growing darkness, their bullets sweeping across the plains to where we were. On the right or west of the pike there were high hills and woods making their advance not so clearly seen.

As we went back through the town we more or less mixed with cavalry and men of the 4th and 10th.

✒ [As usual, Halsey wrote out a complete list of those killed, wounded, and missing and sent it to the *Jerseyman,* where it was published, so that the people back home would know if loved ones were victims. In his report that night, copied into his diary, he noted that the regiment's strength was now 170 men, down from 234 four days before.]

August 19 (Charlestown, Va.)
Dear Sisters,

The last week has been an exceedingly rough one for our Brigade and the wonder is that there is anything left of it. We left our camp near Harpers Ferry on the 10th and reached Strasburg and the enemy on the 13th after a very hot, hard march. On the same evening our line was within about two miles over Cedar Creek and three days ration were issued with orders to have them last four days. Sunday afternoon our Brigade was again moved over to support the skirmish line which was pushed up to overlook the town at dark. The Brigade then deployed or relieved the line. Of course, they had no rest that night. The next morning, the enemy not being in sight, our regiment skirmished this side of town by order of Col. Penrose and came near being caught. How be it, we lost but one man wounded and the line was back in its old position by noon by orders of General Sheridan.

About 3, the rebs forced us back for our audacity by charging our line with about a division of infantry or three pieces of artillery. Crook's command on the left fell back and compelled our left to fall back a little but not far and after about an hour they noticed our men following them up vigorously and at night our line was re-established. The rebs lost eight killed and 40 wounded. They acknowledged including a colonel, surgeon and three color bearers. Our loss was one killed, two captured and three wounded (the 4th and 10th were not engaged) besides what Crook lost.

Tuesday, we were still on picket and undisturbed save by a few shots. It was rumored that the enemy were flanking us and before dark our forces were moving away and our line was safely withdrawn about nine or 10. Then commenced the march to Winchester which we reached about 8 Wednesday morning—18 miles for us—bringing in our rear and two miles farther than the rest.

Here our brigade was detached to support cavalry and make a rear guard fight. It was a most decided outrage considering that we had just been on a skirmish line two days while the rest were lying still, had been rear guard and this made our 5th day on three days rations. However, our Brigade deployed skirmishers with the cavalry and skirmished with the reb cavalry till about 4 when the enemy showed an infantry line which made things more serious. Things now began to look exceedingly dusty.

Our infantry was all gone but us and all the cavalry but one division. The enemy began to show double lines of battle in front and on both flanks. About six, their rush was made. The 15th rallied three or four times, getting back to the town and must have punished the enemy severely. The 10th on the left had to give way first. The 4th on their left came near being swallowed up. The flight to the town was swift with their balls [flying at us]. I collected what I could of provost guards, color guards and such and hurried back to the town and fell in with the cavalry. About 10 up came Col. Penrose, Col. Campbell and what was left of the 15th with straggling men from the 4th and 10th. The 4th went some other way and no one knew where the 10th was.

A halt was made till daylight. [Then] we moved up to where our division was encamped in the Charlestown Road. Here we met part of the 4th, 10th and 12th and got into something like shape. It was found not to be so very bad as was expected. We have lost 57 missing, nine wounded, including one captain wounded and one lieutenant missing. The 4th lost 111 missing. The Lt. Col. and the rest of the 10th are gone but another 100 men and three or four lieutenants supposed to be mostly captured. Our Brigade now numbers about 400 or 450 for duty. Yesterday afternoon, we came back here, about 7 miles, and are awaiting further orders.

It is reported that our three regiments and the 3rd N.J. Cavalry fought a whole Corps, Breckinridge supported by Early, and the wonder with ourselves and with the rest of our corps is that the Brigade was not gobbled up en masse. At one time our men were on one side of a stone fence and the enemy on the other in the darkness. Col. Campbell rallied a rebel line over it. One reb came up to one of our men and was asked "where do you belong?" He said "To Breckinridge's Division."

"Surrender you!" he said.

"Why. I'm a reb," our man said quite innocently.

"Yes, but I'm a Yank," said the reb.

The reb was taken in, the only prisoner who was captured.

The crossing of the plains into the town itself in the back head was a foot race. Rebs on every side but one. I do not take any credit for myself on this fight for I was with the reserve (what was left of it) and moved back as the wings were swept away (though I thought it was nearly as deadly a place as I had seen with balls cutting the dirt around my horse's legs from every direction) but of the regiment I must say they fought like bulldogs and all say they would rather go through two Cold Harbors than over such a place although our loss was the same in nearly both places.

The enemy is said to be in a force of 70,000 with which of course we have no business—Longstreet, Breckinridge and Gordon. We have not seen a newspaper or a letter since Sunday.

Here comes Alanson and I must stop to hear the news.

[Added later]

I enclosed a newspaper picked up on the 15th of August here. In it, Colonel Penrose is reported to have told General Wright he believed if he had two more regiments he could have whipped them. Said the General: "You don't think you could whip their [whole] Corps?"

Penrose said we could have.

August 21 (Near Charlestown)

Rainy. About 8 A.M. we were suddenly amused by the enemy advancing in force. It seems our pickets first fired into their column moving by the flank as though unsuspicious of danger. A Massachusetts regiment was on the picket line armed with Spencers [rifles] and the racket they made was our first alarm.

The rebels closed in on our lines and then a few shells came in over us. Our skirmishers were seen coming in on the double quick but a regiment or two were sent out to hold the line and it was re-established. We set to work at once throwing up a breastwork of rails. The fighting continued all day.

Col. Campbell was corps officer of the day and Major Boeman Division officers of the day (the latter I understood selected by General Wright, not because it was his turn, Col. C being already detailed from the Brigade, but because he was a man who would answer best in the emergency). Col. Cornish was in command of the regiment. Some 30 of the 10th were in our line and nine were wounded.

At midnight, we fell in to fall back and marched through Charlestown as the day was breaking.

September 2

🖋 [Court-martial. Lt. Frank Marley, Fourth New Jersey, pleaded guilty to drunkenness and was cashiered.

THE WAR: John Hunt Morgan, along with Mosby, was one of the South's most important raiders. Operating with a fast-moving cavalry, Morgan struck federal forces again and again in Tennessee and Kentucky and even raided towns in the North, in Ohio and Indiana, doing considerable damage and capturing thousands of prisoners.

The dashing, flamboyant leader was captured in 1863 and put under heavy guard at a state prison in Columbus, Ohio. His legend grew when he and others engineered a bold escape by digging a long, narrow tunnel under the walls of the fort. They evaded captors until they rejoined the Confederate Army. On June 19, 1864, Union forces received word that Morgan was about to rejoin his men in Greeneville, Tennessee. A small force sneaked into town early in the morning and waited for him. Morgan was shot dead in the ambush as he rode into town.]

September 4

🖋 [LESSLAND PLANTATION: A frantic Millie Halsey, who had
girls to their grandfather's in New Jersey in the spring,
junior from her plantation via the "flag of truce" arra
armies used so families on opposite sides of the war cou]
It was one of the very few letters that got through to F

My Dear Brother,

    I drop a line by flag of truce to inquire where Fannie and Annie are, and how they are. I have heard nothing from these dear children since June 22 and feel very solicitous to know their welfare. Hope they are well and under your care and protection. Please attend to their wants and supply them with whatever may be necessary for their comfort and promote their advancement, and keep an account of their bills which will be promptly paid whenever communications are restored.

    All well and quiet at Lessland. Your brother is temporarily near home, and well. Give our love to all the family and write us by flag of truce, directed to Rapidan Station.

Your affectionate sister,
Millie

[Millie received a return letter from Sam junior within a week, saying that the girls had arrived safely and were fine.]

14

THE END IS AT HAND

September 19–November 8, 1864

[The prospects of Union victory in the long, hot summer of 1864 were grim. Union campaigns in Mississippi and Louisiana, under way since 1862, had bogged down. Grant's May-June offensive in Virginia was a stalemate. Northerners complained bitterly that Grant had become a butcher, pressing the bloody Wilderness campaign, which, in a month, brought no real victories and a staggering fifty thousand casualties. The savage fighting at Spotsylvania and Cold Harbor had stunned even hardened supporters of the Union. At Spotsylvania, Halsey's Fifteenth New Jersey Volunteers suffered the second-highest losses of any regiment in the war, 116 killed out of 432 men, or 26 percent of the regiment (only the losses of the First Minnesota at Gettysburg, 28 percent, were higher). Grant then moved on Petersburg and had been stuck outside it for months. Some newspapers began calling for a truce of some kind. The chances for victory in the summer of 1864 were so slim that some aides urged Abraham Lincoln to declare a state of national emergency so he could suspend the election of 1864, which they feared he would lose.

His closest advisers and friends were afraid Lincoln would not only lose, but be badly beaten, especially since he adamantly refused the pleas of many moderate politicians to withdraw the Emancipation Proclamation, which they thought would bring the entire Republican Party down. Orville Browning, instrumental in helping him get elected in 1860, told friends Lincoln was "a failure" as president. Thurlow Weed, one of his top strategists in 1860, told everyone within earshot that Lincoln would be a one-term executive. "Mr. Lincoln's reelection is an impossibility," he said, shrugging. Horace Greeley, the influential editor of the New York *Tribune,* felt the election was over before it began. "Mr. Lincoln is already beaten," he said. "He cannot be elected. We need a new ticket."

The president realized how unpopular the war—and he—had become. Grim and gaunt from four years of war, Lincoln was certain that he would lose the election and in August wrote a note to himself in which he predicted defeat and promised to help the new president hold the country together during the transition period.

That new president, he knew, would be none other than Gen. George McClellan, the army commander he had fired. McClellan's remarkable popularity not only endured after his firing, but grew. In August 1864, the Democrats nominated him for president and called for a cessation of hostilities because the war was not winnable. The Democrats wanted peace under McClellan, who vowed to give it to them. The Democrats were certain that McClellan would carry most Union states by majorities and that he would win 80 to 90 percent of the more than 1 million votes of men in the army.

The war's fortunes turned dramatically as summer faded into autumn, however. After two weeks of fighting, naval admiral David Farragut gained control of Mobile Bay, Alabama, on August 23, bottling up the seaport of Mobile, the last operational port the South had on the Gulf of Mexico, cutting off all supplies that came through that port to much of the Confederacy. The blockade of Southern ports on the Atlantic, more effective as time went by, had, by September 1864, put a stranglehold on Confederate shipping there. England, which Southern leaders had tried to tug into the war on their side, remained staunchly noncommittal.

Most importantly, Sherman captured Atlanta, Georgia, a major city deep in the heart of the Old South, and the Confederacy's railroad hub, on September 2. The capture of Atlanta was not just the taking of a city, but a sign that the North could move wherever it wanted and win and that it could send an entire army deep into the heart of the South to strike any city. It was a military victory, but also an enormous political victory.

Then, finally, in early August, Gen. Philip Sheridan was given command of the newly created Middle Military Division—forty-eight thousand men—and ordered to cleanse Virginia's entire Shenandoah Valley of Confederates. The Shenandoah, a gorgeous valley with its sloping hills, thick forests, early-morning mists, and hundreds of clear, crisp, meandering creeks, had been the foundation of the Confederates' eastern campaigns since the beginning of the war, the stronghold of the late Stonewall Jackson. The valley ran southwest and northeast and was reached via dozens of narrow mountain gaps the rebels knew intimately. The Confederates had used it to move in and out of Virginia and into and out of Maryland, to attack Washington, D.C., and to burn the small Pennsylvania town of Chambersburg. It was protected by the rolling Blue Ridge Mountains, and its hills and thick foliage provided safe hideaways for various guerrilla bands, including the highly effective Mosby's Rangers. The Shenandoah, one of the most fertile valleys in America, also served as the granary of the South. Its food and wheat supplied the Confederate Army throughout the war. Its farms provided animals for meat. Some Southerners felt that no matter how badly the war went, their armies could always hold out in the gentle embrace of the Shenandoah. If Sheridan and his newly formed army, which included the VI Corps and Edmund Halsey and the Fifteenth New Jersey Volunteers, could boot the Confederates under Early from the Shenandoah, they would eliminate all future campaigns out of it against the North, clean out the troublesome guerrillas, and starve the rebel army all at the same time.

Sheridan arrived in the valley in mid-August and sparred with the enemy in a number of small engagements as he drew up a battle plan. Sheridan was reluctant to launch any major attack because military intelligence told him that Early had forty thousand men. Intelligence was wrong. Early only had twenty-three thousand men in the valley and only twelve thousand at Winchester. Early, not knowing Sheridan was ordered to act defensively because of the miscalculation, had little respect for Sheridan, who he said showed no enterprise, and waited while the quick-stepping, bantam general maneuvered around the valley. Finally, in mid-September, Sheridan, now knowing Early had fewer men, met with Grant and outlined a plan to defeat the Confederates. Sheridan was convinced that he should move down the pike in the middle of the valley to get south of the Confederates, who were apparently taking a stand near Opequon Creek, at Winchester. He wanted to hit the rebels there at Winchester with everything he had and drive them out of the valley. He had forty-eight thousand men, extensive supplies, artillery, and some of the best cavalry units in the army under Custer and Averell. After listening to Sheridan talk for a long time in an energetic and animated fashion, his hands constantly gesturing in the autumn air, Grant pulled his ever-present cigar out of his mouth and made a quick decision. "Go in," he told Sheridan.

On the morning of September 19, at Winchester, Sheridan's army, with Ed Halsey's company in the middle of it, went in.]

September 19

Winchester. Clear & Warm.

Review at 3, never at 4. Crossed the Opequon Creek about 9. Charged (second line) at noon. Fell exhausted at 3 and caught up with regiment at Winchester at dark.

Moving westward from the Opequon up a ravine. Twice had a few flankers within range to sight. Arriving at a place when a little hollow came in from the South. [There was] an [area] ahead covered by wood. We lay down. The lines advanced and shot and shell flew around and over us. Directly, we moved up this hollow and to the right, by the flank, into this cover, Colonel Campbell and myself leading. Here the regiment was brought up and by the command "charge front forward in full Company," which it executed handsomely. We were now exposed to a terrific shell fire. I suggested to Col. Campbell going on into the open with the regiment as the ground was better there than where we were. We did go (while I was talking with Colonel C his pants were torn with a shell), coming out of the thick of the woods, we saw the 3rd division way ahead of us on the left. We lay down for a few minutes only.

The men advanced in line of battle, crossing the pike diagonally to the north side. Here we met Gen. David Russell, who, howling aloud, ordered Col. Campbell to "clear the enemy out of that cornfield." We could have done it where we stood but Col. C. ordered us forward into the cornfield. We went about down a little hill and up another to the edge of the field and there commenced firing (I saw Clift wounded and one or two others as we were going down this descent).

All at once we heard a rebel yell and close to us over on our right, Rebs appeared resting their rifles on a rail fence and firing into us at half a dozen yards (the 19th Corps occupying that flank had fallen back, which we could not see on account of the wood. They were afterwards rallied by Sheridan in person who rode ahead of them into the fight).

We were there a mere moment. Cornish hesitated a few minutes and then commanded us back. Milligan, of company "F," was killed here. I got as far back as the high knoll and stopped, seeing a line of 3rd division coming up. A solid shot sliced into the ground in front of me and bouncing plumb over my head killed a man behind me. General Russell was killed to my right. [Russell was shot in the chest earlier in the day but concealed it from everyone. He was killed by an exploding shell five yards from Halsey.]

It was now 3 P.M. and I was played out. Capt. Crater and I went back to the woods and got something to eat and leaving them there, I followed the regiment (which had been back in this woods while I was still in front and came up in two detachments). At camp, Col. Campbell abused me at first for not keeping up in the afternoon. It was then that more men [came] and I did not agree. I was the first man through the woods and the first into the cornfield.

In going back, our men captured a number of prisoners who had gotten around us in our rear. The regiment was not together after the charge in the cornfield and individuals had their own experiences. Earle, Harold and another man lay behind a pile of rails. A shell struck it, killing the unnamed man, wounding Harold and making Earle quit.

The regiment camped that night at the northern outskirt of Winchester.

🦶 [The attack of Halsey's men at the cornfield, just before Russell was killed, was critical. The attack went right into the heart of the Confederate advance and pushed it back. It was one of the rallying points of the day. Gen. Emory Upton cited the entire regiment for bravery. Earlier, dozens of Union wagons and ambulances on the pike had slowed the Union attack, forcing soldiers to walk in fields and over hillsides, and prevented the XIX Corps from taking its position next to the VI Corps. The Confederates poured into the gap and moved across the cornfield, where they were stopped by the Fifteenth New Jersey. In the afternoon, the Union Army pushed Early's men back to the east of Winchester, when Sheridan sent in cavalry under Merritt and Averell to rout them. Early ordered a full retreat shortly after 5 P.M. and took his men down the pike to Strasburg, where he would stage another defense at Fisher's Hill. He was followed by the Federals. Of 37,711 men in the fight, Sheridan lost 5,018 (697 killed, 3,983 wounded, 338 missing). Early took the field with 12,150 men. His casualties were 3,921 (276 killed, 1,827 wounded, and 1,818 missing—over 1,000 captured). The defeat of Early, and the start of the chase of his army through the valley, with subsequent engagements at a half dozen villages, was hailed as a major victory by the press.]

September 20.

Clear. Marched through Winchester, Newtown, Middletown, to hill overlooking Strasburg 18 miles, reaching there about 3 P.M. and overtaking the enemy there. Rebel flags captured from the enemy were carried in triumph behind the different generals and all were in high spirits over the victory.

September 21

We had 100 men on picket this morning (under Major Cornish). About half past one, we marched off to the west a mile or two and advanced against Fisher's Hill. We had six companies in line, each being deployed. We lay for a time behind a little knoll and right on a woods. A cleared field was in front. Our pickets pursued the enemy closely and balance of regiments relieved the others.

Our casualties: Killed: Brewer, Brown; Wounded: Buck, Moser, Voorhees, Corwin, Miller, Wright; missing: Hawk, Sidener, Strait, Staats.

[Major Cornish, stunned but unbloodied, survived.

Sheridan planned a two-stage assault on the heights of Fisher's Hill, just outside Strasburg, which looked impregnable to most of his officers. He ordered a frontal charge of the XIX and VI Corps (the Fifteenth New Jersey) to be aided by a surprise, late-afternoon flanking charge from Gen. George Crook aimed at the most inexperienced troops in Early's lines. The Fifteenth New Jersey was positioned at the left center of a line of attack directly in front of the hill in the morning in an effort to soften up the enemy. The men, pinned down early, wound up in the middle of what became a desperate battle that lasted all day. They were not able to push the Confederates back at all until Crook's men, howling and screaming, charged in the afternoon.]

September 22

Fisher's Hill. Clear.

At midnight, the regiment was moved to the right into the wood and to the front and proceeded to dig a rifle pit, the enemy being very near our front. Lay in the rifle pit all day, the pickets in front keeping up a hot fire nearly continually—the enemy occasionally exploding a shell in the wood in front.

At 3 P.M., the lines were ordered forward—our regiment in the second line. We moved forward in line of battle to about the edge of the wood. From a road on our right flank we could see clear fields to the front. Every shot fired by the enemy passed over us and among us—we were so scared—but no big loss was experienced. Davis was slightly wounded with a shell. Cornish came in from the picket to us here.

Later, from the far (or even) side of the cleared field ahead of us rebels were seen running and behind them Crook's men cheering and pursuing. At once the whole line went forward. As we approached, the rebels ran, leaving guns in position. Crossing the woods, we wheeled to the left and advanced rapidly diagonally towards the pike and across the fields. The plain was covered with men fleeing and pursuing—our men seemed wild with excitement. But our Brigade preserved their order and was about the only one that did. It was dark when we reached the pike back of the rebel position. Here the "crowd" was re-organized—8th Corps this way, 6th Corps this way and each to different sides of the pike. Our Brigade was at the front and in order, ready to repulse any attack of the enemy while our men were in disorder. But they did not think of such a thing.

One officer of the 4th had been under arrest for some little escapade (and had his sword taken away). I remembered him rushing along with a handkerchief tied around his head where he had been slightly wounded, brandishing a hickory stick, cheering and shouting with all his might. His sword was given to him the next day I believe. Men seemed wild with joy and enthusiastic and men of the 8th Corps were warmly cheered by the 6th for the important part they had played.

After a time spent organizing we moved on continually to Woodstock, which [we reached] at daylight.

✍ [Fisher's Hill was a significant defeat for the Confederates. Not only were they beaten badly for the second time in four days and pushed farther up the valley, but they suffered 1,235 casualties, lost 12 pieces of artillery—overrun by Halsey and his regiment—and watched as the Federals took another 1,000 prisoners. Union losses were 528, with only 52 killed.

THE WAR: Lincoln asked Postmaster General Montgomery Blair to resign in order to gain the support of the Radical Republicans in the upcoming election. Blair was replaced with Ohio's Republican governor, William Dennison.]

September 24

Hot. Advanced about 8 and for a time saw nothing of the enemy. At Mount Jackson we came upon their hospitals. They were still in force. From the high ground in which Mt. Jackson is located we could look across a level flat, around which swept the Shenandoah, and see the rebels on the hill beyond. Our artillery practiced on them with some little effect but their right was turned by our cavalry and we were set in motion across the plain, halting once or twice in line of battle at right angles to the pike.

(Averell we heard was superseded by order of General Sheridan for not attacking some or all on the enemy's right. It was the second time Averell was superseded.)

Once across this plain, we fell in [behind the rebels] in full retreat and we pursued them till dark through New Market and Sparta... in all, twenty miles.

This advance was one of the magnificent sights of the war. From the top of the hill we could see their long lines of battle stretching across the valley and moving away from us. Passing men cleared our ploughed fields. Their lines could hardly be distinguished from the ground save by the flashes of their musket barrels in the sun. Behind the lines of battle were their skirmish lines which a line of our cavalry skirmishers continually attacked. Behind the cavalry skirmish line was an infantry line of skirmishers and when the first line was checked it immediately came up and the rebels moved on. Behind the infantry skirmishers was the long black first line of our infantry, behind which was the second line moving by the sight of regiments in the front ready to swing into line. Our artillery ran out to the skirmish line and was occasionally responded to by two or three guns the rebs had. At dark, the enemy seemed to make a stand. We formed new lines and were asked to attack when they moved up again and we went into camp.

September 25

We found the churchyard where Tom Haines [Alanson's brother] was buried by his men in 1862, one of the citizens showing us his grave. They all seemed to know of the Union officer who was killed at the time. The grave was marked "Capt. Thomas R. Haines, Co. M, 1st N.J. Cav., June 6, 1862."

Alanson had of course found the place before us and seeing a proper box, the coffin was battened up still and in excellent preservation. Capt. Seder, a division ordnance officer, made room for it with the supply train should it arrive. [Alanson obtained ten days' leave from September 26 and left September 28 with the remains for New Jersey.]

At night, the appearance of the camps lying all about the town from our hill was beautiful, like that of a great city.

🖋 [In the fall of 1864 both armies were full of new recruits, and some gave the war a dark and sinister side, making it hard to determine who was the real enemy, evident from Halsey's letter home the next day.]

September 26 (Harrisonburg, Va.)
My dear cousin,
 A few minutes ago one of our men was brought in with his throat partially cut. He had been out for apples and some men attacked him from behind, attempted to murder him and took some $300 he had with him. The wound is not considered mortal but the affair is not a pleasant one. He thinks they were citizens who attacked him but I guess it was some of our own men. Possibly men of my own regiment who knew him to have money—his recent bounty. The new men [include] some hard men among substitutes and recruits.

🖋 [The cavalry continued to chase Early's men through the Shenandoah through the end of September and into early October, defeating the Confederates at Port Republic, Weyer's Cave, and Brown's Gap. Halsey and the men of the Fifteenth were moved from town to town, but did little more than wait.

 THE WAR: Centralia, Missouri, was looted and burned by the guerrilla band of Bloody Bill Anderson. The guerrillas, who included Jesse and Frank James, the notorious Old West outlaws after the war, killed twenty-four unarmed federal troops in town and later ambushed a federal regiment chasing them, killing 116.]

September 30 (Mt. Crawford)
 Showers. Put up my desk and went to work at monthly returns, judging from appearances that we would stay some time in camp. Our men were out foraging and some of them I am afraid pillaging.
 Had just completed the tabular back of the returns when an aide came up and said "We move at once, your regiment leads."

🖋 [In late September, Grant ordered Sheridan to destroy everything he could in the Shenandoah to prevent it from ever supplying the Confederates again ("We want the Shenandoah valley to remain a barren waste") and, some charged, in revenge for the burning of Chambersburg in July.

Sheridan followed Grant's orders. His men stole livestock, burned barns and fields. Soldiers and war correspondents reported that for weeks the army saw columns of smoke wherever it went, the signature of Sheridan's burning of the valley. On October 6, Sheridan wrote to Grant that by then he had destroyed "over 2000 barns filled with wheat, hay and farming implements; over 70 mills . . . have driven off 4,000 heads of stock and killed not less than 3000 sheep." Merritt's cavalry alone, sent to ravage nearby Loudon County, burned 1,200 barns, 7 furnaces, 4 tanneries, 1 railroad depot, 71 flour mills, 1 woolen mill, 8 sawmills, 1 powder mill, and 3 saltpeter works and destroyed 947 miles of railroad. His men captured or destroyed 3,772 horses, 545 mules, 10,198 beef cattle, 12,000 sheep, 15,000 swine, 435,802 bushels of wheat, 20,397 tons of hay, 2,500 bushels of potatoes, 450 tons of straw, and 874 barrels of flour.

Thousands of civilians in the area, plus hundreds of children, their farms destroyed and suddenly homeless, trudged along after the Union Army as it moved through the Shenandoah, alongside hundreds of freed slaves. Sheridan's army became a seemingly endless caravan of civilians, white and black, tagging along on a road to nowhere. At one point over four hundred wagons full of people followed the army in a dreary exodus away from their burning farms.]

October 2 (Harrisonburg)

🖋 [Halsey's letter to his sister reflected his feeling that the war would soon end but shows his disgust at the way his own army pillaged the Shenandoah Valley. Then he switched to a lighthearted note to his brother about his grand plans to buy a new jacket.]

My Dear Sister Sue,

This has been anything but a quiet Sunday for us. The paymaster came last night and has been paying off the Brigade today, making every one work though being paid is not unpleasant work. There came the sound of cannonading to the southwest gradually causing noise until it finally ceased at dark. Orders were received to be in readiness to move at short notice and horses were harnessed for any emergency. With the paymaster came the mail and supplies which they have been issuing all day. I was fortunate enough to receive two letters—one from Anne and yours enclosing the tobacco pouch and written I imagine about the time we were "going in" at Winchester on the 19th. Accept my thanks for this and for the *Observor* which came with it.

As yet, we have received no letters written since the battles of the 19th and 22d and feel quite anxious to hear of their effect on popular feeling in the North. Through military telegrams we received Grant's and [Secretary of War Edwin] Stanton's congratulations and last night the news of a victory by the 10th and 18th corps on the Peninsula. I fear so much good fortune will turn the heads of our leaders and the people while our shrewd and yet powerful foe may from his defeats sap still great advantages. Much has yet to be done, but if Grant could as thoroughly demoralize Lee's Army as is that of Early here I would believe that Providence had unmistakably declared itself for us and that the end is at hand. We feel it impossible that slavery and secession will eventually succeed, but no one can tell how much longer we will be tried.

It was a great sight to see the battle of Winchester and the subsequent pursuit. I never saw troops feel better than ours or an army in more complete rout than the rebels. The citizens here seem ashamed of their own men. Many refugees, both black and white, accompany our trains towards the North, alas feeling that this country, beautiful and productive as it is, is no place to live in.

Thursday, we marched down to Mount Crawford and came back Friday. Our cavalry is, they say, going beyond Staunton. As usual, our stragglers covered the country for miles, bringing in forage, sheep, chickens and grain. I cannot pity the small pack of the sufferers much but I am sorry for the women and children who have taken no part in the treason. Soldiers come in lugging honey, pots of preserves, clothes, and many houses are completely "gone through." Everything which they seem to think can be made of use and they are able to carry, they bring in. The rest they demolish. Beds and women's apparel are ruthlessly torn up and the houses ransacked from cellar to garret. Surely, we have no right to act the Pharisee while we sympathize with the people of Chambersburg. Sometimes vengeance follows speedily and the man who works to satisfy his cupidity is gobbled by guerillas and his fate depends entirely upon the humor and nature of his captors. It is said Averell's cavalry had orders when he fell back to burn every mill and grain barn in his route and leave the country as much a wilderness as possible.

It is also said that strong reinforcements have been received by the enemy and in that case our stay here will be short. It is now all but impossible to obtain rations for our force and the many gaps in the Blue Ridge expose our rear to risk of being cut off. No reinforcements of any account have been received by us and there is no object gained by remaining here much longer unless it is the intention to go on to Lynchburg, which it will take a much larger army to do.

October 4 (Harrisonburg)

Finished Col. C's ordnance repairs by working all day and in the evening played whist as we did the night before.

Every building within five miles was burned by order of Sheridan by the murder by guerillas of Col. John Meigs.

🖎 [Meigs, just twenty-two, was one of the boy wonders of the Union. He was the son of Quartermaster General Montgomery Meigs and also an engineer who had graduated at the head of his class at West Point in 1863. He was brevetted for bravery at Winchester and Fisher's Hill. Meigs was a protégé of both Sheridan and Grant. Sheridan told the army Meigs had been murdered and ordered buildings within five miles burned to the ground in revenge. Later, it was learned that Meigs was killed in a fair fight with some Confederate scouts.]

October 6.

Started at 5:30 A.M. and marched till half past five in the afternoon with only a few needed halts to the hill south of Mount Jackson and between it and New Market (about half way).

As we moved along the pike or by the side of it, our cavalry swept either side to the mountains burning barns and driving sheep and cattle. Smoke was seen far southward. As usual, many black and white refugees accompany our trains. Men rested at night for tomorrow. 1/4 rations hard tack. 1/2 ration pork, and three coffee and sugar.

October 8

Very cold with rain in gusts. Left camp at 8 and reached camp between Strasburg and the river about noon, passing over the rebel position of the 21st which we now flanked.

From three o'clock until dark there was cannonading at our rear—which we supposed was the enemy following up our cavalry.

Received a mail and wrote the girls. Five days rations were issued. Reported 224 men for duty.

October 9

Union Cavalry under Custer and Merritt attacked and crushed Confederate cavalry at Tom's Brook, near Middletown, taking 300 prisoners.

🖎 [Custer and Merritt were, with the South's J.E.B. Stuart, the best cavalry officers in the war. George Armstrong Custer was one of the flashiest figures in the conflict. Aggressive, brave, and charismatic, he was one of the most decorated men in the army. He was promoted up through the ranks quickly and became a general at twenty-three. Fearless in battle, he was wounded once and had eleven horses shot out from under him. His panache increased after the war when he was with the Seventh Cavalry in the West. There, as in the Civil War, peers and superiors worried that he was not as composed as he should be when in command of large units. The impulsive Custer was killed and a large part of his regiment wiped out with him at the Battle of the Little Big Horn in 1876.

Wesley Merritt began the war as a twenty-six-year-old lieutenant in the cavalry and ended it as a much decorated general. He went on to serve his country all his life. Merritt stayed in the army after the war and participated in the Indian Wars before becoming superintendent of the U.S. Military Academy at West Point. He returned to the service for the war in the Philippines in 1898 and received the surrender of that country along with Admiral Dewey. He served as military governor of the Philippines for several years. He retired in 1900 after forty years in the military.]

October 10 (Strasburg)

Cold and windy. I am trying to keep comfortable (fires only burning on our side; while the other side froze).

Attended services in the afternoon.

Cannonading to the southward as yesterday but in the morning. At noon, it died away. It seems that yesterday General Torbert reported to General Sheridan that the enemy was following him up pretty close. Sheridan replied: "A good deal closer now—I like to be followed."

With this, General Torbert acted today and laid a trap for the rebel cavalry, capturing 11 of their 12 guns. General Rosser is said to have gone through Middletown in the morning boasting to the citizens that there would be a charge and that his cavalry from the Army of Virginia would not lose. A few hours later, he rode through that same place chased by a squad of our cavalry on a dead run.

October 11

We camped near Front Royal. I rode out to the top of the hill in front of our camp and took a view of the valley. Front Royal is near the junction of the north and south forks of a river, Manassas Gap and Wapping

Heights, and is near the camp of our Corps. It was one of the prettiest pictures I have seen in this region.

In the evening, I foolishly invested in a horse raffle. [These were quite popular. Men on their way home often raffled off their horse for $1 per chance.]

🖎 [THE WAR: State elections in Pennsylvania, Ohio, and Indiana reflected the victories at Winchester, Fisher's Hill, Mobile Bay, and Atlanta. The supposedly weak Lincoln Republicans (now running as the Union Party), bolstered by a tremendous surge of public hopefulness as the prospects for victory improved sharply, won impressively. Staunch Lincoln supporter Oliver P. Morton was reelected governor of Indiana. Republicans made sizable gains in congressional races in all three states. Newspapers formerly critical of Lincoln began to endorse Republicans. Lincoln, who stayed up all night in the War Department to read election returns, was pleased.]

October 12
    [Letter to Sam]

My dear Brother,

I can send but a line. We came here Monday from Strasburg and tomorrow we will likely be getting out of this, whether we know not. If we go back across the Bull Run Valley to Alexandria, the probability is that Petersburg will be our final destination, which our experience paints in anything but glowing colors. What object is to be gained by proceeding farther up the valley or remaining here is not apparent. In short, we are quite in the dark as to what our future movements will be as yourself. Winter is now drawing on fast. The past few days have been very cold—the nights decidedly cold and the sky has the appearance of a coming storm.

Guerillas [Mosby's Rangers] abound in this region. The train which came up tonight brings rumors of the murder of Lt. Col. [Cornelius] Tolles and Dr. [Emil] Ohlenschlager, the latter a splendid officer and man as I know myself. Of course, some of the rascals who follow this business are shot and hung occasionally but every male in the valley will have to be removed before the practice can be stopped.

From the hill in front of our camp is a splendid view: the junction of the north and south forks of the Shenandoah, Manassas Gap and Wapping

Heights, Front Royal and Sunay Valley, all combine in one of the prettiest pictures I have yet seen in this region.

You must have received my letter from Harrisonburg, and the money sent by Major Durith. If convenient, I wish you would send me about 1/2 yards more of the flannel like my shirt in order to make an addition. Tell the girls I will keep the cotton stockings for a month or more, if not all winter. Alanson may perhaps have seen you in time to send my clothes by him but I can hardly hope for that. Our sutler came up with tobacco and other necessaries tonight and from the looks of his wagon I reckon he will have little to take back. The boys are flush and hungry, i.e. for sutlers goods.

✒ [THE WAR: In Washington, D.C., Chief Justice Roger B. Taney, author of the Dred Scott decision, died.]

October 13

Cold.

Lay "in readiness" till ten, when our regiment and brigade was the last to move. Marched through Neurock (four or five small duty houses) and turned off from the Winchester Pike (about ten miles from here and nine from Front Royal) about noon. Passed through White Post and halted for the night at Neilwood after a march of 15 miles.

We were at the foot of the Blue Ridge and expected to cross in the morning but hardly had we made supper when we received orders to move back to Front Royal, the enemy having reappeared in force at Fisher Hill.

✒ [THE WAR: Maryland voters approved a new state constitution, which called for the abolition of slavery.]

October 16

Camped near Middletown. Cold and blustering. Regimental inspection at 9 and in the afternoon a large number of recruits and convalescents arrived.

✒ [The new recruits Halsey mentioned arrived in huge numbers. The tremendous infusion of fresh troops in 1864 was one of the major reasons the war became winnable for the North. The South, by the fall of 1864, had almost no fresh recruits and soaring desertion rates.]

October 17

🖋 [In letters that night, Halsey wrote of the beauty of Cedar Creek, not knowing that the area would be the scene of one of the war's bloodiest battles.]

October 19

Battle of Cedar Creek.

🖋 [Told that Sheridan was out of the area, Early, with a carefully drawn battle plan, decided to attack the Union forces at daylight with divisions led by Ramseur, Pegram, and Gordon. The Federals were taken by surprise and apparently routed.]

Under our orders the Brigade was moved before daylight and stood, each regiment by its color lined up in the darkness. Men shivering with the cold until objects about grew distinguishable and when it became broad daylight . . . the men sent to make their coffee (had the other Corps had or observed the same order, the fate of the battle might have been different).

After we had broken ranks, the picket firing became louder and louder to the East. It soon became alarming. I put very loose wraps on my valise, despite Dr. Hall's saying "it was nothing." I was none too soon. Directly the bugle blew and Col. Penrose called to "pack up." The valises and tents were hurled into the Regimental or Brigade wagons which were rushed to the rear. The Brigade started at once in the direction of the firing past Sheridan's headquarters (in the field).

The stragglers from the 8th and 19th Corps were now streaming to the rear in columns. The line was formed on the ridge beyond. Here Col. Penrose was under Col. Campbell and Major [Lambert] Bowman was killed [leading a charge]. Falling back, a stand was made back of where our camp was. Going through a piece of woods, John Mouder, carrying the state colors, was killed. No one noticed the loss till too late to get the colors. The enemy did not pursue after this last stand of ours and the division moved by the flank of regiments to the rear.

Suddenly the order was corrected marched and we were marching in the other direction. Col. Paul told the men that General Sheridan had gotten back. We found a line in the wood. The brigade moved as one regiment, no effort being made to distinguish companies. Capt. Hufty commanded. Capt. Penrose, who had been on picket, was now up and commanded the 15th and men back of the line.

We halted here long enough to get something to eat. A regiment of the 19th corps came up and formed on our right. Moved by some impulse, they commenced firing by volley and were with some difficulty stopped. Our pickets were in front of them.

Here came General Sheridan along the line with a word to every part of it.

"It's all right, we'll flank 'em" or "We can't be beat" or "You'll be back in your old camps tonight" he would yell.

The men cheered.

About four, the advance was made down through the woods—at the edge of it we could see across to a ridge opposite on which were the enemy behind a stone wall. Their fire checked the first lines and the second came up and merged with it.

Across the field and up the hill the line went the enemy firing at it and we were losing some men, but they abandoned the fence before we even reached it.

Gunderman, carrying the colors, was struck in the right shoulder with a solid shot, which broke the staff in splinters, tore off his sleeve and rolled him backward down the hill. But he was up in a moment and seizing the colors, went ahead with the charge.

The rest of the advance was like the evening at Fisher's Hill on the 22d of September. The whole plain seemed covered with running men. At night fall the only possible order was for every man to find his camp of the morning.

Around at our old camp, fires were built. Large pots of coffee were made and the wounded were searched for and limped in. I think 17 of the badly wounded were around our fires that night. Dr. Hall dressed their wounds and I sought to make them comfortable. It was near morning when the work was done. And yet with the exception of one man, who was shot in the head and became unconscious, dying before morning—I did not hear a groan or word of complaint from one of them.

Wounded were Colonels Penrose and Campbell [his entire left arm was shattered and he was sent home to recuperate and, even though he did not have to return, was back in January], Captains Davis, Travis, Crater, Bullock and Williams. Major Boeman was killed. We had nine killed, 50 wounded and 48 missing. We had 150 men left (this report was corrected afterwards).

[Cedar Creek was the scene of the legendary "Sheridan's Ride." The Union general, at headquarters in Winchester after his quick trip to

Washington and certain Early would not attack, stopped eating breakfast when he heard cannons in the distance, from the direction of Cedar Creek. He and his adjutant raced to their horses and began to ride toward the sounds. Just a half mile outside of town, Sheridan encountered the first of the soldiers retreating from what appeared to be a terrible defeat at Cedar Creek. He encountered hundreds more retreating men as he rode hard up the pike. Taking off his cap and waving it in the air, his fabled horse Rienzi at full gallop, he rallied them: "Face the other way, boys!" "We are going back!"

The soldiers, shocked to see their commander riding among them like a cheerleader, began to shout, "Sheridan! Sheridan!" and turned and moved back toward the fight. Sheridan made it to the battlefield, hundreds of men following him, at 10 A.M. to find most of his army in retreat. Grabbing the reins of Rienzi and waving his hat, he raced from regiment to regiment, constantly exposed to enemy fire, exhorting the men to turn and fight. Halsey was just one of the men he rode past and galvanized that morning in what became a piece of military lore.

"It's all right, boys, we will whip 'em yet!" he yelled above the din of the battle. The regiments turned and, with Sheridan leading them, cheered and roared, their shouts heard miles away. The Union Army turned back into battle, Sheridan under fire in front, and won one of the most dramatic victories of the war. Sheridan's ride was quickly turned into a poem, which was printed in hundreds of newspapers and recited on theater stages and in schools from coast to coast. Dozens of people wrote about Sheridan's ride, including novelist Herman Melville. The most famous poem was written by Thomas Buchanen Read.

CSA general Stephen Ramseur was one of the South's best and youngest generals. He was wounded twice before the battle of Cedar Creek. He was mortally wounded at Cedar Creek, just a day after his wife of a year had written him that she was going to have a baby.

THE WAR: Rumors flew in Washington that the Democrats would seize the federal government the day after the election if McClellan won and not wait until the legal inauguration on March 4.]

October 20

Camp at battlefield, Cedar Creek. Cloudy.

Orders came to move at daybreak, but we did not move. We stood in readiness all day. The 19th Corps went forward and occupied Fisher's Hill.

Our wounded were being taken away in ambulances all day, the last going about 4 P.M. After our own were taken we sent Major Kyle of Baltimore, inspector general of (C.S.A.) Gordon's staff, who was badly wounded and had been taken care of by us. Dr. Hall and I gave him our tent and he repaid us by telling what he knew of the battle. He knew Gill of our class well.

Charley Hall and I went over in the afternoon to see the "trophies." In one line were 47 pieces of artillery [and] close by them were 30 wagons. Some of our own, some high backed farm wagons and ambulances with 2d and 3rd Corps badges were there, and about 1,000 prisoners.

✒ [The fight ended for Kyle at Cedar Creek. The major was eventually taken back to Baltimore to recover. By the time his wounds had healed, the war was over. Kyle never forgot the kindness of the men of the Fifteenth, though, and was in the crowd that greeted them as they marched through Baltimore at the end of the war. Kyle played host to several soldiers from the Fifteenth that night.

Several men who had been in the regiment from its first lusty day of muster back in Flemington died in the Shenandoah campaign. Charles Milligan, who had enlisted at eighteen, was badly wounded in the charge at Spotsylvania and could have gone home but refused. He returned to duty and was killed September 19. Joe Moser, the thirty-six-year-old Tennessee carpenter who was drafted by the Confederate Army and deserted to join the Union, was badly hurt on September 19 and had his leg amputated a few days later. He died in October.]

October 21

Cloudy but raw.

Our state color which was captured on the 19th and recaptured by the 4th cavalry, Custer's division, and was presented to the regiment. Speeches were made by General Wheaton, General Torbert and Custer. The regiment presented a sorry look. Gunderman was in line with his blouse half torn off and holding the other color by its shattered staff. In all, the [speakers] only spoke [well] of the regiment and no blame was attached to them.

I note this same day: Loses stand at 13 killed, 58 wounded, 13 missing. We went in with 250 and we stand now at 178 present for duty. The Brigade had present 25 officers, 100 new officers and 403 men. Aggregate 528.

A subscription taken up for expenses for sending Major Boeman's body home. Capt. Penrose, Capt. Davis, Capt. Haines, Dr. Hall, Adj. Halsey, several men: each $8, Lt. Cole and Lt. Nicholas each $4 = $80 (Lt. Law, Antwerp, Kline and Ivers: nothing).

🖎 [Early's army withdrew from the Shenandoah for good after the battle of Cedar Creek.]

October 22
🖎 [At some point in the war, Halsey carefully clipped the lyrics to the hastily published "Battle of Cedar Creek" anthem, written to celebrate the victory there. The song, along with "Sheridan's Ride," made an instant folk hero out of Sheridan. The ditty was clearly written by someone from the VI Corps.]

THE BATTLE OF CEDAR CREEK

Come, all ye followers of the Cross!
  Come hither, every one,
A little story I'll relate
  About Red Cedar Run.
At Cedar Run's fierce battlefield,
  The Eighth Corps ran away,
The Nineteenth broke and left the Sixth
  To bear the brunt that day.

(Chorus:)

In the Shenandoah low lands, low lands,
  In the Shenandoah low lands, low,
Just watch them as I lead their charge
  Fight as a single man,
For God, their country, their cross,
  And Philip Sheridan!

At lst they yield by slow degrees,
  Outflanked, outnumbered far,
Backward they go, swept by the tide
  Of stern, resistless war.
The battle now seems to be lost
  Up rides a single man,

One, but a host within himself,
    Our gallant SHERIDAN!

(Repeat Chorus)

Come up with me, you Nineteenth, Eighth,
    Come up with me, I say.
Why do you lay so far behind
    We have not lost the day,
Come up upon this crest of hill,
    You'll see a glorious sight,
You won't get hurt, you need not fire,
    but see that Sixth Corps fight!

October 24

Cold. In the evening a meeting of the officers of the New Jersey regiments was held at Brigade headquarters to testify our respect to the memory of Major Boeman, one of the bravest and best loved men in the service.

October 25

[Once again, Halsey spent the day as a judge advocate at the brigade court-martial hearings. The board, lenient in the past, was particularly hard on defendants in the two cases heard that morning. One of them was Case X regarding a deserter.]

Case X
Prisoner: Corporal William H. Erwin, Co. "D", 3rd regiment, N.J. Vols.
Charge: Desertion
Plea: Guilty (except as to being in the face of enemy)
Finding: Guilty
Sentence: That he be reduced to the ranks, forfeit to the U.S. all pay and
    allowances now due and $10 per month of the monthly pay which may
    become due him and to make good the time lost by desertion (one year)
    from the time he joined the 15th N.J. Vols for duty.

October 26

Distant cannonading audible during the day to the southward. Wrote Sam.

My dear brother,

The mail leaves this evening at eight and I drop you a line to say if you have not sent me the money I asked for in my last or more than one install-ment of it, I wish you would send your check for $20 to Marcus Ward, Newark, to the credit of Chaplain Haines. I borrowed that much of him today, money he intended to send home for some men. As a general thing, there are always men having funds to send and there is no need of risking the transportation twice. I thought when I wrote you that Alanson would probably go home with the Major's body (Boeman) but the Major's brother-in-law took the remains to New Jersey in his place. I have a bill for services in court martial made out for $37 which I gave Emerson to get cashed and taking his own account of $15 out sent me the balance but I have not seen him since and wrote to him yesterday to return the bills and I would get them cashed myself, if possible. It is not so easy to get the money as it depends on the state of finance of the ass't quartermaster, who pays and is seldom flush.

Yesterday, the officers of the Brigade assembled to pay their respect to the memory of the Major. You may see the resolutions in the *Observor*. The full proceedings will be published in his county papers. His loss is a heavy one in the division and Corps, as well as in the regiment where the absence of the two colonels and him leaves a great void. We have one field officer left in the division and but one Brigadier General in the Corps. General Wheaton commands our division. Col. McKenzie was wounded twice and is no doubt now in Morristown. The command of our Regiment is disputed. Capt. Penrose assumes it but Davis claims seniority and Wheaton has been a week without seeming to care which holds it. Capt. Travis was wounded but he, I hope, will get the majority if anyone. It is said to be a fact that the 40th N.J. is coming to our Brigade. If so, it will relieve our anxiety lest the Brigade should be broken up.

✍ [Halsey was so unhappy with Captain Penrose, the younger brother of Colonel Penrose, that he and several others wrote a letter to superi-ors to prevent his promotion. He was promoted anyway, to the dismay of many.]

Perhaps I wrote you before about it but whether I did or not I must tell you that our state color was recaptured. It was lost in the morning [at Cedar Creek] when the bearer was killed and half the guard wounded. We felt rather sore about it the next morning when along came Custer with a lot of Reb flags and among them our old tattered colors. General Sheridan sent Torbert, Wheaton and Custer to return it and the two men in their speeches so far from censuring the Regiment paid us the highest compliments. Every flag we have had has cost at least a life. The bearer of our first flag was killed at Salem Heights. Rubadeau took it off. Last September, that flag was sent to N.J. and a new one substituted. Rubadeau lost his life in May, 1864, carrying the national color and Mouder, who had just returned from absent—wounded at Spotsylvania—was killed bearing the state color on the 19th [at Cedar Creek]. In the afternoon charge a solid shot struck the staff of the national color and shivered it on the shoulder of its sergeant, making a bruise but no permanent injury. Our losses now took up one officer and 12 men killed. We have 188 muskets still for duty. Battles of Aug. 17, Sept. 19 and Oct. 19—our losses have been about the same, though in the first more were captured and in the last more were killed than usual.

Of course, we do not know what they are going to do with us, but Petersburg still looms up in all its dreary magnificence.

PS: I enclose a reb blank [bullet] which is a curiosity, [a] compound with no elaborate forms.

🖋 [Halsey was much enamored with the flamboyant Custer, as were most of the troops. Custer loved to collect flags. He collected everything he could grab, from flags to guns, and immediately let his superiors and newspaper reporters know of his achievements. This often landed him in trouble. The day after the victory at Cedar Creek, Custer wrote to headquarters that he had captured *all* of the forty-five Confederate cannons the Union Army had obtained there. He then told the *New York Times* the same thing and the story was played prominently in the paper, much to the chagrin of Col. Thomas Devin, whose men had captured twenty-two of the forty-five.

Halsey wrote about the regiment's emotional memorial service for Boeman at great length in one of his articles for the *Hunterdon Republican*.]

The officers of the brigade were assembled this morning to show their respect to the memory of the late Major Lambert Boeman, Fifteenth New Jersey Volunteers, who was killed in the recent engagement while commanding the Tenth New Jersey.

Chaplain Haines arose and said: "A good and brave man has fallen; one that we shall miss from our society, from our councils, and from the battle's front. We come together a band of mourners, and when such a one as Lambert Boeman dies, it is not unmanly for his companions in arms, who have known and loved him as we have, to drop the tear of regret. The sorrow that fills our hearts is not peculiar to us, but is shared by the entire brigade. The soldiers in the ranks honored and loved him and they mourn for him as for a near and dear relative. The same sorrow extends throughout the corps.

"That he was a brave man, we who have seen him in the thickest of the fight cannot doubt. When duty called, he shrank from no exposure; and while the battle raged seemed, as a soldier said to me 'never to think of himself.' He was a true patriot. It was of his own wish that he was present in this campaign. As you know, in the spring he was detailed on duty at Trenton, where he was relieved from the hardships of field service and free from danger. His services there were most valuable, and it was desired to retain him, yet he made application to be returned to his regiment, saying: 'If there's danger to be incurred, I am willing to take my share of it.'

"He had a home and family, which, to one of such warm affections as his, were most attractive. When asked if he had any thought of resigning before his term of service expired, he replied 'not if I am needed here.' He was willing, if his country required it, to remain with those who stand to arms till the blessed morn of peace breaks upon our now distracted land.

"He is dead, yet his death was beautiful and attractive. He fell in the heat of action, with his face to the foe, in the noble discharge of duty. We have sent his remains to his native state, there to sleep beneath the green sod, the sweet and blessed sleep of the patriot, but his spirit has found repose in the bosom of his Father and His God.

"Sad are the desolations of war, and we realize them when thus they come home to us; but by such costly sacrifices as these is our country to be redeemed and saved. In former days the blood of the martyrs was the seed of the Church. God grant that the blood of our brethren who have fallen in this conflict, holy martyrs to liberty and law, may not be spilled in vain. May it be the seed which shall bring to future generations a rich and lasting harvest of prosperity, happiness and independence."

Mr. Proudfit, chaplain Tenth New Jersey, remarked:

"I have been greatly struck with the warm affection with which the Major had inspired the men during the short period in which he had been associated with us. Among my acquaintances I know none more conscientious in the discharge of every duty. He was always ready to sacrifice his personal ease and comfort, when they seemed in the least opposed to the most prompt and efficient execution of his office. On the morning of the battle, he left his breakfast untasted, hurrying out to see his men in readiness, anticipating the call which every one saw could not long be delayed."

—E. D. Halsey

October 27

🖎 [Halsey, an outdoorsman, liked to take long walks through the woods and valleys where the army camped. As a youth, he had explored hundreds of caves in the hilly Rockaway, New Jersey, area, his exploits chronicled in great detail in a 167-page diary he kept at age thirteen. When he heard there were beautiful caves in the Shenandoah, part of the Luray Caverns chain, he took a day off from the war to go exploring with two other soldiers. His love of caves is evident in the lush descriptions he included in a letter to his sisters and again shows his ability to separate himself from the awful war raging around him.]

My Dear Sisters,

I enclose a sketch which I think quite good of army headquarters and the mountains beyond us seen from the door of our tent. The genius who executed it [Pearce] I understand would have drawn more but unfortunately he was detailed to ornament the books of Brigade headquarters.

The day before yesterday, the Doctor [Hall], Alanson and myself went exploring [when] learning of certain extensive caves in the vicinity. The first one we went to was near the picket line. We climbed down a hole about ten feet, then down a passage about thirty feet long and four or five feet wide, coming to a chamber which was perhaps twenty feet by thirty, in some places twenty five feet high. Next we came to a low cave which gradually got lower till we reached a stream of water which rushed through and had evidently done the work of excavation. We afterwards learned that by squeezing through we could have gone two or three hundred yards further but seeing no opening we gave it up and came out. The walls were of limestone but there were no stalactites. We fell in there with an old citizen named Matthews who said he had lost $16 by the war already but who said he was a good union man. He was very amiable and volunteered to show us another. This was on the bank of Cedar Creek which [the bank] rises at this point almost perpendicularly about a hundred feet. The cave was perfectly dry but had no chambers, simply a passage four or five feet wide branching off in spurs which grew impassable after a short distance, the sides almost coming together. It was very high and in places reminded me of the pictures of Weyer's Cave in its formation. Stalactites and stalagmites resembled in shape the ice on a mill dam. I broke off a piece and took it in—it is not very pretty in itself but seems a relic. I have a piece in my valise which a lady of Harrisonburg took from Weyer's Cave.

The whole county seems to be undermined with these caves as they tell us of four or five about here.

The third brigade of our division which has been at Winchester since the battle there came up today, which seems to augur a move. The doctor suggests they have come up to take our places to let the Jersey men go home to vote—the standing joke here [the administration wanted the men to go home and vote for Abe Lincoln]. The rebels are said to be at New Market where they took off after the fight. They will need some more artillery before they try that dodge again.

It is very lonely here without our field officers. Colonel Penrose has gone home. Colonel Campbell is at Winchester and doing well. The Major's body was set home at our expense. He leaves a wife and two children who were very much attached to him as everyone here. His death has made a deep impression and to us who remain his fearless discharge of duty and his patriotism speak in loudest tones for more energy and courage on our part while his example makes a similar fate less grievous to be borne.

I received the testament, also the handkerchiefs, four shirts. I am pretty well off at present and I will try to get along with cotton socks, if I can. They will be better I think. Alanson and I talk of our getting out together in December but for myself I think there is great doubt.

PS: I will send you a little hymn book (from a rebel) which is attractive for its size. It has in it "The Balm of Gilead" hymn.

Added: I thought I had finished my sheet but soon am left to tell you of an incident of guerilla warfare. The major and other officers of the 3rd N.J. down in the valley stopped at the house of an old man who professed to be conservative and with his two daughters entertained them very handsomely. Sometime after, the Major, wounded, made Harper's Ferry in an ambulance. They were attacked by guerillas and the Major was robbed of his watch and other valuables. Some of our cavalry came to the rescue and fought the guerillas and captured some of them away from the secesh. The major recognized his former host. He with seven others were taken out and two were shot and the rest hung.

The mail is waiting and with this story I leave you . . .

🖎 [THE WAR: On October 28, Confederates recaptured the South Side Railroad outside Petersburg against a much larger Union force and would hold it all winter. Twenty-one-year-old naval lieutenant William Cushing torpedoed and sank the Confederate ironclad *Albemarle* at Plymouth, North Carolina.

Confederate cavalry under Gen. Nathan Bedford Forrest captured the Union boat *Mazeppa* with a cargo of nine thousand pairs of shoes and the following day damaged the gunboat *Undine* and captured two Union transports. Forrest then sailed his makeshift "navy" south on the Tennessee River and plagued Federals at Johnsonville, causing $6.7 million in damage.]

November 7
🖎 [By November 7, the Fifteenth New Jersey was inactive, in winter quarters. Halsey spent most of November and December serving as judge advocate in more than a dozen courts-martial, once again carefully keeping records of sentences, which ranged from severe prison terms to the loss of a month's pay.

THE WAR: Confederate president Jefferson Davis, in what would be his last major speech, told the Confederate Congress that the war was still winnable and then recommended that the government purchase slaves from planters for work in the army and suggested that, if needed, they might be used as soldiers and, when the war was won, be given their freedom (earlier efforts to get slaves to volunteer had failed).]

November 8
Cloudy. In Camp.

🖎 [THE WAR: Election day. In one of the most remarkable comebacks in political history, Abraham Lincoln, himself certain of defeat just nine weeks before, was reelected president in a landslide. Lincoln won 55 percent of the popular vote to McClellan's 45 percent and carried every state in the Union except Kentucky, Delaware, and New Jersey. The military vote was heavily Republican. Lincoln won over 90 percent of the soldier vote from many regiments in the field and was the overwhelming favorite of soldiers who who were furloughed to vote in their hometowns. McClellan won 52 percent of the vote in New Jersey and carried Morris County, Halsey's home county. McClellan, who lived in West Orange at the time, stayed in the friendly confines of New Jersey and was elected governor in 1877.]

15

GOING HOME

December 25, 1864–January 20, 1865

[The Fifteenth New Jersey was transferred back to Petersburg in December. Sometime during the train ride to the Union Army camp outside of Petersburg, where Grant's men were still laying siege to the city, Halsey decided it was finally time to leave the army and go home.

Edmund Halsey never tired of the war, and his ardent patriotism never flagged, but by December 1864 he was sick just about every day. The old "soldier's cough," which he had picked up during the first winter of the war, became worse. By the winter of 1864–65 it had weakened him and affected his voice and started to seriously worry him. He was certain he had pleurisy, the illness that had plagued his father all of his life. He was developing severe respiratory problems, chest congestion, and had trouble breathing. A tough soldier to the end, he never checked himself into the hospital. Worse, he constantly received letters from Sam Halsey Sr. that *he* was very sick. His father was running the family farm and business by himself and, at age sixty-eight, was not able to handle it. His wintertime pleurisy was getting worse as he grew older, and the winters of 1862, 1863, and 1864 had been three of the severest ever in New Jersey. Sam senior also had to help his daughter Cornelia care for Anne, who by Christmastime of 1864 was bedridden all day. Sam junior, who used to help, was himself a father now and busy trying to raise his own children and run his growing law practice. Edmund was afraid the workload would kill his father. His father needed him home. He had served his country long and well, and now it was time to serve his family, too.

On December 20, 1864, Ed Halsey, who had lived through Fredericksburg, Chancellorsville, Gettysburg, the Wilderness, Spotsylvania, Cold

Harbor, Petersburg, and the Shenandoah Valley campaign, who had fought for McClellan, Burnside, Hooker, Meade, and Grant, who had been close enough in parades and battles to have seen the eyeballs of both Abraham Lincoln and Robert E. Lee, who had been an eyewitness to Pickett's Charge and Sheridan's Ride, resigned from the United States Army.

Colonel Penrose, who did not want to lose his valuable "temporary" adjutant, turned down the request, but Halsey went over his head, using his many connections at headquarters, and got Capt. Baldwin Hufty to pressure Penrose into changing his mind.

Halsey was given an unusually heavy caseload of courts-martial to try during November and December, thirty-three in all, as the army tried to tighten up discipline. Some of the sentences were harsh, such as a year's jail term for John Scott and a three-year jail term for William Reed, but in many cases Halsey, tired of the war, went out of his way to downgrade the severity of offenses for the soldiers hauled into court.

• Pvt. Henry Zimmerman, sent out to procure food or supplies, wound up being charged with desertion after he was gone fifty-five days. Halsey convinced the court-martial board that Zimmerman was probably unfamiliar with procurement procedures and misunderstood his orders. The board was lenient and merely fined him $30.

• Leander Snider was to be sentenced to three years' hard labor, but Halsey told the board that Snider's record until the offense had been spot-less and that his superiors said that Snider was a man of good character. The board, on Halsey's recommendation, reduced the sentence to three months.

• Lt. John Chandley, charged with conduct prejudicial to good order, was drummed out of the service, but not imprisoned because Halsey asked for a recommendation of mercy, which the board honored.

• George Somers, a sixteen-year-old Pennsylvanian, deserted on May 12, 1864, and was captured on October 16. Halsey pleaded for leniency for the boy, who could have been shot, reminding the board that he was only sixteen and probably did not know what he was doing. They agreed and the sentence was merely a loss of pay for a year.

• Thomas Lanahan had three different courts-martial condensed into one. He was not only charged with desertion, but with disobeying orders and being drunk on duty. His punishment was just the loss of pay for ten months and the carrying of a weighted knapsack in front of the guard-house for ten days.

• Lt. E. G. Weaver sneaked out of his tent on December 1 and went home for three days to see a very sick family member. Halsey recommended leniency, citing "strong inducements," and Weaver's sentence was just a reprimand by his commander.

• Lt. James Hill was tried for disobeying orders, conduct prejudicial to good order, and being drunk on duty. He was kicked out of the army but spared prison time.]

December 25 (Christmas Day)

I wrote Sam of my resignation and to say to the family . . . that my cold is gone, but leaving a cough peculiar to our family and to which I am peculiarly subject in winter.

January 1 (New Year's, 1865) Sunday

I attended church and did little work.

January 4

Snow.

January 6

. . . witnessed the execution of Cox of the 4th N.J., who was shot in the presence of the Division. I acted as adjutant, reading the order.

On return to camp I found Lewis, who gave me a copy of the orders discharging me from the Army.

🖋 [John Cox arrived in the army for the first time in October 1862, as a colonel in charge of the Twenty-third New Jersey Volunteers, but promptly resigned after he became drunk and tried to assault several of his own officers with his sword. Cox, who should never have been permitted near a regiment again, was allowed to reenlist in the army in 1863 with the Fourth New Jersey. Unhappy, he deserted during the battle of the Wilderness in 1864 and joined the Confederate Army. He was captured in late 1864 near Petersburg. His execution was ordered because he had not only deserted but had gone over to the enemy and fought against his own men.

To Halsey's surprise, his resignation was forwarded through channels with remarkable swiftness for the Army of the Potomac, and he began to receive orders relieving him of various duties. On January 7, he was relieved of his duties as judge advocate after fifty-seven trials, thirty-three of them during the previous two months. That same day he was told to finish up all of the ordnance papers he was working on. The next day he received his formal order of discharge. January 9 was to be his last day in the army, and on January 10 he was scheduled to go home. The rebels had one last volley for Ed Halsey, though.]

January 9

Cold. The rebels again attacked our picket line. To protect the line from these sudden incursions [artillery] batteries were taken out to the line. The rebels saw these being placed for a while quietly, but suddenly opened fire—wounding Lt. Earl in the leg.

Quite a jubilee at Brigade Headquarters for me. Dr. Sullivan and Cornish coming up from the 39th. I gave Dr. Sharp my silver watch.

[The going-home party for Halsey was attended by dozens of officers from different companies and different regiments throughout the Army of the Potomac. They were certainly sorry to see their comrade go but glad that, having survived every major battle in the eastern theater, he was finally going to be out of the line of fire.

The Army of the Potomac and its bunglers had one last present for Ed Halsey, too. The next day he got up bright and early and went to City Point to find passage to Washington and then on to Newark, New Jersey, but there was none that day. He was told to come back in a day or two. Disappointed, he planned to take a train back to Petersburg, but was told the only passage the army could provide was to put him into a freight car with six other people. He grumbled and got into the car. Halfway to Petersburg, the army train broke in half, and the half carrying Halsey rolled, without any power, more than a mile down the tracks and finally came to a stop in a hollow where the tracks dipped down and then went up. The train rolled back and forth between the inclines until it came to a rest. Halsey and the others, victims of yet another army screwup, did not get back to camp outside Petersburg until late that night.]

January 12

Left City Point on the boat with Hufty, Davis, Kline and one of our men who was furloughed.

🖋 [Like many in the army, Halsey considered his trusty horse, Ned, with him for eighteen months, part of himself. He had no intentions of raffling off his horse, as some soldiers on their way home did. He hired Predmore of Company D, also on his way home to Rockaway, to bring Ned back to Halsey's home and paid him $75 for his efforts and train expenses.

Halsey arrived in Washington, D.C., with the others on Friday to collect his back pay, but the department was shut down because of the death of noted orator and former vice-presidential candidate Edward Everett. The men were told to come back on Monday. After a visit to a bar, which Halsey referred to as "a low, mean place," the men registered at Willard's Hotel, where they stayed until Monday. Halsey went to church Sunday morning and again on Sunday evening. On Monday morning they were told to come back on Tuesday.

Halsey finally received his back pay on Wednesday morning and saw a play with his friends at Ford's Theater, where Abraham Lincoln would be murdered three months later. He caught a 7 A.M. train for New York in the morning and arrived there at night. Instead of going directly home, though, he saw another play, on Broadway, *The Shamrock,* and the next day took a train to Brooklyn to see his uncle and to deliver a message to best friend Alanson Haines's relatives.]

January 20
    ... To Rockaway with the afternoon train.

🖋 [Edmund Halsey's Civil War was over.]

EPILOGUE

The Fifteenth New Jersey Volunteers, still led by Colonel Penrose, fought on through the battle of Petersburg, winning it after Halsey's departure. The men of the Fifteenth fought through the spring campaign in 1865, as the Southern armies weakened and then collapsed, and were at Appomattox Court House with Gen. U. S. Grant on April 9, 1865, the day Robert E. Lee, their longtime nemesis, surrendered the Army of Northern Virginia to just about end the Civil War.

Colonel Penrose, the commander of the regiment, was a good soldier. He decided to stay in the army and spent the rest of his career there, retiring in 1896. Major Cornish went to New Mexico to become a gold prospector. Colonel Campbell hung in the shadows of army life after the war as a veterans' pension agent. He died in Colorado in 1913. Alanson Haines returned to New Jersey to become a minister and wrote his memoirs in 1882. He died in 1891.

John Vanderveer worked as a clerk for the New Jersey Senate in 1866 and then moved to Colorado. Vanderveer, who had managed to escape all the typhoid fever epidemics in the army, died in 1866 . . . of typhoid fever.

Lewis Van Blarcom became prosecutor for Sussex County, New Jersey, after the war and later the chairman of the Sussex County Republican Party.

Edmund Halsey, the Fifteenth's "temporary adjutant," did not slow his pace when he returned home. His experience as a judge advocate in fifty-seven army courts-martial convinced him that he did, indeed, want to be a lawyer and not an engineer, farmer, or gold prospector, and he passed the bar exam in 1865 and became a partner in his brother Sam's Morristown law firm. His arrival seemed to bolster the sagging law firm's business, and it prospered. Edmund practiced corporate law, not trial law, because his life-long respiratory problems, caused by the sickness he'd suffered in the war, prevented him from doing courtroom work.

Joseph and Ed patched up their heated political differences within weeks of the surrender. From January until June 1865, Ed personally took

294

over the care and supervision of Joe's daughters, Fannie and Annie, making sure they received an education and stayed healthy. He took them to plays, out to dinner, and, with girlfriend Mary Darcy, on extensive shopping trips in Morristown, Newark, and New York. The girls were enchanted with their uncle Ed. The end of the war, and slavery, meant the end of the political differences between Joseph and Edmund. All fiery letters ceased, and Ed visited Joe often at Lessland.

The entire Halsey family continued to thrive. Sam junior kept up his interest in politics and served several terms as mayor of Morristown. Ed dabbled in politics, too, serving a single term in the New Jersey Assembly in 1875–76. The Northern and Southern wings of the family patched up their differences rather quickly, and regular visits resumed shortly after the war. (Joseph's two daughters returned home to Lessland in the summer of 1865, after living almost a year with their grandfather.) Ed's older brother Abe remained in California and became an assistant district attorney and later wrote a book about San Francisco. Ed's older sister Susan remained married to Dr. Beach, who went on to become one of New Jersey's most prominent physicians. Their son Fred, to whom Halsey wrote letters of encouragement from the war while Fred was in grade school, grew up to become a lawyer, too, and joined Ed and Sam's Morristown law office in 1880. He also went into politics, like so many of the Halseys, and became mayor of Dover.

Sam senior died in 1871, at age seventy-five, pleased that his sons had survived the Civil War and that afterward he was able to visit Joseph, Millie, and their family and mend all family feuds. Anne, who thrilled young Ed with her organ playing in the family home and was bedridden throughout the war with rheumatism, deteriorated after the end of the war and died in 1868.

Joseph Halsey was a dogged and relentless patriot for the Southern cause. He remained in the Confederate Army until the very end, putting in four long years of service, and watched, along with thousands of others, Lee's surrender at Appomattox. As soon as the surrender was signed, Joe Halsey got on his horse, turned its reins toward Lessland, and rode home, making it to the edge of the Rapidan by early evening. As darkness fell, Halsey trotted slowly alongside the river, turned, and headed up the low-sloping hill to Lessland Plantation, where he was greeted by a tearful wife, who hugged him hard, and his two small sons, buoyant that their father was home for good.

From 1865 to 1870, Joe Halsey worked hard to restore his plantation as a working farm without slaves. Some of the slaves who had stayed on after the Union Army invaded Virginia worked at Lessland for years as paid laborers and, later, tenant farmers. The plantation struggled to get on its feet, and the progress Joe had hoped for was delayed when a fire burned down most of his home in the winter of 1870. It took several years to rebuild it, which he did with financial help from his father. Joe made his money from small profits from corn sales at Lessland, splitting proceeds with his black laborers, and from his law practice. He still had contacts throughout the county and state, thanks to his wartime efforts to maintain a part-time practice, and although he never thrived as a lawyer, he made a decent living at it. Joe's fortunes improved dramatically in the late 1870s when his son Morton married Irene Stearns, the beautiful daughter of Franklin Stearns, their neighbor, who by then, through shrewd investments in railroads and whiskey, had become one of Virginia's wealthiest men. Joe died in 1907, at the age of eighty-four. He and Millie, who died in 1903, were originally buried at Morton Hall but were later interred in Graham Cemetery in Orange, Virginia, just a few miles from Lessland.

Fate was not kind to Joe's father-in-law, slaver Jeremiah Morton. The strident secessionist was so certain the South would win the war that during the war he unwisely sold Morton Hall and its 5,500 acres to Franklin Stearns, a young businessman, and was paid entirely in Confederate money, which was worthless after the war. The war ended slavery on the three Morton plantations. He had to sell all of his land and homes to avoid bankruptcy. The end of the slave trade crippled his business empire. The slave trade had netted him $30,000 a year ($500,000 in today's money) and provided all the money for his diverse investments. He lost all of his money, most of his property, his homes and buildings, and his shares in various businesses. Morton was ruined.

He had to sell off all of his possessions and lived just above poverty for years in a small house on his one remaining piece of property. He wrote his brother George in 1867 that he was broke, could not buy clothes for his family, and did not even have a single dollar: "We are all still home in abject poverty and want. The two children share one sickbed. I am tired of life . . . have lived too long. All is dishonor and gloom before me. My life now has no happiness or charm." He added in a note to a friend that "I am a blasted stump in the wilderness of life."

Morton was so destitute that he could do nothing to help Joseph Halsey rebuild Lessland after the 1870 fire. Morton wound up living at Lessland with his son-in-law Joseph during his last years and died in an upstairs bedroom there, penniless, in 1878, a bitter and broken man.

Back up north, Edmund Halsey did not enjoy his one term in the state legislature. His real interest was not in national or state politics but in service to his hometown of Rockaway, just as it had been for his father, grandfather, and great-grandfather before him. Ed enjoyed a sense of heritage and service to the small town he had grown up in and much preferred to work for Rockaway and his friends and neighbors than for people he did not know somewhere else.

Ed served as a town councilman in Rockaway for seventeen years and served as a trustee at the Presbyterian church for twenty-nine years, doubling as Sunday-school teacher for many of those years. He was one of the founders of the Morris County Children's Home in 1881 and served as president of the Iron Bank in Rockaway. As a veteran, he became a member of the Loyal Legion, the Washington Association, the Society of the Army of the Potomac, and the Grand Army of the Republic. He continued writing and was one of the key contributors to *The History of Morris County*. He helped cousin Alanson Haines write his memoirs about the Fifteenth New Jersey in 1882. He never again served as the gardener of the Presbyterian church cemetery where 135 of his friends were buried.

Mary Darcy, Ed Halsey's girlfriend throughout the war, and perhaps the main reason he was able to get through it, did not marry him upon his return from the army. She put off any engagement for over a year. Finally, unable to take her waffling any longer, Ed wrote her a passionate letter on November 12, 1866, asking her to make up her mind and marry him.

"For years, I have had but one ambition—the attainment of such a position and competency as would permit me the honor to ask your hand. I could consider it nothing but a beautiful hope. . . . I feel a hesitancy in asking you to engage yourself to one whose circumstances are so unprepossessing and who asks so much. I do so, Mary, because such as I am, I am entirely yours. You are the first—the only one—I ever loved. Where the heart is so deeply interested human language has but the simple words—I love you. Do you love me?"

She did. Ed and Mary were married a year later.

While Ed was successful in his professional life, he suffered even more pain in his personal life than he did amid the dead and the dying in the Civil War. Five of his seven children died before they reached the age of eight. Henry died at four months, Fred and Marion at ten months, Anne at one year, and Mary, the darling of Rockaway, at seven. His first son, a Princeton graduate whom Ed had such great hopes for, died at twenty-six, never marrying. The only survivor of the Halsey line in Rockaway was Ed's daughter Cornelia, a gorgeous young woman. She married Frederick Kellogg, one of the most successful young lawyers in New York, and lived in New York and Morristown until her death in 1967. Sadly, six of her eight children died in childhood. Her two surviving sons carried on the Kellogg name.

After the death of Samuel Halsey, Ed and Mary Halsey moved into the Rockaway home where Ed had grown up. By that time, Sam senior had demolished the west wing of the large, sprawling white clapboard manse, even though Ed had argued against it because that wing was the original Stephen Jackson home where George Washington had spent so much time during the Revolution. Ed and Mary lived in the Rockaway home until their deaths. Later, when Cornelia moved to Morristown, she and her new husband held on to the house. Eventually it was leased to several different families and given to the Sacred Heart Roman Catholic Church in the 1960s. The church turned it into a convent for the nuns who taught at the church's new school, built on what was once Ed Halsey's beloved garden, where he and his father spent so much time together.

Ed was an invalid during his later years and died in 1896 at the age of fifty-six. Ed Halsey insisted that he be buried in the Presbyterian Church cemetery, where he had served as gardener as a teenager and where he could lie in rest forever with the more than one hundred soldiers of the Fifteenth New Jersey Volunteers and other Rockaway men who fought in the Civil War. Every year on Memorial Day, prayers are said and tribute read to the Halseys who served their country—all of them.

BIBLIOGRAPHY

The Halseys

Frelinghuysen, Rev. Theodore. *A Sketch of the Life and Character of Edmund Halsey*. Newark: New Jersey Historical Society, 1898.

Halsey, Edmund, Ed. *The History of Morris County*. New York: W.W. Munsell Co., 1882.

Halsey, Edmund. *A Sketch of Colonel Joseph Jackson*. Rockaway: Privately Printed, 1882.

Halsey, Edmund. *A Sketch of Samuel Beach Halsey*. Rockaway: Privately Printed, 1886.

Halsey, Edmund. *Rockaway Township in the War of the Rebellion*. Dover, N.J.: The Iron Era Co., 1892.

Halsey, Edmund. *The Continental Army in Morris County, 1779–1780*. Rockaway: privately printed, 1892.

New Jersey

Baquet, Camille. *History of the First Brigade: New Jersey Volunteers from 1861 to 1865*. Hightstown, N.J.: Ron R. Van Sickle Military Books, 1988.

Bilby, Joseph. *Three Rousing Cheers*. Hightstown, N.J.: Longstreet House, 1993.

Bill, Alfred. *Revolutionary War in New Jersey*. Princeton: D. Van Nostrand Co., 1964.

Campbell, Edward. *Historical Sketch of the 15th Regiment, New Jersey Volunteers, First Brigade, First Division*. Sixth Corps Trenton: Wm. S. Sharp Publishers, 1880.

Christiano, Terry. Ed., *Rockaway Borough—A History*. Rockaway, N.J.: Rockaway Borough Bicentennial Committee, 1975.

Cooleu, Henry. *A Study of Slavery in New Jersey*. Baltimore: Johns Hopkins University Press, 1896.

Cunningham, John. *Newark*. Newark: New Jersey Historical Society, 1966.

Cunningham, John. *New Jersey: America's Main Road*. Garden City, N.Y.: Doubleday, 1966.

Foster, John. *New Jersey and the Rebellion: A History of the Services of the Troops and People of New Jersey in Aid of the Union Cause.* Newark: Martin R. Dennis & Co., 1868.

Gerlach, Larry. *Prologue to Independence: New Jersey and the Coming of the American Revolution.* New Brunswick, N.J.: Rutgers University Press, 1975.

Gillette, William. *Jersey Blue: Civil War Politics in New Jersey, 1854–1865.* New Brunswick: Rutgers University Press, 1995.

Gilman, Charles. *The Story of the Jersey Blues.* Red Bank, N.J.: Arlington Laboratory for Clinical and Historical Research, n.d.

Haines, Alanson. *The History of the 15th New Jersey Volunteers.* New York: Jenkins & Thomas Printers, 1883.

Knapp, Charles. *New Jersey Politics During the Period of the Civil War and Reconstruction.* Geneva, N.Y.: W. F. Humphrey, 1924.

Longacre, Edward. *To Gettysburg and Beyond: The Twelfth New Jersey Volunteer Infantry.* Hightstown, N.J.: Longstreet House Press, 1988.

Lundin, Leonard. *Cockpit of the Revolution: The War For Independence in New Jersey.* Princeton, N.J.: Princeton University Press, 1940.

Miers, Earl Schenck. *New Jersey and the Civil War.* Princeton, N.J.: D. Van Nostrand Co., 1964.

Mitros, David. *Slave Records of Morris County, New Jersey, 1756–1841.* Trenton: New Jersey Historical Commission, 1991.

Siegel, Alan. *For The Glory of the Union.* Cranbury, N.J.: Associated University Presses, 1984.

Toombs, Samuel. *New Jersey Troops in the Gettysburg Campaign from June 5 to July 31, 1863.* Hightstown, N.J.: Longstreet House, 1988.

Wright, Giles. *Afro-Americans in New Jersey: A Short History.* Trenton: New Jersey Historical Commission, 1995.

Wright, William. *New Jersey in the American Revolution.* Trenton: New Jersey Historical Commmission, 1969.

The War

Anderson, Nancy Scott and Dwight. *The Generals: Ulysses S. Grant and Robert E. Lee.* New York: Vintage Books, 1987.

Bigelow, John. *The Campaign of Chancellorsville.* New Haven: n.p., 1910.

Boatner, Mark. *The Civil War Dictionary.* New York: David McKay Co., 1959.

Bruce, Robert. *Lincoln and the Tools of War.* Indianapolis: Bobbs-Merrill, 1956.

Buel, Clarence, and Johnson, Robert. *Battles and Leaders of the Civil War.* 4 vols. New York: Century Co., 1884–1887.

Catton, Bruce. *Bruce Catton's Civil War.* New York: Fairfax Press, 1984.

Commager, Henry. *The Blue and the Gray: the Story of the Civil War As Told By Participants*. 2 vols. Indianapolis: Bobbs-Merrill, 1950.

Donald, David. *Lincoln*. New York: Simon & Schuster, 1995.

Downey, Fairfax. *The Guns at Gettysburg*. New York: David McKay Co., 1958.

Foote, Shelby. *The Civil War—A Narrative: Red River to Appomattox*. New York: Random House, 1974.

Frassino, William. *Grant and Lee: The Virginia Campaign, 1864–1865: The Army of the Potomac and the Army of the James*. New York: Charles Scribner's Sons, 1883.

Freeman, Douglas Southall. *Lee's Lieutenants—A Study in Command*. 3 vols. New York: Charles Scribner's Sons, 1934–35.

Hattaway, Herman, and Jones, Archer. *How The North Won: A Military History of the Civil War*. Urbana: University of Illinois Press, 1983.

Jones, Virgil. *Eight Hours Before Richmond*. New York: Henry Holt & Co., 1957.

Leech, Margaret. *Reveille in Washington, 1860–1865*. New York: Harper & Brothers, 1941.

Lewis, Thomas. *The Guns of Cedar Creek*. New York: Harper & Row, 1988.

Long, E.B. and Barbara. *The Civil War Day by Day: An Almanac, 1861–1865*. New York: Doubleday, 1971.

Matter, William. *If It Takes All Summer: The Battle of Spotsylvania*. Chapel Hill: University of North Carolina Press, 1988.

McPherson, James. *The Battle Cry of Freedom: The Civil War Era*. New York: Oxford University Press, 1988.

Montgomery, James Stuart. *Shaping of A Battle: Gettysburg*. Philadelphia: Chilton Company, 1959.

Official Records. *The War of the Rebellion: A Compilation of the Official Records of the Union and Confederate Armies*. Washington: Government Printing Office, 1882–1927.

Smith, Gene. *Lee and Grant*. New York: New American Library, 1984.

Smith, George Winston and Judah, Charles. *Life in the North During The Civil War*. Albuquerque: University of New Mexico Press, 1955.

Trudeau, Noah. *Bloody Roads South*. Boston: Little, Brown, 1989.

Warner, Ezra. *Generals in Blue: The Lives of the Union Commanders*. Baton Rouge: Louisiana State University Press, 1964.

Warner, Ezra. *Generals in Gray: The Lives of the Confederate Commanders*. Baton Rouge: Louisiana State University Press, 1959.

Wert, Jeffrey. *From Winchester to Cedar Creek: The Shenandoah Valley Campaign of 1864*. Carlisle, Pa.: South Mountain Press, 1987.

Wiley, Bell. *The Life of Johnny Reb*. Indianapolis: Bobbs-Merrill, 1943.

———. *The Life of Billy Yank*. Indianapolis: Bobbs-Merrill, 1952.

INDEX